THE TIGER HAS MANY LIVES

The story of

ROD WELLS

THE TIGER HAS MANY LIVES

the story of

ROD WELLS

compiled by

PAMELA WELLS

SEVENPENS

The Tiger has Many Lives: The Story of Rod Wells
Copyright © Pamela Wells, 2022

First published 2022

Published by Sevenpens Publishing
Harcourt, VIC 3453, Australia
Email: kseppings@castlemaine.net
Web: https://sevenpenspublishing.com/

All rights reserved. No part of this publication may be reproduced, stored in or introduced into a database and retrieval system or transmitted in any form or by any means (electronic, mechanical, photocopying, recording or otherwise) without the prior written permission of both the publisher and copyright owner.

National Library of Australia Cataloguing-in-Publication data:
Creator: Wells, Pamela 1940 – author
Title: *The Tiger has Many Lives: The Story of Rod Wells*
ISBN 978-0-9954144-9-5
Subjects: Wells, Pamela 1940 – Biography, History, WWII

Contributors: Lynette Ramsay Silver AM, historical adviser and senior editor
Katherine Seppings, preliminary and liaison editor
Front Cover: Photograph of Rod Wells by Francie Young, Melbourne, 1940
Photo courtesy of Pamela Wells' collection
Photograph of Outram Road Gaol courtesy of Silver Papers
Back Cover: Photograph of Tiger courtesy of Pamela Wells' collection
The Princess Anne Banner given to the Royal Australian Corps of Signals 1986
Cover Design: Katherine Seppings
Book Design: Katherine Seppings

This biography is based on rigorous historical research, the facts of which are believed to be true but some cannot be fully substantiated.

To all those who suffered and all those who still remember

Author Profile

Pamela Margaret Ann Bennett was born in Melbourne in 1940, and at the age of 18 months moved to Echuca in country Victoria where she enjoyed a happy and secure childhood with her parents and three sisters. After completing her education to Matriculation level in 1957 she began an apprenticeship in an Echuca pharmacy and in 1960 transferred to the Victorian College of Pharmacy, Parkville, completing the Diploma course in 1963. After qualifying she managed a large group of pharmacies in the Toorak, East Prahran, and Glen Iris area and was active in the Women Pharmaceutical Chemists Association of Victoria for many years.

In June 1974, Pamela Bennett married Rod Wells. On moving to Rushworth in 1983, she continued work as a relieving pharmacist in Echuca, Tatura, Kyabram and Rushworth. During this time, she undertook several executive roles in the Tatura Business and Professional Women's Club and became the first woman to be elected to the committee of Hill Top Golf and Country Club.

Previous writing efforts have been reports, articles, newsletters, and various trivial 'poems', more accurately described as doggerel; they might be compared to 25-metre sprints. Finishing this book, which was started soon after she and Rod were married, has been, to Pamela, like suddenly embarking on an ultra-marathon without any previous training.

Pamela loves keeping up with her family and friends, walking the dog and reading, reading, reading.

Mentioned in Despatches

This book has been many years in the making with a significant number of people contributing in various ways. I documented the early part of Rod's life soon after we were married. His memory at that time was phenomenal; he recalled details that made events come alive and our friends became accustomed to his beginning one anecdote and finishing half an hour later on a completely different subject. I never knew Rod's father but his mother Margot, or Maggie as she was variously called, remembered her early days of arriving in Australia and the strangeness of life on the farm, such a contrast to her life in England.

The biggest vote of thanks goes to Tim Bowden AM, author, radio and television broadcaster and producer, and oral historian. Tim recorded eight tapes of Rod's time with 8 Division Signals in Malaya, his subsequent imprisonment and his survival. The transcript, despite its backtracking, digressions, 'ums', 'ahs' and 'ers', diligently typed by Norah Bonney, as well as Rod's own memories of his imprisonment, were major sources of information. Tim Bowden's tapes, *Prisoners of War: Australians Under Nippon*, which he produced and presented, Hank Nelson's book based on the radio series with the same title, Ray Quint's video recorded interview and an interview by UK author Christopher Somerville for his book *Our War: How the British Commonwealth Fought the Second World War*, all added details which lifted the narrative.

Brothers Sherriff and John Probert undertook a large amount of research with a view to completing Rod's story but, for various reasons, mainly due to my lack of time to commit to the project, it was never completed. However, I am grateful to them for unearthing several relevant facts of Rod's army days. Tatura historian, Tony Ford, was instrumental in discovering the details of Rod's first marriage to Ellen Ashby.

So the project lapsed for many years until I decided to revive it. About four years ago, wanting to test what I had written so far, I joined the Goulburn Valley U3A Writing 4 Pleasure group in Shepparton. I am very grateful to the members for their encouragement and patience in listening to random chapters, or parts thereof, and insisting that I must finish the book – thank you all.

In May 2019, a series of serendipitous events led me to Katherine Seppings of Sevenpens Publishing, Castlemaine. What had seemed to be a huge exercise in finding publishers, editors, artists, promoters and proof-readers turned out to be a one-stop-shop, so to speak, with Katherine taking all of these tasks under her parasol. A previous experience with an interfering editor, who wanted to put in his own inaccurate account of events, had made me wary of the race as a whole. Katherine's gentle and sensitive professional guidance came as a great relief to my doubts and apprehensions about the project; she has actually made the publishing experience an enjoyable one.

On the same weekend that I met Katherine, I visited 'The Mill' complex at Castlemaine. I could hardly believe my eyes when, towards the back of a shop selling antique Japanese artefacts, I came across the wooden blocks, similar to those issued to prisoners as 'pillows'. It is also ironic that the present-day Mill complex was previously the Castlemaine Woollen Mills where Rod's fellow prisoner, Gordon Weynton, worked as an accountant.

The front cover photo of Rod as a young lieutenant was also a miraculous find by an army friend of Rod's in a second-hand shop, where it had been left by his second wife after the break-up of their marriage.

Another happy sequence of events resulted in much needed help being offered by Ken O'Connor. While my research efforts have a habit of going off track, Ken's ability to stay on target, and his enthusiasm for getting the book over the line has been a huge help, as are his photos of the present Wells' farmhouse, producing the time-line and typing up the ChiDE interview. And Lottie, the resident Kelpie, thoroughly enjoyed the treats that Ken brought on his visits. Thank you to Paul Kerrins for details of the Kerrins family and to John Basile, present owner of Cuthbert Hall, for allowing us to visit the old Wells' farm.

To my good friend Dr Barbara Nichol and National Archives of Australia staff, Andrew Griffin and Kathryn Graham, thank you for your persistence in accessing relevant files. Justin and staff at Rodney printers, Tatura, also achieved great results from some very ancient texts and photos.

I have always found the mysteries of setting up the text, pagination etc, a bit hit-and-miss, and this project brought on many of what I call 'headless chook' moments. To Lois Orr my sincere thanks for calmly and logically dealing with missing text, taming rebellious headers and banishing something called 'shortcuts', which were anything but and wasted a lot of time when they deleted whole pages of writing, all of which Lois successfully recovered. She also deciphered the very poor copy of the Kuching trial and speedily typed it up.

Thank you to military historian Lynette Ramsay Silver, my historical adviser and editor who made sense of the chronology of Rod's wartime experiences.

A special thank you to my niece, Emma Jamvold, and life-long friend Dr Barbara Nichol, for proofreading the manuscript.

My final thanks to Rod – soldier, scientist and diplomat – whose wide-ranging experiences allowed me to meet so many fascinating people, to share his story, and who enriched my life in so many wonderful ways.

Pamela Wells

Contents

Author Profile ii
Mentioned in Despatches iii
Introduction by Rod Wells viii
Introduction by Pamela Wells x
Roderick Graham Wells – Time Line xiv
Invictus xvii

Prologue - THE CAGE xviii
Ch 1 - IN THE BEGINNING 1
Ch 2 - BIRTH, SCHOOL, EXPERIMENTS 10
Ch 3 - A SCIENTIST'S LIFE 36
Ch 4 - APPRENTICESHIP, ENLISTMENT, TRAINING .. 57
Ch 5 - MALAYA 68
Ch 6 - IN THE BAG 82
Ch 7 - SANDAKAN 90
Ch 8 - THE UNDERGROUND 104
Ch 9 - ARREST AND INTERROGATION 116
Ch 10 - OUTRAM ROAD 134
Ch 11 - BACK TO CHANGI 154
Ch 12 - WAR ENDS 161
Ch 13 - HOMECOMING 169
Ch 14 - FRESH START 188

Ch 15 - MARALINGA 194
Ch 16 - MY CAREER TAKES OFF 202
Ch 17 - THE 1970s 211
Ch 18 - RETURN TO BORNEO 222
Ch 19 - COUNTRY LIVING AND BEYOND 234
EPILOGUE 247

APPENDICES 255

APPENDIX A – Report on Clandestine Radio 1945 256

APPENDIX B – Fall of Singapore Surrender letter 259

APPENDIX C – Kuching Trial Records 260

APPENDIX D – Eyewitness Statement 269

APPENDIX E – Wells' Self-Sufficient Home 271

APPENDIX F – ChiDE interview by Rod Wells 1995 276

BIBLIOGRAPHY 287
LIST OF ILLUSTRATIONS,
PHOTOGRAPHS AND MAPS 289
INDEX 293

Introduction by Rod Wells

In writing the story of one's life, it should be easy to decide where to begin and in which order to set things down. But to recall the events of childhood in their chronological order is not easy. After 50 years they have a habit of slipping out of line and re-appearing in unexpected places.

Looking back on my life, until I was perhaps 15 or 16, I feel myself sitting before a fire, becoming transfixed by its moving patterns. As I move closer to the fire, I feel the warmth of family life and the security of its love. In the growing flames is the brightness of farm life, holidays and outings, which illuminated our lives. Sparks of my hot temper spit out, and die away just as quickly. The hottest coals hold the anger and frustration. I smell the bitter smoke of hurts and disappointments that sometimes permeated my soul, and touch the cold, wasted ashes of pessimism. But if the fire changed its shape from day to day or year to year its heart remained, a heart of love banked up by my parents' examples of self-discipline, hard work, honesty and steadfast loyalty to family, country and king.

The experiences of childhood may have fused into the impression of a fire, but my early manhood and subsequent years are best described in terms of astronomy. I can identify each event from those times as if they were as steady as the stars, each year's events being clearly discernible. So, in this book I have recorded my early years under several topics rather than in accurate order. Conversations are a general record of the way we would have spoken, but this is not to deny the authenticity of the events described. The later and largest part of the book begins to fall into sequence, which appeals to my logical mind and scientific training. Another aspect of the book, which evolved as the work progressed, was the inclusion of a brief family history. I firmly believe that a happy and successful life is a matter to two things – good genes and, even better, luck. The former has brought me excellent physical and emotional health, and the persistence, energy and ability to pursue my ambitions and careers. Good fortune has allowed me to survive.

Turning over life's memories is like peeling off the layers of a bulb. Some memories are closer to the surface and quite clear, others have been forgotten until we peel off another layer and the next one is revealed: each layer hides and discloses long forgotten events, each of which has shaped our lives. Most of my family and friends will recognise some of the events in the book and how they defined me.

Rod Wells   March 1987

Introduction by Pamela Wells

It was in 1972, that I was introduced to Rod Wells. I had just shaken off Hal, a persistent pest of a man, a liar, boaster and con man who kept bobbing up in my life until, when I threatened further action, he finally took off. I would be very careful of the next man who came along. So I kept Rod at arm's length, telling him I was busy. This was quite true; I had a demanding career as a pharmacist, had a busy social life and at 31 was happily independent. If he is really interested, I thought, he will be in touch.

Eventually, I condescended to accept Rod's invitation to dinner. I must admit, the difference between Rod and Hal was quite a relief. Instead of tiresome boasting, here was a man who was far too modest. Rod's nervous stammer, heavy smoking and edgy manner were quite a contrast; his fair complexion and short but upright bearing were a pleasant change. I was more interested than I had intended and, as was my usual habit, I left things to fate. It was after our second outing, as he eased the car into the kerb outside my flat, that Rod said, almost casually, 'I'm going to marry you one day.'

This was certainly a change from the usual proposal. At least with others I had had a choice, but here I was being told that I would be married. What cheek and what assurance from a man who I thought lacked confidence. I reminded myself what I had said about the next man who came along. Well here he was and telling me that we would be married. He would just have to wait. First let him prove his reliability and integrity.

'Did you hear me?' Rod asked. 'I said that we will be married one day.'

'That's very nice,' I replied at last, 'but I'm not interested in marriage.'

'Well, I can wait,' and he gave a confident smile.

'That looks like the smile on the face of a tiger,' I said absently, remembering a limerick by William C. Monkhouse:

There was a young lady from Niger
Who rode on the back of a tiger
They returned from the ride with the lady inside
And a smile on the face of the tiger.

From that time onwards he became 'Tiger'. I did not realise at the time just how appropriate the name was. Like the tiger, Rod was an expert in the art of survival, courageous in adversity, tenacious and clever in the pursuit of his objectives. A strong sense of loyalty and patriotism made him, like the tiger, one of a vanishing breed. My refusal of his proposal did not deter Rod in the least, in fact he would have been disappointed had I capitulated immediately. Because if there is one thing Rod loved above all else it was a challenge; he thrived when things were against him, becoming bored and restless when life was smooth. The other thing I did not realise at the time was that the manner of Rod's proposal was a repetition of a small piece of family history: his father had proposed to his mother in almost the same way.

So it happened, that, in June 1974, I found myself married to Rod Wells, a man almost 21 years older than I. As with each of us, Rod's personality presented a series of contrasts. Why, I used to ask myself, does he spend patient hours over a tedious job and yet become impatient over a minor setback? How can he remain unruffled over a major crisis yet become so incensed at the fallibility of his fellow humans? If he had such an excellent memory, how was it that after nine years of living in Sackville Street, Kew, could he drive past our street and then wonder where he was? Despite these paradoxes the qualities that stood out in Rod's character were his enthusiasm, his persistence and his sheer physical energy.

After being associated with radio and communications for his whole life, he still received a thrill from listening to a short-wave broadcast –

what seemed to be a crackling mess of poor radio reception to others was, to Rod, a miracle of physics and science.

The horrors of the POW experience in Borneo in World War II are not as well known as those of the Thai-Burma Railway. The main reason for this is because, of the 2,500 Allied prisoners who were sent to Sandakan, Borneo, only six survived. Their story had little publicity until West Australian author Peter Firkins published From Hell to Eternity *in 1979. Many others have followed, some accurate, some wildly inaccurate. One author, writing in 2012, has Rod in World War I infantry, with us being married, and then Rod serving in Signals during World War II. Rod was not born until 1920, and I was born in 1940!*

That Rod survived his treatment at the hands of the Kempeitai (Japanese Military Police) and subsequently became a world expert in electronics and communications was due to his own determination, self-discipline and abilities. His post-war life was full of achievements and was always exciting, but he remained modest about his capabilities. Despite his POW experiences, Rod was eternally optimistic; yes, he was sometimes anxious but, unlike many of his army colleagues, never depressed or suicidal. He was always good company.

This narrative has been many years in the making – life just kept getting in the way. Sorting through over almost 1000 documents has not been easy. There were also 200 pages of transcript of taped interviews with Rod. Newspaper articles, letters, speeches and interviews present conflicting facts, dates do not always correspond, memories differ. Reference books were many and varied and, again, do not always agree on dates or facts. Names, especially Chinese and Japanese, have different spellings, as do place names, eg. Johore/Johor, and in some cases have changed, eg. Jesselton is now Kota Kinabalu; Burma and Rangoon are now Myanmar and Yangon. I have left out a lot of the details of the Sandakan underground, which is a huge subject in itself. Punishments, tortures, escapes and camp setup have been documented in greater detail by other authors.

Following the trail of Rod's life was like dealing with a basketful of eels: just as I thought I had grasped one episode, other facts would slither into view to put a different slant on things. I have concentrated on Rod's life, its fortunes and misfortunes, its luck both good and bad. The following account is as accurate as I can ascertain. No doubt there will still be some discrepancies from other peoples' points of view. Here at last then, is Rod's life story, as it was told to me by him, over 29 years of a very happy marriage.

Pamela Wells, Tatura, March 2022

Roderick Graham Wells – Time Line

01.01.1920	Born at Dhurringile to Richard John Wells and Dorothy Margaret Wells (nee Hall).
1926-1935	Attended Convent of Mercy School, Tatura. Completed Intermediate Certificate.
1936-1937	Commenced apprenticeship at Government Ordnance Factory at Maribyrnong.
1937	Completed Leaving.
23.11.1938	Completed Matriculation by correspondence.
1939	Tutored at Taylors College, Melbourne. Joined Victorian Education Dept as a Student Teacher.
23.11.1939	Enlisted in Australian Imperial Force (AIF).
04.05.1940	Selected for Officer Training at Seymour.
01.11.1940	Transferred to Bathurst for signals training – Commissioned as a Lieutenant.
25.01.1941	Married Ellen Ethel Ashby at Bathurst Cathedral.
29.07.1941	Sailed from Sydney to Fremantle on SS *Katoomba*.
08.08.1941	Sailed from Fremantle to Singapore on SS *Sibajak*.
15.08.1941	Arrived Singapore.
08.12.1941	Japanese forces invaded Malaya.
15.02.1942	Taken prisoner of war by the Japanese Army at Singapore.
08.07.1942	Transported on *Yubi Maru* from Singapore to Sandakan, Borneo, as part of 'B' Force. Commenced construction of radio receiver and transmitter.
24.07.1943	Arrested at Sandakan POW Camp and handed to Kempeitai.
25.10.1943	Transported from Sandakan to Kuching.
29.02.1944	Military trial conducted at St Teresa's Convent Hall, Kuching. Sentences to be confirmed.
02.03.1944	Lieutenant Wells sentenced to 12 years' penal servitude and solitary confinement. Captain Lionel Matthews executed at Kuching.

04.03.1944	Transported from Kuching to Outram Road Gaol to serve sentence.
11.03.1944	Arrived at Outram Road Gaol, Singapore.
03.04.1945	Transferred to Changi when close to death – weight 20 kilograms.
15.08.1945	Japan surrendered.
Sep 1945	Recovered at Changi by Allied Forces.
04.01.1946	Discharged from the Army.
1946-1949	Completed Science Degree and Diploma of Education at Melbourne University.
1950	Head Science Master at Shepparton High School – teaching Physics and Maths.
17.05.1950	Marriage to Ellen Ethel Ashby annulled.
06.01.1951	Married Linda Barton King.
01.09.1951	Re-enlisted in the Australian Army and returned to Army HQ Signals Reg. and completed Engineering Degree. Admitted as a Fellow of the Institute of Radio and Electrical Engineers.
1953	Attended the Royal Military College of Science, Shrivenham, UK. Undertook post-graduate studies, and also at King's College, Cambridge.
1954-1955	Seconded to the UK Ministry of Supply.
Late 1955	Returned to Australia attached to HQ Department of Supply.
Jun-Sep 1956	Attended atomic trials at Maralinga.
Feb 1957	Promoted to Major.
Mar-Jul 1957	Went to the UK, by way of RAF Hastings transport. Attended the Atomic Weapons Research Establishment, Aldermaston, Berkshire.
1957	Returned to Australia. Continued with the Department of Supply.
1959	Transferred to the Army Reserve List of Retired Officers.
1960	Appointed to the Defence Department as a scientific officer and returned to the UK for further training.

1963	Participated in trials for Britain's first nuclear submarine, HMS *Dreadnought*.
20.08.1964	Death of Richard John Wells (Rod's father).
24.03.1974	Divorced Linda Barton Wells.
29.06.1974	Married Pamela Bennett at Scott's Church, Collins Street, Melbourne.
27.03.1977	Death of Dorothy Margaret Wells (Rod's mother).
01.01.1978	Resigned from the Defence Department.
24.01.1978	Commenced work as a private consultant with the business name of R & P Consultants.
1981	Involved in the planning for the Commonwealth Heads of Government meeting held in Melbourne. Technical security and communications adviser to the CMI Group, Australian Bankers' Association.
1983	Built an entirely self-sufficient home at Waranga Basin, Rushworth.
Oct 1987	Retired due to ill health.
1995	Final visit to London. Interviewed by historians at the Centre for the History of Defence Electronics, Bournemouth University. Met Eric Lomax again.
1996	Awarded Life Membership of the Royal Australian Corps of Signals.
Jun 1999	Admitted to the Rushworth Nursing Home due to declining health.
Apr 2002	Awarded Life Membership of the RSL.
12.10.2003	Death of Roderick Wells at Rushworth.
Sep 2007	New building of 126 Squadron at Holsworthy Army Barracks opened and named 'The Rod Wells Wing'.

Invictus

Out of the night that covers me,
Black as the pit from pole to pole,
I thank whatever gods may be
For my unconquerable soul.

In the fell clutch of circumstance,
I have not winced nor cried aloud:
Under the bludgeonings of chance
My head is bloody but unbowed.

Beyond this place of wrath and tears
Looms but the Horror of the shade,
And yet the menace of the years
Finds and shall find me unafraid.

It matters not how strait the gate,
How charged with punishments the scroll,
I am the master of my fate,
I am the captain of my soul.

William Ernest Henley
Echoes, Book of Verses (1875)

PROLOGUE

THE CAGE

The door to the cage clanged shut. I stumbled onto the platform and sat hunched on its bare boards. My head sank between my knees. The trial had left my mind confused and exhausted. Death was certain. I had cheated it on several previous occasions, but partly through fate and partly through my own resources I had managed to escape. Escape was impossible now. The Japanese Military Police, the Kempeitai, was invincible and its execution squads infallible. My mind wandered to Captain Lionel Matthews, who had become a trusted and admired colleague and close friend. I knew that his last thoughts would be for his wife Lorna and his son David.

For the first time in my life I was defeated, desperately weary and completely alone. I sat for some hours until a cool breeze, coming through the barred corridor windows into my wire cage, told me that the sun had set. I raised my head and stretched my limbs. Over the past four months I had become used to the two planks that comprised my bed and the wooden block provided as a pillow. It is the 29th of February 1944, I thought. I have lived just 24 years. They had been hard and exciting years and soon my life would be extinguished. I had no regrets about the things I had done since imprisoned by the Japanese, but I felt a deep sadness that I would never again see my wife, Ellen, nor my parents and sister. I felt sadder for my parents than I did for myself. My father, Dick Wells, and my mother, Maggie, had worked hard and lived sensibly and honestly. They had brought me up to be resourceful and straightforward. Now their hopes and efforts would be wasted. They would never know how I died, or why. I prayed that they would all somehow know that my last thoughts had been of them.

A single guard patrolled the perimeter corridor. Through the outer window I could see the stars twinkling brilliantly in the blackness of the tropical night. They will be shining over the farm, I thought. They will shine over the farm long after I am dead. I calculated that it would now be about 8.30 pm; that meant it would be 10.30 pm at home. The afternoon milking would be long since finished. The cows would be back in the paddocks gently stirring up clouds of insects from the cool clover with the sweet pungent smell, peculiar to irrigation areas, that I could smell so clearly, even now.

My parents and sister would be sitting on the veranda before turning in and trying to sleep in the warm house. They would have listened to the evening news, but the news they wished for was not broadcast on impersonal national bulletins. Statistics of troops killed, of battles won or lost meant little to the thousands of families waiting at home. Like my family, they waited for news of just one or two special people – news that might shatter their lives and hopes – but news that they would bear with courage and pride.

I deliberately closed my mind to my execution and thought of home and family. Eventfully, I fell into a sleep, which brought not refreshment but an even deeper exhaustion.

Frontispiece: Dick Wells, just before leaving for WWI.

CHAPTER 1

IN THE BEGINNING

Dick Wells was bored. Fancy sitting here like a crow on a post, he thought, with all these stuck-up English girls. Not a decent one amongst them. Why should they be so unfriendly? It was all Paddy's fault, he reckoned. Paddy O'Byrne, his best mate. They had enlisted together in Australia. On their first leave from the battlefields of France, Paddy had persuaded him to go to Brighton to spend time with the O'Byrne family, instead of going to Ireland to seek out some of his own distant relations. Dick had been keen to visit Ireland: his mother had been born there, his patient dark-haired mother who had reared ten children on their small farm at Murchison in Australia. Far better to be in Ireland, he mused, where at least he would get a warm welcome and not have to put up with these aloof English girls. Who do they think they are? Can't they even say hello to a fellow without being introduced?

'What are you looking so miserable about?'

The soft voice with its blurred Sussex accent sounded strange to Dick's ears; but it was soothing and understanding. He looked up. She was not, he decided, what he would call a good looker, but her plump face with its friendly smile comforted him and he relaxed. The endless war with its crowded trenches and oceans of mud and ceaseless noise and turmoil of conflict and death were not part of her life. Her face reflected a soul at ease.

'Come and sit and talk to me,' he said.

Perhaps Paddy was right after all, and his friends really were a decent lot. Dick's melancholy began to lift. After all, he was not one to brood and, if there was some fun or a party going on, he was always the leader. Her name was Maggie Hall; her father had owned The Cuthbert Inn at Brighton. When he died in a cart accident in 1902, Maggie's mother, Isabella, kept the inn running as well as rearing her ten children. After their mother's death in 1912, Maggie, aged 24, found work in the office of a large butchering business and Maggie's eldest sister Flo cared for the children who were still at home.

All of these things Dick learned as they talked together. He also discovered that, despite her shy exterior, Maggie Hall had a bright sense of fun and a calm outlook on life that appealed to him. At the end of the evening he announced, 'Maggie I'm going to marry you'.

Maggie's reaction was neither surprised nor surprising.

'Don't be silly, Dick,' she said calmly. 'We don't know each other properly.'

'I'm not silly, Maggie. We can be married on my next leave.' And he gave her the smile, which she had already noticed changed his face from being somewhat stern and tight-lipped into looking rather cheeky.

'Well, let's wait and see,' Maggie replied.

On a picnic outing, the next day, Dick repeated his proposal and met with the same calm refusal. A refusal meant only one thing to Dick Wells – a challenge; he dearly loved a challenge. He was always at his best when life was against him. His bounce and confidence were barely ruffled by what he considered to be a very good offer. Dick's cheerful farewell to Maggie at the end of his leave led her to believe that his proposal had been made in a fit of loneliness. If Maggie thought of Dick at all during the next few months it did not prevent her from going about and enjoying herself as usual.

Six months later Dick managed to obtain a short leave and went straight to Brighton and to Maggie.

'Well now, Maggie, are you ready to marry me?'

Still she hesitated, but Dick had things well planned.

'We must be married, Maggie. You see, the only reason I could get leave was because I told the commanding officer (CO) I had a special marriage licence. No marriage, no leave. If I go back to my unit without being married, I'll be on a serious charge.'

The idea of Dick being on charge did not appeal to Maggie; she capitulated and they were married a few days later at St Matthew's Church, Kemp Town, Brighton, on 21 November 1917 by Vicar Robert William Odell.

Throughout their married life, my parents always recalled the bluff with affection and without rancour or regret. After a brief honeymoon in London, Dick returned to France. In 1918, at the end of the war, he managed to make the system work in his favour again. As a non-commissioned officer, my father had worked hard and been promoted to lieutenant. This was quite an achievement those days, as the majority of officers came from the officer training schools. As a transport officer, assisting with demobilisation, Lieutenant Wells could not immediately return to Australia. He managed to convince his superiors that the best place for him to operate from would be at a demobilisation camp near Plymouth, which was conveniently nearer to my mother in Brighton than was France. The de-mobbing took some weeks. He eventually returned to Australia on 27 January 1919 on the troop ship *Port Hacking* via the Cape. My mother, wishing to have a last Christmas with her family in England, sailed in January via the Atlantic, crossing Canada by train and boarding another ship for the long Pacific route to Australia.

My father met the ship in Melbourne in March 1919 and, after a few days in the city, they travelled by train to Murchison. As the hills of the Great Dividing Range settled into flat unending fields, Maggie became silent. Before leaving England, she had tried to picture the Australian countryside. The green hills and well-established farms of the Sussex landscape were comfortable and re-assuring. But nothing she had tried to imagine had prepared her for the impact of panic and loneliness that spread through her as the train took itself noisily and awkwardly about its business.

There were so few villages and the farmhouses, which appeared infrequently, looked shabby and deserted. The autumn land was harsh and dry, not soft and moist like England in autumn, and the monotonous gum trees were a dejected green, not splendidly red and yellow. She felt stifled and alien, as if she had crept into this strange autumn landscape by mistake. But there was no going back. She tried to cheer up for Dick's sake. He talked enthusiastically of the land that he hoped would be allocated to him under the Soldier Settlement Scheme. Maggie made an effort to listen but felt she could never be part of his plans.

Their arrival at Toolamba station was signalled with a sigh of steam from the engine. As she stepped out into the hot March sun, Maggie's sigh was one of dejection at ever having left her former home, rather than a cry of triumph at having arrived at the new one. She was relieved when Dick's brother Ernie, who had come to meet them at the station, greeted her quietly after a rowdy reunion with Dick. As the gig rattled over the dusty road to Dhurringile the brothers talked cheerfully of family and local news. Maggie was silent. She had been miserable enough on the voyage out and the parched flatness of the countryside did nothing to relieve her heavy mood. A knot of panic began to pull and tighten inside her.

She wanted to run to the horizon of that cheerless landscape and tumble over its edge into relief and escape. Instead she sat quietly on the hard seat, her fingers biting into her hands until deep red marks appeared on their hot and sweating palms. From the men's conversation she gathered that irrigation water would soon be available to more parcels of land. Well at least, she thought, it will be green and pleasant in summer in a few years' time. After all, she could have been much worse off. Many of the women with whom she had started out from England had married Canadians. Some of them were probably snowed in right now, feeling just as homesick and regretting their decisions as much as she was. She began to cheer up. Dick had assured her that it never snowed at Dhurringile so she would be able to get out and about even in winter.

By the time they reached Dick's parents' home she was feeling more composed and was prepared to fit in with her new life. One comforting thought was that her brother Harry had promised to pay her return fare back to England if she should find things too difficult. She would wait and see.

Dick's mother welcomed her warmly enough and his several younger brothers and sisters were anxious to meet the newest member of the family. The Wells' home was a rambling collection of rooms, which scarcely fitted together. Dick's block of land under the Soldier Settlement Scheme had been allocated and he had begun clearing it. Until they could organise a house they would stay with his family. Dick's mother ran the farm with the help of his three younger brothers and the four of his six sisters who were not yet married. Catherine Wells coped cheerfully with the endless chores and the worry of trying to raise the family on the meagre amount of money that was left after father Wells had distributed the larger part of his earnings to the local publicans and bookmakers. He was a building and labouring contractor, a tireless and competent worker, but quite irresponsible in supporting his family.

Dick, the eldest son, had left school at thirteen to help support the family. A few years later, in early 1914, he joined the Militia, like many young men of his time. Aged 19, he then decided to leave home for a new life of adventure. Travelling on horseback, he was in country New South Wales when war was declared so he immediately returned home to enlist in the Australian Imperial Force, or AIF. Since he was under age his mother wrote giving her permission for him to enlist. There must have been hundreds of parents who, at the time, wrote similar letters with great dread of what the future would hold. Dick duly enlisted and served in the Middle East then in France. His soldier's pay, sent home regularly during the war, helped keep the family fed and clothed.

Now, on that first night, as Maggie tried to sleep in their hot little room, she worried again over her situation. How foolish she had been to come so far from home with a man she scarcely knew. How strange and crude this country seemed after Brighton. She would write to her brother Harry tomorrow. The humiliation of going back would be small compared with the loneliness she would endure by staying. As she came to this decision, a long wailing cry from the fields echoed her loneliness. She started up in bed. There it was again, the cry of a child in distress.

'Dick! Dick! Wake up! There's a child out there!'

'What's that? What's going on?' Instantly he sat up in bed, frightened and confused. Like so many former soldiers his immediate response was to prepare for action.

'There's a child out there crying. Listen.' The cry came again quietly but clearly.

'It's alright, Maggie,' Dick said, relieved to find he was not in danger. 'That's just a curlew. It's a bird we have around these parts. You'll soon get used to them.'

As he patted her hand and settled back to sleep Maggie felt ashamed at her lack of thought in waking Dick. She should have remembered why he often cried out in his sleep, why he started at sudden noises and why he preferred to sleep with the kerosene night lamp softly shining. Would she ever become accustomed to these things? Perhaps she might, in time, but the curlew's plaintive cry had touched her heart and whenever she heard it afterwards it stirred her feelings of that first lonely night at Dhurringile.

Each day for the next few weeks, Dick and Maggie drove 3 kilometres to their own block in the gig. She had to admire his unfailing energy and enthusiasm as he cleared thistles, erected fences and prepared the land for irrigation, which would soon make it habitable and productive. It was a momentous day when a house arrived. With his unfailing inventiveness Dick had arranged for an old house to be brought the 13 kilometres from Murchison on a large sled-type arrangement towed by several horses. He saw the place as their livelihood with their home, sleek stock, a dairy, orchard and garden. It would be called, rather grandly, 'Cuthbert Hall' – encompassing both the Cuthbert Inn and Maggie's family name. But Maggie still looked on it as an alien place with no amenities, the misery of loneliness, and the heat, which even now, in the late autumn, she found extremely trying.

Some weeks later as they sat on a log one day, finishing their lunch in the winter sunshine, Dick took Maggie's hand as he explained to her some new scheme for the farm. She could not look at him, keeping her eyes caste down, watching some ants struggling in the dust.

'I'm sorry Dick, but I'm not staying,' she said at last.

'But Maggie, you're not going back to England. How can you? We have no money for the fare,' he argued. Still she kept her eyes down.

'Yes, I have Dick. You see before I left England my brother Harry promised me that if I didn't like it out here, then I should let him know and he would send the money for my fare home.'

He smiled as he asked, 'Yes, but there was a condition to that wasn't there.'

She had to admit that, yes, there was the condition that she should not be pregnant. Dick, true to form, had things well in hand.

'Well then, it's all settled,' he said, 'because you are pregnant aren't you?'

Maggie had to admit that, yes, she was.

'You see, Maggie, before we left England, your brother told me what he had said to you, so, of course, I made certain you would have to stay.'

Maggie, realising that she had been out-manoeuvered by experts, capitulated gracefully and stayed. It was an incident they recalled throughout their married life without rancour or regret.

Thus, the pattern was set for their married life. My father made the major decisions and my mother staunchly and loyally supported him. It was not in her nature to quibble but to accept with patience and good grace whatever he decided. This must have brought her many moments of anguish but, if it did, she never allowed it to show or linger and she remained unruffled through many difficult times. One of the first of many crises I was to cause her was the event of my birth.

Cuthbert Hall, Tatura, 2018.

The township of Tatura is about 20 kilometres west of Shepparton, 190 kilometres north-east of Melbourne, Victoria.

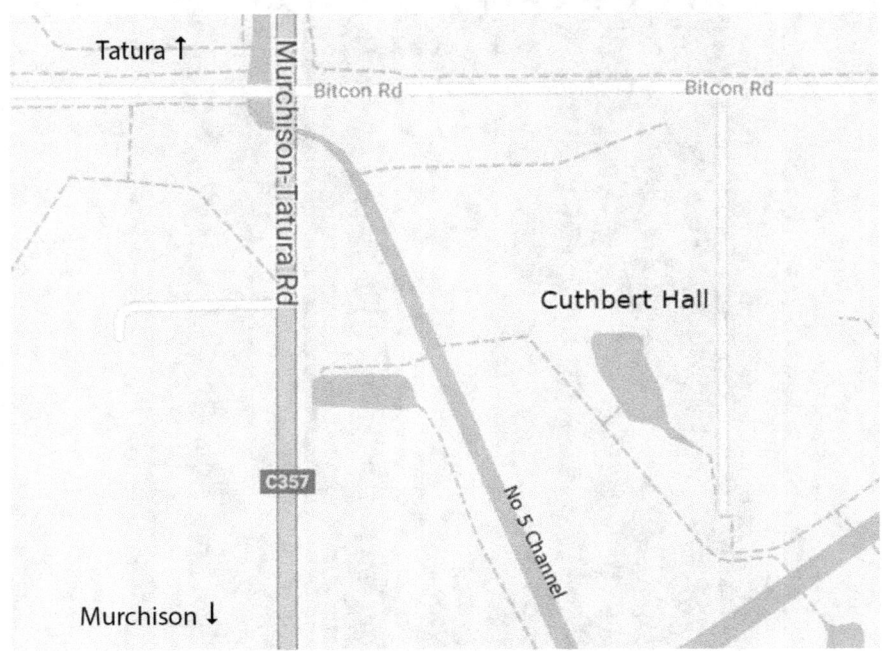

Wells' farm: Cuthbert Hall, Tatura.

CHAPTER 2

BIRTH, SCHOOL, EXPERIMENTS

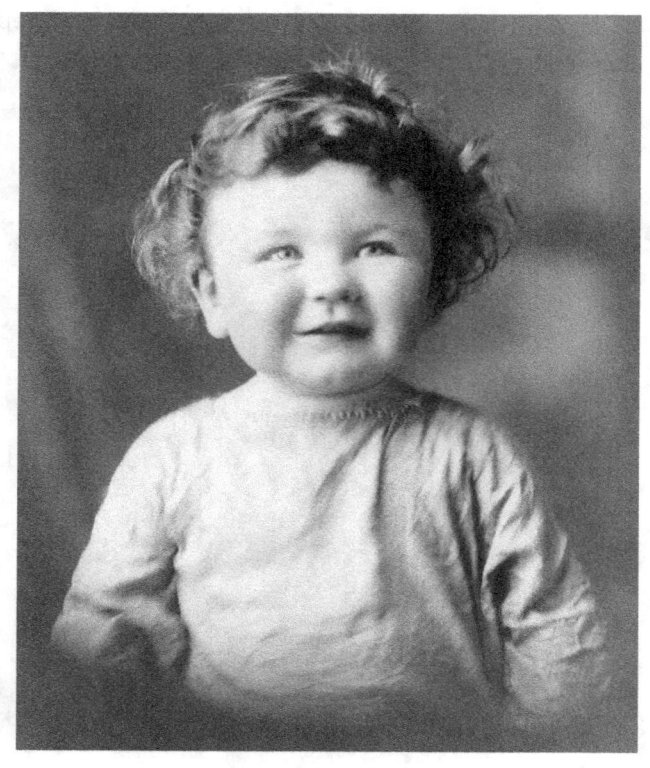

Rod Wells, early 1922.

Like many women of her time, my mother was unsure of the business of procreation and birth and, without the comfort of a mother or sister, was bewildered as to what lay ahead. Fortunately, Miss Virtue or Virtch, a friend who was a midwife, arrived from England at this time and was invited to attend the birth.

'I had little idea of what to expect,' my mother recalled. 'It was summer and the fruit was at its best. Apricots were my favourite. I enjoyed them because they were very sweet and plump, the best I had ever tasted, and I had eaten far too many. It was New Year's Eve and we were sitting in the evening cool on the veranda. Suddenly I felt a pain, but thinking it was caused by too many apricots, I said nothing. As the evening went on, the pains became more frequent and severe, so I mentioned it to Virtch.

"The baby must be on its way," she said. "It's time to go for the doctor."

I protested that it was just the apricots and there was no cause to call him yet. They wouldn't listen to me and your father set off in the horse and gig to alert the doctor. I was still convinced it was the apricots causing all the trouble, but the doctor confirmed it was more than apricots. You eventually arrived at six o'clock the next evening.'

The quiet way my mother used to tell this story belied the long and difficult time she had in labour. Many years later I learned that the doctor had had to stitch her internally without the use of an anaesthetic. During this procedure she bit through the flesh of her hands to prevent herself from screaming out and worrying my father.

Such was my arrival into the world on the first day of a new year, 1 January 1920. I was eventually christened Roderick Graham Wells. According to family legend, my father used to recite a poem about Roderick, or Red Erik – an apt name, as my hair eventually turned into a deep red colour. The guardian angel in attendance at my birth must now be even more grey and old than I am. Had he known what a hectic time lay ahead, I doubt he would have taken on the job. But perhaps he could see the course my life was to follow and that I would need the utmost of his strength and vigilance. I am very thankful that he decided to stay.

The township of Tatura presents itself boldly about 20 kilometres west of Shepparton in the Goulburn Valley district of Victoria. However, in that flat landscape it has no alternative but to present itself boldly – there is not one hill to provide shelter from the June frosts, no river to bring relief from the scorching summers, not even a creek bed where the town could tuck itself away from the dusty winds that blow from the north. Irrigation came to the district in the mid-1880s and the township, established in 1873/74, grew quickly.

Irish settlers built the first church and renamed the main thoroughfare, formerly Goulburn Street, after their principal benefactor, Thomas Hogan. William, Albert, Thomson, and Casey soon followed, along with Ross, Fraser, O'Toole, Walshe, Brown and Wilson. After World War I, the Victory Hall was erected in Hogan Street and in 1921 my father became first secretary of the Tatura branch of The Returned Sailors and Soldiers Imperial League of Australia, and now known as simply The Returned Services League or RSL.

Our property had previously been part of the Winter-Irving family's Dhurringile Estate, about 6 or 7 kilometres to the south of Tatura on the corner of Bitcon and Murchison Roads and allocated after World War I as soldier settlement blocks. The southern boundary of our farm bordered the home paddocks of Dhurringile Mansion. The block Dad was assigned was completely undeveloped and there was much work to be done. He had to clear the ground of endless thistles, erect out-buildings, a dairy, house and fences and prepare the land for irrigation.

If I have any ability as an engineer, it is because my father was a naturally gifted builder, able to tackle everything from plumbing to bricklaying. He carried in his head the dimensions of his various projects, the positions and sizes of doors, windows and pipes in the house and sheds, the quantities of wire, nails, timber and concrete down to the last centimetre. At 13 years of age he had been forced

Rod, Maggie, Madge and Dick Wells.

to leave school to help out with family finances. A year or two afterwards, the shire engineer, noting his quick brain and practical ability, had offered to pay for his education to enable him to become an engineer, but his father, suspicious of education and with an eye to the more immediate prospect of his son earning some money, refused permission. My father's talents were certainly not wasted, and like many of his generation who did not have the opportunity of an advanced education, made good without it. Every job that he tackled was done thoroughly and was built to last.

In the 1950s, when I was home at the farm, he suggested that I should see a new property he had bought and the house that was being built.

'Where are the house plans?' I asked.

He pulled an old envelope from his pocket with rough pencil drawings on the back.

'You mean that's all you've got?'

'Yes, I just go along each day and tell the builder what's to be done and then check it that night. Work's well so far.'

When I visited the new place and spoke to the bricklayer he was quite incredulous at Dad's supervision.

'It's all in his head,' he said. 'He tells me how many bricks long, how many rows high and where to leave spaces for doors and windows and pipes. So far he hasn't been wrong. I've never seen anything like it.'

'It's no good doing a thing unless you do it properly,' Dad would say, hammering a nail into another solid project. One of my earliest memories was when a travelling salesman called to see him.

'Good day, Mrs Wells, is Dick about?'

I peeped from behind my mother's skirt as she replied.

'You should have seen him on the way in. He's up at the gate digging a new post hole.'

The salesman pushed back his hat, scratching his head.

'That's strange, I didn't see him there. I'll go back and have a look.'

'Mum, can I go too?'

'Yes, and tell your father his dinner's ready when he's finished.'

We walked off along the track that ran about 200 metres from the house to the road. As we approached an enormous hole we heard singing, accompanied by the rhythmic sound of the regular rise and fall of a shovel.

'Are you down there, Dick?'

'Yes, I'm coming up now,' and he emerged from the hole which eclipsed him in height and girth. The stout red gum post, which he subsequently erected, still stood some 60 years later.

Dad was one of ten children and his brothers and sisters were scattered around the district. His mother Katherine Thompson's family had come from the village of Killybegs in County Donegal, Ireland, and her life was a constant struggle to keep the family fed and clothed. Dad's father, John George Wells, although a hard worker, spent most of his wages on drink and gambling. Dad escaped this life; I think he was naturally quick witted, and the discipline and experiences in the Great War gave him the impetus to make something of his life.

The Thompson grand uncles were an interesting lot. John, a water bailiff, warded off quinsy and other ailments with a large red spotted handkerchief tied around his throat. Instead of a pocket watch he used a small alarm clock carefully wrapped in an old singlet and stored in his coat pocket.

'What's the time please, Uncle John?' I would ask.

Extracting the clock from his pocket he would solemnly unwrap it.

'Half-past-eleven, young man,' he would reply, before carefully re-wrapping the clock and restoring to his pocket.

About 10 minutes later, after a whispered argument outside with my sister Madge, who was two years younger than me – 'It's your turn Rod' – 'No it isn't, I asked him last time' – Madge would ask him the time and the entire process was repeated. It was not until he had done this three or four times that he would realise we were asking the time purely for the entertainment of seeing the clock being wrapped and unwrapped and send us on our way.

However, he never tired of displaying his skill of spitting accurately into the fire.

'See that big coal at the back,' we would say, sitting before his open hearth. 'See if you can hit that,' and, to our intense and never-ending delight, he would oblige with his usual accuracy.

Dad's brothers also had their uses. I would have been about seven or eight when I was out with Uncle Ernie one day. As we passed a paddock, not for the first time, I noticed our bull behaving in a very strange way. When I had questioned my mother about this I was usually given a vague reply. But Uncle Ernie was made of sterner stuff and gave a crude but more enlightening description of reproduction as practised by cows, sheep, dogs, and humans. He added that my own appendage was for the same purpose, suggesting that one day I would be similarly occupied, 'only not necessarily standing up.' I was absolutely fascinated, if somewhat incredulous, to think that I would ever wish to behave like the bull.

As always, I was anxious to share my knowledge. At the tea table that night I repeated my conversation with Uncle Ernie. Mum was flustered and made embarrassed remarks to Dad about 'that dreadful brother of yours.' Dad made strange choking sounds and rushed from the table. Madge stared in open-mouthed wonder at such colourful information.

Many people would probably consider that our life on the farm was hard but, if it were, we certainly did not consider it to be any harder than that of most of the other farmers in the area. My father was a stern disciplinarian but, being of a hot tempered, argumentative and teasing nature, I probably needed a strong hand to keep me in order. Most of my early outbursts of temper came from striving to be a perfectionist and from frustration that I lacked the skills and patience to carry out experiments and projects perfectly at first try.

From an early age, I was expected to help with chores around the farm; feeding the chooks, gathering kindling sticks and later bringing in the cows for milking. Dad's discipline was stern but fair; he was a fairly hard taskmaster, but the self-discipline I learned from him stood me in good stead later in life. I inherited many of his characteristics and he instilled in us all the values of self-reliance and duty. He insisted that I be practical, resourceful and thrifty. I should be curious to find out how things worked and then make them for myself. He advised me not to expect too much help from others; when I did a job, I should do it thoroughly, preferably at the first attempt. He encouraged me to be enthusiastic and not do things by halves. Loyalty to King and country and unwavering self-discipline were prized but, above all else, never, ever give up.

I am not sure where my hot-headedness came from; certainly not from my mother who was always placid and gentle. Affectionate, gracious and uncomplaining, she was probably a product of her English Victorian and Edwardian upbringing and a little innocent about the ways of the world. Both my parents had a good sense of fun and our house was often filled with neighbours for social evenings, cards and sing-a-longs. Dad loved a party and was a great practical joker. Despite his short, overweight build, he was immensely strong and his favourite party trick was to remove the crown seal from a bottle of beer between his thumb and forefinger while holding it at arm's length.

Like my mother, there were several English women in the district who had married Australian soldiers and travelled as war brides to this remote country, to unknown families and a strange new way of life. A family named With lived near us. Mum became very friendly with Mrs With, and her son Tom and I soon became firm friends. It is unfortunate that many of the soldier settlers were not suited to agriculture. They had no experience of running a farm, let alone knowing how to go about starting one from scratch. On top of this, often their health was poor and finances were a constant source of worry. Unfortunately Tom's father was among this group, and when he died as a result of a piece of shrapnel being left in his body, Mrs With and Tom were left pretty much destitute. Dad helped sort out the business side to enable them to leave the farm and then organised fund-raising events to help pay their fare home to England.

Madge and Rod Wells, 1928.

Like many English women, Mum considered the state primary school was too rough for her children, so we were sent to Tatura Convent. For the first few years I travelled to school with our neighbour's children, with the eldest girl, Kitty Kerrins, placed in charge of their horse and jinker as well as her various brothers and sisters. However, by the time I was 9 years old, it was my responsibility to take my sister Madge to school. Every morning I would catch our pony, Codger, harness and hitch her to the jinker. Once at school, I unhitched her, making sure that her nosebag was in place, before leaving her under the peppercorn trees with the other ponies.

The convent school was run by the Sisters of Mercy, though after some years under their care and discipline it was obvious that they were quite inappropriately named. All of the classes were held in one room, then seemingly vast, now when revisited not at all intimidating. The younger students were in one corner, the older

Convent of Mercy, Tatura, now St Mary's College Hall, 2010. Boarders were upstairs; the school room below.

primary students were in another, while the secondary students up to Leaving Certificate standard fitted into the rest of the space. At the time it did not seem congested or confusing, but it must have presented the nuns with many difficulties and no doubt contributed to their regular canings and outbursts. Since most country schools were one-room, one-teacher, the situation at the convent was not unusual, and many children of my generation received an excellent education under similar conditions.

The nuns gave a sound education to Form 5, or Leaving Certificate level. They looked after my formal schooling, but if I pass over this rather briefly it is not because I did not enjoy school, but because my main interests lay outside the classroom. The things I did in class remain rather vague; I was no better or worse than most students and survived the usual reprimands, punishments, praise and fights. By the time I reached Form 4, the nuns were unable to help me much with science and maths subjects: their talents ran more to English, History and Geography. I think they were at a loss to understand my constant quest for facts and figures. As for a science laboratory, that was totally non-existent.

However, they didn't mind profiting from my talents on fund-raising days. One of my contributions was to put a silver two-shilling piece in a metal bucket of water, through which I ran a low electrical current. Customers paid a penny to see if they could retrieve the coin. The small shock they received deterred most people and we made a good profit, much to the nuns' satisfaction.

If hours spent in class remain misty, time spent outside school is etched clearly in my mind. I must have been about 9 years old when I built my first crystal set, and from that time onwards I became addicted to the science of radio.

The 1920s were exciting times. Although the charm of horse-drawn vehicles remained, motor cars were becoming more common, and communication was gradually speeding up. The latest wonder was the science of sound waves. Telephones, radio-telephones and wireless sets suddenly transported people from the hum-drum existence of their homes into the magic world of instant contact. The 1920s saw the birth of a new science and the beginnings of a powerful industry – communications.

I was greatly excited by these developments. Determined to be part of them, I decided to learn as much about radio as possible. A children's magazine to which I subscribed had simple scientific experiments, which I enthusiastically carried out and was supremely happy from dawn to dusk. The farm, with its paddocks, dams, channels and sheds, provided the perfect laboratory.

One of my earliest experiments was to make a pressurised diving suit. I found an old 15-litre kerosene tin, cut out small segments to fit over my shoulders and a small piece out of one side, over which I fixed a piece of glass with putty as an observation hole. As the launching was to take place in our very muddy dam this was a needless refinement. From my scout belt I suspended several large rocks on pieces of string along with my scout knife. The idea was that the rocks would help my descent and the knife would be used to cut them free when I needed to rise to the surface. My friend and neighbour, Jack McIntyre, was coerced into manning the car tyre pump, attached to some long pieces of old dairy tubing, to supply air to this advanced piece of equipment.

One sunny afternoon, we were ready to test the wonderful contraption. I waded into the dam in swimming trunks and an old shirt. I had padded the sharp edges of the tin with rags to stop it cutting my shoulders, checked that the scout belt was secure, the knife at the ready and the tubing firmly attached at both ends.

'Now don't forget to keep pumping as hard as you can,' I reminded Jack as I squelched through the mud.

'Don't worry Rod, I'll keep her going alright.'

The water rose to my armpits. I waded on until it was above my chin, then right over my head. I couldn't see a thing through the glass, and my nose, mouth, eyes and ears were rapidly filling with water. No doubt Jack was pumping manfully but it was a losing battle. I grabbed for the knife but, in my panic, I couldn't find it.

'Keep calm,' I told myself, 'you know it's there. Start walking backwards to shallow water and keep trying for the knife.'

At last I found it, cut the rocks loose and by that time my head was above water.

'Gee, you didn't stay under for long, Rod,' Jack commented.

'Well, I nearly stayed under for good. I don't think it worked very well.'

Looking back, I was not in much danger as the dam was not very deep, but it had given me a considerable fright. I would have to think out my experiments more carefully in future.

One of my earliest experiments, which I am sure is still demonstrated on the first day of the first term of Form 1 science, was to make oxygen. After carefully rigging up some simple apparatus in my bedroom, I heated the ingredients and passed the gas through water until I was sure that I had a test tube full of oxygen. Ready to prove it, I raced to the kitchen where Dad was comfortably smoking his pipe and reading the paper.

'Look Dad. I've made some oxygen!'

Before he could respond I had inverted the test tube over the bowl of his pipe. Immediately the tobacco erupted into flame. Sparks and ash flew over his face and hair, while the paper caught fire. At first, he was quite angry but eventually saw the funny side of it and just cautioned me to be more careful with my experiments in future. Years later, I realised that the explosion had triggered memories of his time in the trenches. It was also one of the first of many times that my family ruefully and patiently suffered the results of my experiments.

My interest in radio came when I made a crystal set and, using a cat's whisker detector, managed to receive a signal. It is hard to say what fascinated me so much about the science of sound waves.

Firstly, its logic appealed to me. It was a new and developing science, covering a wide range of other subjects – mathematics, physics, magnetism and chemistry. With its increasing scope and sophistication, its range for communications seemed endless. Because of my father's wartime experiences in Egypt and France, and my mother's family in England, my world extended beyond the farm fences. To receive radio programs, telegrams and telephone calls heightened my anticipation that something exciting could happen at any moment.

From quite a young age, using my bedroom for sleeping became secondary to its use as a laboratory. Most indoor experiments were fairly harmless to my way of thinking but my room was constantly full of fumes, the walls blotched with chemicals or smoke, the bedspread pocked with acid burns and, on one spectacular occasion, the brass on my bedstead was tarnished with nitric acid fumes. Photography was another hobby that I took up, developing the photos myself.

My idol at this time was the Tatura postmaster, Mr Ray Dudley. It was my job to collect our mail after school. I always hoped that, when I called, the postmaster would be wearing his headset and taking down Morse code from incoming telegrams.

'Just a moment young man,' he would say. 'There's a telegram coming through for your father.'

Then, while directing his staff, keeping an eye on customers, and sorting mail with one hand, he would take down the message with his free hand, never hesitating as the pips came through on his headphones. When I plucked up enough courage to ask if I could listen, I was left breathless at the rate at which the messages came through; it made me determined to practice my Morse code.

When it was my turn to be served at the post office, Mr Dudley would walk over to the pigeon holes and extract the 'W' mail. He would return to the counter, sort the Wells letters from the pile in a flash and return the remainder to the compartment. This operation intrigued me. His hands sorted the mail so quickly it was like watching a magician. My intrigue turned to admiration when I noticed that, while sorting the mail, he invariably had an ear tuned into a Morse sounder. More surprisingly he would go over to a table on which a machine stood and from there produce a telegram. One day, while he was sorting the mail, I noticed that the sounder held his attention, but he continued with the sorting and asked me to wait. Walking over to his table, he wrote down a telegram, sealed it in an envelope, and told me to give it to my father, not my mother, when I arrived home. This I did; the telegram contained the news that my mother's sister in England had died.

Curiosity soon gave me the courage to ask if I could see the equipment at close hand. I was in heaven. Mr Dudley would sort the mail and while doing so remember a long telegram word for word at a speed of about 30 words a minute then, at a convenient time, accurately commit it to paper. No tape or other record of the incoming messages was made. He also had to recognise the call sign for Tatura telegrams from the constant 'click, clickety, click' of messages meant for other post offices. Later I learned that the country telegraph systems, and no doubt the city ones too, consisted of a sounder and Morse key connected in a series at each post office through several towns as a single wire loop. In our area, the loop was completed in Bendigo. Each station, in this case Tatura post office, was looped out with a switch across the Morse key so that the sounders of the other stations on the loop could operate. Of course, only one message at a time was sent. People wrote more letters in those days and telegrams were mainly for urgent matters. The sounders clicked away all day in every post office, although mostly the messages were for other places.

It was Mr Dudley's ability that inspired me to become a telegraphist. One of my biggest thrills was to sit for the Boy Scouts telegraphists badge. The test was conducted on the Bendigo loop, in no less a place than at Mr Dudley's table at the post office one Saturday afternoon. To be able to send and receive a proper telegram by myself, no doubt agreed to by Mr Dudley and the other stations on the loop, was a memorable occasion.

I later found out that Ray Dudley had enlisted at the age of 17 in World War I, and served in France under 2nd Australian Division Signals Company. The Officer Commanding was Stan Watson, whom I came to know when I joined the 2nd AIF and was posted to the Royal Australian Corps of Signals. My interest in telegraphy was partially responsible for the posting, and I appreciate the influence that Ray Dudley had on the direction of my life.

To complete my wireless badge, I presented myself to Dr H Lyell Andrews, another of my early mentors, who helped me fully understand 'anode bend' detection aerials, rectifiers and the like with graphic and mathematical explanations. Dr Andrews, a medical practitioner, was a keen constructor and operator of amateur radio equipment. After my father, he was the person who has had the most profound influence on me. Having no children of his own, he helped me to explore the world of science, as he was also an expert in advanced chemistry and physics. We spent hours poring over science magazines, medical journals and catalogues. Often I would ride my bike the 16 kilometres to Murchison where, under his direction at first and then by my own efforts, I carried out many experiments and projects. He tutored me in physics, chemistry, mathematics and astronomy and also allowed me to help with pathology tests.

'Come on lad,' he would say. 'Here's a sample of Mrs ...'s urine. We're going to see if there is any sugar in it.'

He showed me how to accurately measure and mix the two Fehling's solutions, add the specimen and then gently heat the test tube, noting the colour changes. The centrifuge was another piece of equipment I was allowed to use, spinning samples of blood then helping him to conduct the various tests. When it came time for my tonsils to be removed, we conducted the operation under the guise of a scientific experiment. Each Saturday afternoon, for about six weeks, I rode my bike to the surgery at Murchison, where the offending tonsils, alternating left and right, were coated with an anaesthetic paint and then zapped with a wonderful new piece of equipment that Dr Andrews had acquired from America – a diathermy machine. But the thing that appealed most to me about Dr Andrews was his passion for radio; he could see its potential. One of my earliest joys was to build crystal sets, a wireless and even a rudimentary two-way radio. Lyell Andrews must have been one of the first doctors to enjoy the benefits of a mobile radio when he installed one in his car in the early 1930s.

Jock Stark, another person who influenced my future, was the local radio repairman. He happily allowed me to spend many hours at his work table, which I worshipped as a mysterious blinking, crackling, wire-enshrouded, valve-cluttered shrine. Sorting and identifying various parts of the radios, learning how to mend them and, importantly, learning how to use a soldering iron, were skills that Jock not only taught me but served me well throughout my life. Jock later enlisted in the RAAF in South-east Asia as a radio operator.

One of the more ambitious projects I tackled was to build a short-wave radio receiver. This was inspired not only by my interest in radio but by the fact that my mother's family was in England. If we had a short-wave receiver, we could tune into the BBC broadcasts. Dr Andrews encouraged me in this but I did all of the calculations and construction by myself. I would have been about 14 years old.

Although my father did not exactly foster my interests in chemistry and physics, he always encouraged me to be practical and it was during the building of this short-wave receiver that I realised how inventive he was. I had assembled most of the equipment required but I needed a dozen insulators and asked him for sixpence to buy them.

'Sixpence! I can't afford sixpence just like that!'

'I want to buy a dozen insulators for the short-wave receiver, and they are a halfpenny each.'

'What are they like?'

'Well, they are made of thick china with wire coiled around,' I explained.

He thought for a moment. 'I can't give you sixpence. Things are so bad with the depression; we have to save every penny. But I think I can show you how to make them.'

I was rather dubious about this but at his insistence we went down to the dam and fished out some old bottles from its boggy edges.

'Now I'll show you how to cut off the necks.'

I watched, fascinated, as he placed a piece of wire in the kitchen fire. When it was red hot he held each end with a piece of rag and carefully drew it through the neck of a bottle, severing it neatly.

'There you are. Now you can coil the wire around it and make the insulator. You must learn to make everything you need whenever you possibly can. It's the best way to learn how things work.' And with that piece of advice he left me to deal with the rest of the bottles.

After some weeks of planning, designing and assembling, I was ready to test the set one Sunday afternoon. Mum, Dad and Madge had decided to pay a call but I wanted to stay home. All I needed to complete the project was a valve, so I decided to 'borrow' one from our radio set. The house was enveloped in the hush of a Sunday afternoon. Only the crackle of the receiver disturbed the peace as I twisted the knob searching for a signal. It must work, I thought; I've checked the valves and wiring several times and everything is connected and soldered correctly.

Then I heard it.

BONG! BONG! BONG! 'This is the BBC and here is the news.'

It was Big Ben. 17,000 kilometres away and I heard it more quickly and just as clearly as if I had been right there in London. I shall never forget the excitement of my first taste of the wonders of short-wave radio. Even now I marvel at being able to pick up a radio signal from remote parts using only the atmosphere as a transmitting medium. When the family returned, I launched enthusiastically into an account of the results of my project.

'Are you sure it was the BBC?' my father asked.

'Gosh, yes, Dad. Let's try again.' I tuned in again and we spent some time listening to the BBC.

'Well you've certainly managed that quite well,' my father said at last. He tried to sound casual but I know that he was as excited as I, and really rather proud of my achievement. But it was not in his nature to praise me too much. After all, he mustn't give the boy a swollen head. He was only 14 and too full of confidence. Just keep him in his place for a while yet. Of all the exciting work and projects I became involved in over my lifetime, I still count this as the most thrilling and rewarding.

Another practical project I set up was a simple 12-volt lighting system for the house, which was a short distance from the milking shed. This involved installing a Vauxhall generator, modified to operate from the engine of the milking machine, which I had already connected to an old car engine to charge batteries for night use. Another innovation was to rig up a small engine to drive the grinding stones to make flour from our wheat. Anything and everything that could be modified, invented or improved was a source of inspiration to me.

It would have been at about this time that I built a radio transmitter. It was very powerful and used 10 watts of power. I used it to send messages to my friend Jack McIntyre, who lived 800 metres away on the south-west corner of the cross roads. Because the signal was so broad, it interfered with all other radio reception in a radius of about eight kilometres.

The most important event of a farmer's working day was to tune in to the weather report on the evening news and it was invariably at this time that I called Jack to discuss homework, Scouts or some other important matter. Instead of the news, all that could be heard on radios for kilometres around was an offending crackle. My father had warned me about this and told me to dismantle the set but I conveniently 'forgot' and continued to transmit messages to Jack. However, Dad never wasted his breath on threats or shouting. His way was subtle and far more effective.

'By the way Maggie,' he said idly one evening, glancing over the top of *The Weekly Times*, 'I saw a couple of strange men in town today. Great big fellows they were too.'

'Oh! Who were they?' my mother asked, not even looking up from her darning.

'They tell me they are inspectors from the post office. I should think they're looking for the person who is causing all of this interference on the wireless.'

I pricked up my ears while pretending to be absorbed in my homework.

'Do you think they'll find him?' she asked.

'Well they are usually very good at tracking down that sort of thing. They have special equipment you know. I wouldn't like to be the culprit. It's a £500 fine. Probably a spell in gaol too,' he added.

My stomach churned. A £500 fine. At my present rate of pocket money, I would be an old man before even the first £100 was paid off. When my homework was finished, I slipped into my bedroom and sadly began dismantling the transmitter.

Astronomy became another of my interests; the clear night skies around the farm were perfect for viewing stars and planets through my father's binoculars. I also ground down a watch glass to make a rudimentary microscope, spending many hours examining insects, leaves, flowers, frogs, water from the tanks and dams or anything else that I thought would be of interest.

As well as being interested in the physics of radio, I enjoyed the thrills of chemistry. My experiments covered a wide range, their frequency depending on the amount of money I could save to buy the chemicals and apparatus. One of my boyhood idols was Miss Quinn, who owned the chemist shop in Tatura. My days at school were not always spent entirely in the school grounds. From the age of about 13, during the mid-day break I would frequently run the few hundred yards up Hogan Street to the chemist shop. None of the mysteries of the chemist's art was revealed by the dignified façade, whose immaculate brass surrounding the window, in which bulbous glass carboys filled with coloured water were on display, gave an air of distinction to the establishment. On pushing open the door, the hushed atmosphere promoted a feeling of discretion and authority, which was embodied in Miss Quinn as she came forward to deal with prescriptions, minor ailments, and a host of other problems. On the highly polished counter, bottles of Evening in Paris perfume and containers of Cashmere Bouquet face powder were flanked by hot water bottles and a box of knobbly bath sponges. Sliding wooden doors on the shelves behind the counter hid most of the items but an occasional glass cabinet displayed invalid cups, Sloan's liniment, Balsam of Horehound, tightly rolled bandages, fragrant ovals of Morny bath soap, Warm's Wonder Wool and boxes of antiphlogistine poultice.

It took me almost a year of expeditions to Miss Quinn's to buy chemicals, test tubes and litmus paper before I squeezed up the courage to ask if I could see into the dispensary. What a thrill for a budding scientist – an Aladdin's cave of chemicals and such excitement to see the large brass scales and the more delicate beam balance in its glass case. What potent drugs lay in the rows of drawers each beautifully labelled in gold leaf with a mirrored glass knob? Gum Asafoetida, Cinchona Bark, Myrrh, Buchu Leaves, Quassia Chips, Senna Pods and Black Sulphur. Maroon coloured earthenware pots of various sizes contained ointments, plasters, powders and pills. Tincture presses, infusion pots, mortars and pestles of all sizes, demi-johns of cough mixtures, liniment and tonics jostled for place amongst the ointment slabs, chrome suppository moulds, sieves and funnels.

Miss Quinn with her dark, good looks became my idol as she compounded mixtures with the mortar and pestle, deftly cut out pills and rounded them on the pill machine, and produced an endless array of tinctures and infusions, syrups and extracts to be used in the mixtures and ointments. Miss Quinn encouraged my interest in chemistry and eventually allowed me to help make up some of the solutions. Parrish's Syrup was an iron tonic fed to anaemic children until their cheeks showed a healthier colour. To make it, I obtained iron filings from Pyke's Garage. These were carefully washed and cleaned with alcohol, then weighed and added to phosphoric acid to make ferrous phosphate. This, in turn, was made into a syrup. Miss Quinn must have dispensed gallons of Parrish's Syrup, much to the disgust of its recipients. Even now I can taste the lingering metallic flavour barely disguised by the syrup base. I was also allowed to manufacture Fehling's solution, used as a test for diabetes.

It was while browsing through a chemistry book one day that I came across the formula and method for making nitroglycerine and immediately decided that I must make some. The basic ingredients were concentrated nitric acid and glycerine, both readily available from Miss Quinn, though purchased on separate occasions in case she should realise the ultimate purpose. The main difficulty with the manufacture of nitroglycerine was that it had to be made without a trace of impurity, otherwise it would explode spontaneously, especially on percussion. I decided that, in the event of an explosion, the fowl house and its occupants were more expendable than our house and my family. So the nitroglycerine was manufactured there, with practical help from Laurie Diamond – the manager of the Commercial Bank's son – and the uncritical supervision of some nesting hens. The dirt and feathers in the fowl house, not to mention an occasional demented hen, added difficulties to the project, but we finally managed to produce a sauce bottle full of the stuff.

On a Saturday morning, Laurie rode his bike out from Tatura for the testing. Laurie was a tireless holder of test tubes, an adept passer of tools and an enthusiastic supporter when I became gloomy over some project. Laurie's father, Mr Diamond, was a tall, overweight figure, a florid, puffing testimony to his love of good food and drink. By contrast, Laurie's long, thin frame looked as though it received less than its adequate share of nourishment.

'Do you think it will work, Rod?' Laurie asked anxiously.

The sun, piercing through the holes in the iron roof, made his black hair gleam. He had recently started to use Californian Poppy Brilliantine and its strong scent overpowered even the smell of the fowl house.

'Well, it should. We've spent a lot of time on it. But I'm a bit disappointed. It doesn't look very dangerous. It's just like heavy water, it can't be all that terrible.'

'Aren't you going to try it out?'

'Yes, I'd like to, but I'm wondering where the best place would be.'

'What about the channel bank?'

'No, that's too close to the house. If it does work it might block up the channel and Dad would kill me.'

'You'll think of something Rod, you always do.' Laurie's faith in my ability to carry out our schemes always cheered me up; the hens clucked encouragement while I thought.

'I know,' I said after a minute or two. 'Let's go out to Waranga.'

'Gee, yes, that's a good idea. We could take some lunch with us.'

'Alright, I'll ask Mum for some sandwiches. But don't tell anyone where we're going.'

When I asked my mother for some sandwiches she asked where we going.

'Laurie and I thought we might go rabbiting,' I replied.

'Well you be careful,' she said, 'and make sure you're back by 6 o'clock for tea.'

The white lie bothered my conscience, but I settled it by rationalising that even my placid mother would panic at the mention of explosives. It would save her needless worry if she thought we were rabbiting. Waranga Basin, some 14 kilometres south-west of Tatura, is a storage area for the Waranga-Mallee Irrigation Scheme. My grandfather, John Wells, had been one of the contractors when it was excavated in the early part of the 20th century. His teams of horses and men had scooped and banked the clay helping to form the wall around the lower part of the basin. Grandpa Wells was a skilful carpenter, builder and odd job man. The most vivid memory I have of him is nailing floor boards to our house. With the nails in his left hand, he worked swiftly along the floor accurately placing each nail with one swift blow from the hammer. The work would proceed smoothly until a nail, which happened to be the wrong way up, would become embedded by its head, causing Grandpa to bellow out words quite new to my ears.

I thought of these things as we pedalled along the dirt road. During the building of the basin, several quarries had been excavated and, as we headed towards them, puffs of dust rose as we bounced over the potholes. The sauce bottle with the nitroglycerine also bounced along, suspended in a basket, which I had tied onto the handlebars of my bike.

'Isn't it a bit dangerous if it gets a knock?' Laurie asked.

'No, it won't explode by percussion unless it's impure,' I explained with renewed confidence. After all, a scientist whose technique has been faultless should have no doubts even if his laboratory was a bit unconventional. 'We need a detonator though. I've brought some string for that.'

Two or three crows jeered our arrival at the quarry, otherwise the world left us to ourselves. We tackled our lunches first, leaning against the rough trunk of a drooping gum. Mum's cooking was of the plain but nourishing variety and we ate in silence. It was very hot and only the ants breached the stillness carrying off our crumbs as they dropped.

'Where do you reckon we'll put it Rod?' Laurie's voice roused me. I had been mulling over the same question.

'We could try the crevice by that rock over there. Let's see if some water will stay in it first.' We splashed some water from a bottle into a crevice that had formed between a rock and a hard-baked mound of earth. The water held perfectly, seeping away very slowly into the hard soil. I carefully carried the sauce bottle to the spot.

'Be careful.' Laurie was not sure now whether to be enthusiastic or terrified. Making nitroglycerine was one thing but testing suddenly became a serious business. If anything went wrong our fathers would finish off those parts of us which the explosion left untouched.

'Of course I'll be careful,' I said, cautiously pouring the nitroglycerine into the crevice. 'Here, pass me that string.'

'What's on it?'

'I wet it and rolled it in gunpowder. Put one end in the hole and we'll ram some earth on top of it.' We gathered up some lumps of clay, pounding them to close the crevice.

'Trail the string out over here, Laurie.'

'Don't you think we'd better get out of the way?'

'Yes, I suppose so. We'll light the string and then run over near our bikes.'

Laurie struck a match. The string fizzed and hissed as we raced off to crouch behind the cover of the bikes, about 200 metres away.

'It's probably a dud,' I said, trying to sound modest. The flame on the string inched towards the crevice. 'Still, it was worth …'

The crescendo of a terrifying bang swept up the rest of my words. Tonnes of earth and rock shot into the sky, danced about and then plummeted down in cascades of debris, splitting apart as they bounced off the ground. My head thumped and popped; I pressed my hands to my ears and shielded my head in my arms on the ground. A few seconds later there was silence. It was more sickening than the noise. Laurie's fingernails bit into my arm. I looked up.

'Oh my God,' he whispered. 'What have we done? Our fathers will kill us. We'd better scram before someone comes.'

Laurie's face was white and my hands shook as we snatched up our things and fled for home. I looked back over my shoulder at the devastation. We must have moved about 10 tonnes of earth. For a kilometre or two we pedalled furiously and then by tacit consent flopped on the grass at the side of the road. Laurie was panting. My chest was scorching and I wiped the sweat from my face with the back of my hand.

'My gosh, Rod, it sure worked,' he gasped.

'Yes, it sure did. But if anyone ever finds out, we've had it. You've got to spit your death.'

We mustered up what little spit we had left and swore to die if either of us ever told about the episode.

'Gee, we're lucky it didn't explode on the bike. We'd have both been dead – especially you.' Laurie said gloomily. I was much too aware of our escape to reply. My knees wobbled and I felt sick in the stomach, as picking up our bikes, we rode silently home.

'Did you get any rabbits?' Mum asked when I arrived home.

'No … we saw a couple, but missed them.'

News of the unscheduled explosion spread through the district with the same force and rapidity as the explosion itself. Little groups of farmers gathered in Hogan Street, speculating with authority as to the motives and identity of the culprits. Two or three nights later we were having tea in the kitchen when my father looked up from his meal.

'Oh, by the way Maggie, I saw a couple of new policemen in town today,' he remarked in a loud voice. 'Great big chaps they were, too.'

'Fancy that. What were they doing?' my mother asked.

'I hear they are looking for those fellows who blew the hole in the quarry out at the Basin.' He paused eating his soup, the spoon marking time between the bowl and his mouth, his eyes looking at me sternly. My mother put the question I dared not ask.

'Do you think they'll catch them?'

'Most probably, these Melbourne policemen are very good you know.'

'What would they do to them if they caught them?' I asked, trying to appear casual.

'Probably hang them. I certainly wouldn't like to be in their shoes. Yes, it would definitely be a hanging for that sort of crime. I'm glad it's no-one in our family,' he added, giving me another stern look.

I suddenly displayed great interest in my soup, silently praying that Laurie would keep our oath. Through my own attention to detail I had escaped being killed by the nitroglycerine. But my father's wrath, combined with the persistence of the police force, would leave me no hope if a word were breathed about the incident. I'd better behave myself, I thought. I want to live to do some more experiments. I'd better lie low for a while.

CHAPTER 3

A SCIENTIST'S LIFE

Rod Wells' schooldays, 1930s (Rod: back row, 2nd right).

Our farming community at Durringhile was close knit and our nearest neighbours were the McIntyres and the Kerrins. Jack Kerrins, an irascible Irishman, farmed on the north-east corner of the cross road in a rather haphazard way. His farm was called 'Shamrock Vent', which rather puzzled me, and he loved abusing his neighbours, especially my father.

'Damn Proddy bastard, spying Freemasons,' Jack would storm at my father after some perceived slight.

But my father, knowing Jack's ways, would merely laugh. However, when it was time for the doctor to be called out for yet another of Mrs Kerrins' confinements, and she had ten altogether, Jack's bigotry was quickly forgotten. One of the Kerrins' children would come racing over with the message.

'Dad says can you come quick Mr Wells. It's Mum again,' and the horse would be quickly hitched up for the five-kilometre dash into town. When we became one of the first farms to be connected to a telephone it at least saved my father a trip to Tatura to alert the doctor. Later on, when Dad became one of the first people in the district to own a car, Jack Kerrins was delighted that Mrs Kerrins could be rushed into hospital; no doubt Mrs Kerrins found the trip over the rutted road very uncomfortable, though she would have had the luxury of a few days in hospital.

The incident of the Kerrins' gate illustrates very well the different natures of my father and Jack Kerrins. It must have been when I was about 10 years old that Dad and our other neighbour, Ernie McIntyre, went possum shooting one night. When climbing through a dilapidated wooden gate on the Kerrins farm, it collapsed at their feet. Before we had finished breakfast the next morning, Jack stormed over to our place.

'Thieving Protestants! Rotten neighbours! Wrecking a man's property like that. I'll sue you for this,' he bellowed.

'It's alright Jack, calm down, I'll fix it up for you,' my father said, quite unruffled.

'Well you'd better.' He stamped off muttering about rotten neighbours and filthy British.

For the next few days, Dad was busy hammering and sawing in the workshop; I enjoyed helping and seeing how the gate was constructed. The timber was new oregon; I enjoyed its sleek feel and the fresh smell of the shavings as they curled from the plane. We made it with notched joints, stout bolts held the crossbars; there was not one nail in it.

'Why are you taking so much trouble, Dad? His gate was so old it would have fallen down anyway.'

'Oh, you'll understand one day son, you'll understand,' he smiled. When the gate was finished, we painted it bright green and Dad added what I thought were several orange clover leaves on both sides of the top rail. He explained that they were something called shamrocks. It was the most splendid gate I had ever seen.

'I think we'll give Mr Kerrins a nice surprise,' he said, well satisfied with the effect. 'I'll get Ernie McIntyre to help me put it up tonight.'

'Won't he be glad you've made such a good gate,' I remarked.

'Probably son, probably.'

They hung the gate that night. Mr Kerrins was over at our place before we had finished milking the next morning.

'I'll sue you, Wells! You'll hang for this.'

'What's the matter Jack? Don't you like the gate?'

'Like it! It's an insult to a man. Shamrocks on a gate!'

'Oh, I thought you'd like them. Gives the gate a touch of class.'

'Well it's a terrible blasphemy, insulting a man's religion.'

'Well I'd hardly call it blasphemy. Anyway, you can paint them over if you don't like it.'

'Paint them over! I wouldn't touch the bloody thing,' and he stormed off.

'What a shame he didn't like it,' I said, thinking my father would be hurt. But he just laughed.

'You'll understand one day, son, you'll understand.'

Episodes such as this taught me to respect other peoples' views and to be tolerant of their foibles. Despite the occasional ruction, our families remained good friends and Jack or one of the boys was always ready to help out with our harvest or other jobs around the farm. Pat, Jack's son, and I became lifelong friends.

John and Jim Stewart, Jock Steen, Bernard McNamara and the Barker family – Roy, Peter, Josie and Molly – were my close friends at the convent. Being the youngest and slimmest, Peter Barker was cajoled by Roy and me into climbing trees to collect birds' eggs. We were careful to take only one egg from each nest and, thanks to Peter, who eventually became Master of the Courts in Victoria, I managed to complete a comprehensive display, carefully blowing out the contents and storing the shells in cotton wool, marveling over the delicate patterns.

One of my regular chores was to take Mum's grocery order to the local shop.

'Good morning, young Wells. What can I do for you today?' Mr Williams smiled at me from behind his counter with its juicy hams stored under damp cheesecloth.

'Mum wants some groceries; I'll collect them on the way home tonight,' I explained.

'Right, let me see now. Cheese, sugar, nutmeg, baking powder, stove black. Right, no flour today?'

'No thanks, Mr Williams, Dad makes our own now. I hitched up an old car engine to the grinding stones so that makes it easier than doing it by hand.'

'That must save some money with the way things are at the moment. They tell me you do a bit of inventing as well.'

'Yes, just a few things – like crystal sets. I've built a radio receiver and I'm working on a short wave one now, but it's a bit slow because I have to save up for the parts.'

'Yes, it must be an expensive business that. There's not much

Williams' shop exterior, c 1910.

money about now with this Depression going on. Never mind, patience has its rewards they say.' Mr Williams clearly understood my dilemma.

'I hope so,' I responded cautiously. 'Anyway, I think I'd better get along to school now, Mr Williams.'

'Right-o, young man. Do you think you can manage a 20 pound [10 kg] bag of sugar on the bike?'

'Yes, that's alright. Madge and I drive the horse and jinker to school now.'

'Well, I'll see you after – GET AWAY YOU BLOODY GREAT MONGREL!'

Mr William's face changed from ham pink to tomato red. He rushed from behind the counter and dashed to the door grabbing up a sturdy broom on the way. The weapon was thrust at the head of a shifty-looking dog, which had just relieved itself on the spotless brass of the shop window.

'Too late, again. I'll kill him one day!' Mr Williams exploded.

Clearly the incident had left its mark. Only a soul-shattering event would transform Mr Williams' placid self into such a dervish of wrath. Meanwhile the mongrel had sauntered off, his tail at a jaunty angle and followed by an assortment of canines.

'Does he do it often?' I asked.

'Often?' he bellowed. 'Often? Every day. And it's worse when I close at dinner time. The whole bunch gets going then.'

The brass on the grocery store window was Mr Williams' pride and joy. It was carefully polished every day. The Lifebuoy soap message embossed on its surface glinted when the sun shone on it. Action was necessary.

'I think I could do something about him,' I volunteered, when Mr Williams had calmed down a bit.

'You? How?'

'I could give him an electric shock, just tape some wire around the window and join on a battery, then when he does it … Bang!'

Mr Williams seemed doubtful. 'It wouldn't be dangerous would it?'

'Oh no, not to people. It would just give the dog a terrible fright.'

'It wouldn't kill him, would it?' He asked, looking a little remorseful.

'No, but I could make it kill him if you wanted to. You said a while ago that you would like to kill him.' My passion for truth and accuracy could not be neglected even during this serious discussion.

'Well, not really.' Mr Williams looked somewhat ashamed. 'I'd like to give him a thorough fright though,' and he brightened at the thought at besting that miserable dog.

'Alright, you leave it to me, Mr Williams, and I'll be back when I've got the equipment ready. I must run now.'

'Thanks a lot,' he called, as I scooted off to school.

What joy. At last I could put my talents to legitimate use. The path of a novice scientist was not easy. Ready cash to buy books, apparatus and chemicals was a constant source of bother to me. Some of the more advanced experiments were beyond me, but I persisted until I had perfected them. The worst thing was that some recent experiments, involving nitric acid, had gone haywire in a spectacular manner, scorching my newly painted bedroom to a splattered mess and corroding the brass on the bed head. My father had absolutely forbidden me to carry out any experiments for one month. I fretted and fumed against this ban but he was adamant in its imposition. However, being full of enthusiasm, I had to tell my father about my plan to restore Mr Williams' pride.

'Are you sure you can make it work?' he asked.

'Of course I can, Dad. It's very simple, just a wire and some battery. There's nothing to hurt anybody,' I explained easily.

No doubt he shuddered inwardly as he recalled previous efforts of 'just some wire and a battery.'

'Well you make sure that it is quite safe. But you can't do it until the end of the month when the ban is lifted.' I had to be content with that, but I could see that behind his gruff exterior my father was really rather proud of me.

The equipment needed for the job was very simple and could be obtained without expenditure of anything other than my own energy. Pyke's Garage was an oily jungle of tools, wire, batteries, scrap metal, nuts and bolts – hours of fossicking through their scrap heap yielded endless grubby treasure which I would cart home, patiently clean and restore, making useless scraps into workable units. Every potential scientist should have an Archie Pyke's garage.

I had soon scrounged enough wire for the job and my next requirement was an induction coil to increase the voltage of the battery. Jock Stark, the wireless repairman, was a willing instructor for my many projects. When I explained what was needed, Jock's eyes lit up like his crystal sets, and under his guidance, I had soon put the coil together. The ban was duly lifted and early one Saturday morning I cycled into Tatura. Mr Williams greeted me heartily.

'Have you got everything ready lad?'

'Yes. I'll take this wire along the brass then bring it into the coil and battery just inside the door.' I then attached a simple switch that I had made at home and we were ready for action.

'Do you think he'll come this morning?' I asked. It would be a pity not to see some results for my efforts.

'Yes, he's bound to. He never fails on Saturdays; he seems to know that I'm extra busy.'

Thus reassured, I took a look around the grocery shop. It always smelled special. Sacks of bran and pollard mixed their heavy scents with the lighter aroma of spices. Biscuits tins, when opened, wafted a sweet delicate smell that helped to overcome the pungent fumes from bags of onions. I was always fascinated by the enormous set of scales and their chrome weights poised ready for action next to the high, ornate cash register. I could have looked at the shelves for hours – they ran from the floor to the ceiling with an array of jams, pickles, polishes, sardines, dried fruits and dozens more items.

It was tantalizing but I must keep my mind on the job. A quick look outside showed the enemy sauntering into view. He swaggered along with the mob trailing respectfully behind. They paused to sniff appreciatively outside the butcher shop. Pyke's Garage offered little of interest and they sauntered across the road. The smell of ice cream was better though and they lingered outside the lolly shop next door to Mr Williams.

I slipped inside and turned on the switch, calling to Mr Williams to come and watch. The black mongrel sniffed his way to the grocery shop. He paused and struck a confident pose near the window, smirking at his followers. He lifted his leg. The result was instantaneous. The dog shot into the air, his body rigid, giving an outraged yelp as he hit the ground some six feet from the window. He lay paralyzed in the dust, legs pointed heavenward. There was an awed silence. Tentatively the gang crept towards the black dog; they sniffed at him expecting at any moment to be put in their places. Since there was no response, they became bolder and poked at him with their noses. Jerking to his feet the wretch trembled for a second then bounded off with another yelp. His tail clenched between his legs completed a picture of shame and humiliation.

The mob held a quick consultation then scampered off to find another leader, preferably one who was made of sterner stuff.

For once, my tongue could find nothing to say. Mr Williams was stunned and his usual cheerfulness was quite inadequate for this spectacle.

'By Jove,' he whispered at last. 'Well I never, by Jove, by Jove, did you see that?' in tones of increasing admiration. I was overjoyed. The experiment had worked perfectly. Mr Williams continued to be amazed.

'Did you see him? What a fright you gave him. Well done lad, well done. I bet he won't be back here in a hurry,' and he rubbed his hands with glee.

I packed up the gear as Mr Williams bustled about the shop attending to some early customers. When I was ready to leave, he called me over to the counter.

'Now, young Wells, what do I owe you?'

'Owe me?'

'Yes, all of that wire and stuff must have cost you something.' It had never occurred to me that Mr Williams was prepared to pay me; it had been thrilling enough to put the whole thing together and to see the results. Although I was keen to earn some money, I could not, with a clear conscience, ask for payment for such a small effort.

'Oh, no, Mr Williams, I couldn't take any money for it. I had the wire and battery at home. I enjoyed doing it, really I did.'

'Well perhaps you might like to take a few sweets,' he suggested.

'Oh, yes please, that would be good.'

He filled an ample brown paper bag with sweets, smiling and 'by Joving' to himself all the while.

'Thanks a lot, young man. You've really done me a good turn. I won't have to worry about my brass so much now.'

'No trouble, Mr Williams, no trouble at all.'

'Right-o, now don't eat all of those at once. Better watch out that your sister doesn't get at them too,' he added helpfully. Here was a man after my own heart; when it came to sweets and girls, you couldn't be too careful.

'Too right, I'll be careful,' I called out as I left.

I pedalled home happily. This was treasure indeed. I could eke out the sweets, thus saving precious pocket money for my short-wave radio project. I might give Madge one or two. Jack McIntyre and Laurie Diamond, my best friends, could certainly have some.

Then a wonderful thought struck me. I could sell the rest to the kids at school. With such a large bag I could afford to be generous; I would offer them six a penny (a cent) instead of the usual four a penny that they charged at the lolly shop. I whistled my way home. Not only was my fortune assured but my short-wave receiver was closer to being a reality. And for the first time in my life, science had made a profit, which also made me extremely happy.

If Mr Williams became an admirer of the wonders of science as practiced by me, then George Robbins, Dad's farm hand, frequently declared his wish for my immediate and preferably permanent removal from his hot-tempered presence. On the

Williams' shop interior as Rod would have known it, c 1920.

whole he was good fun, but his temper matched his red hair and I frequently found myself doused with a bucket of water after one of George's outbursts on 'meddling kids' or 'those blasted wires' or any one of my projects that impinged on his dignity and patience. He lived in an old cabin set firmly into the clay near the milking shed. One of my earliest memories is of being scolded by my mother for the illicit use of her hand-operated meat mincer. I had attached it to a stump of George's cabin and was happily employed in mincing lumps of clay when she suddenly descended.

George worked on our farm for many years. When my father could no longer pay his wages during the depression, George elected to stay on without pay, reasoning that he was lucky to have board and keep. The depression made less of an impact on us than many other families. We had ample milk, cream, butter and eggs. Dad had planted an orchard and a large vegetable garden; we had pigs, chooks and ducks for meat. A barter system operated for lamb or beef and there were always rabbits to be shot or fish to be caught in the Goulburn River or the irrigation channels. New clothes arrived if and when finances permitted and my father repaid his farm loan as he could afford it.

Wednesday afternoons were half-day holidays in Tatura. George was one of the classier players in the local football team and would bribe me into doing his work on that afternoon. Washing out the milking shed and feeding the pigs were heavy work for a 10-year-old and the sixpence he paid me to do the chores was a clear case of exploitation. When my father heard of the arrangement, he brought it to a halt – I should have done it willingly, for nothing.

Jack McIntyre, Laurie Diamond and I pestered the life out of George over the years and his constant cry was 'those young devils, I'll kill them one day. I swear, I'll hang for them.'

It was after a particularly trying time with George, when I must have been about 12, that Laurie and I decided we had to take a firm stand. It was the evening of the dance at the Dhurringile Hall and

George had taken a proper bath instead of the weekly wipe over with the flannel.

'All right, you young twerps,' he called as we were messing about near his cabin after tea. 'Get me some shaving water from the house, and hurry up. I don't want to keep Francie waiting.' He was courting Frances Ferguson from a nearby farm.

We took his shaving mug up to the kitchen where the huge black kettle was simmering quietly away on the dying heat of the wood stove.

'Here Laurie, let's make it good and hot. It'll serve him right.'

We put a couple of pieces of wood into the stove and raked up the coals. The kettle soon steamed. We warmed up the mug with some boiling water, discarded it in the sink and then refilled the mug.

'Okay Laurie, run it down now. Don't spill it.'

I raced ahead calling to George that the water was on its way.

'It had better be just the right temperature,' he snapped snatching the mug from Laurie.

'Just right,' we assured him, waiting in the doorway for the outcome.

He plunged the shaving brush into the water, soaped it on the shaving stick and splashed it onto his red whiskery cheek. We dashed for cover as his pained cry hit the air.

'You young bastards! It's boiling hot. Jesus Christ, I'll murder you both!'

When he set out shortly afterward a scowl had been added to the burn on his cheek. By that time, we were well out of sight. We hoped it would make him even less appealing to Frances. Calling to Codger to gee up, he drove off muttering about blasted kids and filthy little swine.

'Hey Laurie, I've got a good idea to make him really mad,' I said as we watched the jinker disappear along the road.

'What's that?' Laurie asked enthusiastically.

When I told him of the scheme he grinned with delight. It was a hot summer evening and still quite light as we set off on our bikes.

'Where are you going to?' my mother asked as we left.

'Oh just for a ride.' We might go and see Jack McIntyre.'

'Alright then, but be back by 9 o'clock. You must be up early for Sunday school tomorrow.'

I was a confirmed Anglican attending a Catholic school and usually went to Christ Church Sunday School. However, curiosity had prompted me to rotate my devotions around the various churches to which my best friends belonged. The Presbyterian Church that Jack McIntyre attended was currently competing for the chance to save my soul; hence my mother's interest in seeing I attended Sunday school.

'Right-o Mum, we'll be back by then,' and off we peddled.

The Dhurringile Hall stood on private property with a track running in for half a kilometre or so from the main road. A fence skirted the track from the road to the hall. Jinkers, gigs and a few cars sprawled around the hall; the horses surveyed each other patiently, snuffling into their nose bags for an occasional feed of

The Wells' jinker and horse, Codger, 1930s.

oats. From the hall came the steady thump of dancing feet and the rhythm of the band. We found our jinker and Codger swished her tail at the unexpected diversion of seeing some friendly faces.

'Laurie you hold her still while I unhitch the jinker.' I patted Codger talking to her softly and she was soon free.

'While I'm away Laurie you wheel the jinker over to the fence and put the shafts through.'

'OK Rod, don't be too long.'

'No, I'll be as quick as I can.'

It was becoming darker as I rode Codger along the track. On reaching the main road I soon found a gate into the adjoining paddock and followed on the other side of the fence back to the hall. Laurie was waiting, the shafts of the jinker protruding through the fence.

'Won't he be mad? He'll really have something to go crook about now' Laurie speculated.

'Gee yes. He probably will kill us this time' I said slipping back through the fence leaving a bemused Codger on one side and the jinker on the other. It was risky to stay longer; a burst of applause and laughter signalled a break in the dancing. We pedalled home, revelling in our daring and speculating gleefully as to the end of the episode.

'I wonder what he'll do to get even this time? Serves him right though,' Laurie mused.

'Yes, just when he's trying to show off to Francie. Won't they get a shock when Codger won't move?' We laughed at the thought of Francie sitting alone in the gig near the deserted hall while George brought Codger back with only his choicest swear words to keep him company.

When I overheard George telling my father about the episode the next day our speculations were not half as colourful as his description. Since there was no retribution from my father or George, Laurie and I decided that the score had been evened.

George eventually married Francie and moved away from the farm. Ian Ferguson, Francie's brother, took his place and his fate at my hands was much more exciting than George's had ever been. With the wireless-interfering transmitter dismantled, I had rigged up a simple telephone system over to the McIntyre's farm. An ear piece and mouthpiece attached to an old axe handle served as the hand set, which made it quite an advanced piece of equipment on the old PMG wall set. Not only was I forbidden to use our telephone unless in an emergency, but for me there was the added humiliation of having to stand on a chair to reach the mouth piece. My system was far more convenient. Jack McIntyre at his end had only a head phone on his axe handle and was obliged to twist it backwards and forwards to alternately speak and listen.

One problem with this simple system was that we had no way of signalling when we wanted to speak to each other; we needed to rig up an electric bell. So, I put an ignition coil from an old T-model Ford (scrounged from Pyke's Garage) at my end, connected it to some equipment that I had made to increase the voltage and joined the wires from the phone to the top strand of our barbed wire fence. To take the wire across the main road to McIntyre's farm, on the south-west corner of the cross road, we floated an insulated wire in the channel under the bridge; a short run along the fence then took the wire to the house and into Jack's bedroom. When I wanted to call Jack, I pressed a button and the headphone rang at his end. It was a simple and efficient arrangement. The one drawback was that the wire had to go across one of our farm gates, so I made a connecting plug and socket to join the wires. I asked my father and Ian to disconnect the wire when opening the gate and to reconnect when closing it. The wire on the fence would have carried about 12,000 volts and on dark, frosty nights, if I called Jack, a beautiful, purple corona ran along the fence creating an eerie glow across the paddocks.

The whole arrangement was quite safe but Ian was always muttering about 'new-fangled telephones' and 'kids messing about with wires.' He was an untidy fellow; instead of wearing a pair of working boots on the farm he wore his old, low-heeled patent-leather dancing pumps, with the frayed cuffs of his trousers constantly wet and muddy from trailing in the mud and dirt. Inevitably, I pressed the button to call Jack one day, just as Ian was disconnecting the plug across the gate. His damp shoes and trousers made a perfect earth for the system. Every one of the 12,000 volts streaked up one arm, across his chest and down the other arm before he was thrown clear, landing stunned and enraged in one of those enormous puddles that invariably form at farm gateways. His fury knew no bounds as he ran bellowing up to the house about 'that bloody little fiend.' I thanked God that it was Ian and not my father who had been the recipient of all those volts.

If there is one scene that still stands out in my childhood memories, it is the sight of the steam chaff-cutting machines. Dad had his own header, but in autumn the chaff-cutters would arrive to deal with the stubble. It fascinates me still that such cumbersome machines could be manoeuvered so delicately, puffing away gently as they turned the hard stalks into sleek bags of chaff. The team of four or five men with their brown, well-muscled arms added a charm and colour to the farm. It was hard work and gave the men enormous appetites, so chaff-cutting time was also very busy for my mother. Occasionally I was employed to run the morning and afternoon teas down to the men – spicy slab cakes and hot buttered scones, helped down by gallons of strong tea. It was essential that the midday dinner should be ready on time, as the machines were kept steaming while the men ate and there was not a moment to lose. Just before dinnertime my father would come up to the house to make sure that all was ready. He would frequently find my mother lost in a dream world of women's magazines or a romantic novel.

'For goodness sake, Maggie,' he would shout, 'isn't dinner ready yet? The men will be here soon and we can't keep them waiting.'

My mother would placidly look up from her book and assure him that all was ready, while Dad would rush back to work shaking his head at the unshakability of women. We triumphed over the magazines when Mum was in town one day.

'Quick son,' he called. 'Let's get going before your Mother gets back. Run these down to the boiler.'

'What will Mum say?' I queried.

'She'll never miss them. There's enough to fill a dray with this lot.' For half-an-hour or so I raced stacks of magazines down to the boiler in the dairy, which burned them up gleefully. I doubt that my mother ever missed them and they were soon replaced by others.

At the age of about 14, another of my interests was to help the projectionist at the local picture show. The Victory Hall in Tatura served as the local theatre with a new film being shown every Saturday night. Talkies were the latest thing to thrill the audience and it was an even greater thrill to be in the projection box. With the reels whirring and clanking, the flickering of the arc lamp produced weird, dancing shadows on the walls of the stuffy, cluttered room. Professional pride required the reels to be changed smoothly and I was constantly being warned to have the arc primed ready on the takeover projector to keep the reels running seamlessly. I was always ready but on one terrifying occasion I had forgotten to change the carbon rods in the projector. With just seconds to spare I managed the changeover, narrowly avoiding the humiliation of being booed and whistled by a disgruntled audience from the blackened theatre. Concentrate, I reminded myself. Never be distracted from the task at hand and always be ready for action.

Our first car, a second-hand Rugby, rattled into our lives in about 1926. It was a solid car, with wooden-spoke wheels and a fold-down hood. Oilcloth side curtains, which could be clipped on and off, formed the sides of the car with a piece of Perspex in each curtain for a window; a flap in the driver's window allowed his hand to protrude for hand signals. Heating and cooling for the comfort of passengers was simple. In summer, the hood remained up for shade and the side curtains were removed to catch the breeze. Spring and autumn saw the hood rolled back, whilst in winter all coverings were firmly clipped in place.

Madge and I felt very grand sitting up so high in the back and we would pretend that we were Eastern potentates, visiting royalty or persons of consequence. I was intrigued with the engine and it wasn't long before I knew the function of all the working parts. The Rugby opened up new delights to us as we bounced our way along the track into Tatura, dodged between the trees on trips to Rushworth, and on hot summer evenings set off for a dusty drive to the Goulburn River at Murchison or Toolamba. Here the river flowed slowly; even now if I close my eyes and picture the dark cool scene, the slightly stagnant smell of the water and the fragrance of eucalyptus from the gums is strong in my nostrils. Plunging into the river after a scorching day soon revived us, sharpening our appetites for sandwiches of cold meat, tomato and cucumber and large pieces of slab cake, helped down with raspberry vinegar. We played games after tea and, if there was time, had another swim until the mosquitoes forced us to pack up for the trip home. On the way we would sing songs with Dad giving impersonations of well-known singers, punctuating each act with a honk of the bulbous horn. In 1928 or 29, a sleek new Dodge replaced the Rugby, and over the years a series of new cars gave us added comfort, speed and reliability, but they could never replace the excitement of our first car.

A trip to Melbourne to see my godparents, Paddy and Ruby O'Byrne, was something that was not undertaken lightly in the early 1930s. The 65-kilometre stretch down to Seymour was a rough track that wound between the trees. From Seymour to Melbourne it was a dirt road. The highlight of the trip was always the laborious climb up Pretty Sally.

'Come on girl, you can do it,' my father would say as he coaxed the car along. Slowly we would proceed to the top of the hill and then, at last with a view of Melbourne in the distance, would coast down at a reckless 65 kilometres an hour. In summer, there was the added excitement that the car might boil and, in winter, that we could get bogged. Punctured tyres, which had to be repaired on the spot, were always a possibility as well as flat batteries, loose wheels bowling off into the trees and lamp globes blowing. We loved it all.

Holidays were spent at Brighton with the O'Byrnes or at Point Cook Air Force Base with the Eatons. Charles Eaton and my father had met during World War I. He was a Royal Flying Corps' veteran and was in charge of air-force training at Point Cook. Time spent there was a sheer delight with the sea nearby, the air force band playing each morning for parade, and planes manoeuvering overhead.

It was on one of these holidays that we almost went home fatherless. Uncle Charles, as we called him, had taken Dad up with him in a small aircraft. We were inside the house with Mrs Eaton and her children and some other visitors. Suddenly one of the men moved towards the window.

'I hope you don't mind if I pull down the blind, it's rather sunny in here,' he said.

If he looked anxious, nobody took much notice. A plane was buzzing close by but that was a common sound on the base. Some minutes later he pulled up the blind and, looking rather relieved, rejoined the party. Some ten minutes later, Dad and Uncle Charles returned, very pale and calling for a stiff drink.

'What's the matter?'

'Did you nearly crash?'

'Are you alright?'

They explained that they had climbed to 300 metres and were beginning to enjoy the view when the engine stalled. Charles' frantic efforts to restart it failed and the plane plunged into a spin. With only seconds to spare, he managed to revive the engine and lift the aircraft from its plummeting course. The visitor, realizing what was happening, had pulled down the blind to prevent us from witnessing what could have been a tragedy. I am sure that none of us realized just how desperate the situation had been, but my father was very subdued for several days afterwards.

Charles Eaton had a distinguished and interesting career in the Royal Australian Air Force. One of his most harrowing experiences was in April 1929 – the search for Lieutenant Keith Anderson and Robert Hitchcock in north Western Australia. The two pilots had set out in their plane, *Kookaburra*, to look for Charles Kingsford Smith and Charles Ulm, who had become lost in their plane, *Southern Cross*, and had been forced to land in the desert when their fuel ran out. Uncle Charles helped to conduct the search for Anderson and Hitchcock, and eventually found their bodies himself.

He inspired another of my hobbies, keeping homing pigeons. After our visits to Point Cook we would sometimes bring home several of his pigeons in a basket and release them at the farm. One of his pigeons had gradually been taken further and further from Australia and trained to return home. Eventually it was taken to England and succeeded in finding its way back to Point Cook. It fascinated me that these gentle docile creatures had the stamina and instinctive ability to bear a homeward path irrespective of the weather conditions or the distance to be travelled.

On one breathtaking occasion, we heard an aircraft buzzing over our house and circling lower and lower. Suddenly a small basket suspended on a miniature parachute fell from the plane and several pigeons made a safe landing. It was thrilling to be part of the new wonders of flying and we often received parcels from the Eatons in a similar manner. Our visits to Point Cook were stimulating for a small boy – the excitement of aircraft taking off and landing, the airmen in their uniforms and the bustling order of the base provided endless fascination. I could soon identify most of the aircraft. The worst aspect of our holidays, which usually took place in summer, was that with my fair skin and deep auburn hair, I quickly became sunburned and spent a considerable amount of what I considered to be wasted time lying in a darkened room covered in vinegar and brown paper.

It must be remembered that, before World War II, farms, on the whole, had no electricity. Within towns such as Tatura, the local butter factory supplied limited and unreliable power: if the factory shut down anytime during the day or night, the electricity simply went off. Milking on the dairy farms was done by hand and the old car motor I had rigged up to generate power for the dairy made the job easier for my father.

Boyhood was not all happy sailing. One of the saddest incidents involved my dog Buster who was an enthusiastic companion in my many experiments. When he contracted distemper, for which, in those days, there was no cure, Dad made me put him down. I pleaded with him not to make me do it, but he insisted.

'You might have to do this one day, son,' he said.

Grieving, greatly unhappy, and for once truly hating my father, I took the rifle and carried out the deed.

CHAPTER 4

APPRENTICESHIP, ENLISTMENT, TRAINING

Rod Wells, 1938.

By the end of 1935, when I was almost 16, I had completed my Intermediate Certificate at Tatura Convent. Although we were not poor, Dad could not afford to keep me at school any longer. I desperately wanted to do electrical engineering at university, but this luxury was out of our reach. Besides that, he was very keen for me to be a farmer. I knew that, as much as I loved farm life, I could never be content with it as a lifetime career. A compromise was reached and it was decided that I should become an electrical trades apprentice at the Government Ordnance Factory at Maribyrnong.

So it was, that in 1936, I went to live at Essendon with the Gladstones. Mr Gladstone had been Dad's batman in the war. During the day I worked at the factory and at night went to Footscray Technical College to study trade subjects and to do my Leaving Certificate. Apprentice wages were very poor, but I just managed to scrape by and my needs were few. For recreation I would ride my bike 35 kilometres or so to Point Cook at weekends to visit the Eatons or 25 kilometres around the bay to Brighton to visit the O'Byrnes. The years 1936 and 1937 were fairly uneventful but they served to sharpen my wits to the ways of the world.

The factory foreman viewed me with suspicion. It was unthinkable in those days that an apprentice should seek an education other than a practical trade. Studying for extra maths subjects for my Leaving Certificate at Taylors College in Melbourne at night made me rather unpopular with him. He was an omnipotent person who strutted around the factory in a suit, showing that he was better than the average worker.

The episode that stands out in my mind at this time was when some VIP visitors, probably government inspectors, were being shown over the factory by the leading hand, Charlie Lovell. As the visitors approached the area where I was carrying out some electroplating, one of them asked me what I was doing. I explained the process, adding that it would be more effective, efficient and less costly by changing the concentration of the solution. In other words, it was more concentrated than necessary for the process.

The visitor was interested and I launched into more technical details, forgetting in my enthusiasm that I was merely an apprentice. Eventually the party moved on and I forgot the episode, but not so Charlie Lovell. He was enraged at my audacity in suggesting that the process was inefficient, and humiliated that I had shown up his lack of knowledge of chemistry to the VIPs. I had to be cut down to size. For the next month I removed insulators from kilometres of wire, a task that was carried out on the top of a hill in the middle of a Melbourne winter. I sat from 7.30 am until 5 pm deflecting the freezing westerly winds and trying to keep my numb fingers at work.

'I must not be so hasty,' I reminded myself. 'Be clever but not cheeky and don't waste time up here.' So I smuggled a maths book under my boiler suit and occupied my mind with that. My fingers might be frozen but I would keep my brain on the move.

One morning, while working in the workshop, whistles blew, sirens shrieked and all work ceased.

'What's happening?' I whispered to someone near me.

'Come and see,' he replied quietly.

In the factory grounds, a miniature train running on rubber wheels was being slowly and gently wheeled from a shed to a storage depot; in front walked a man carrying two red flags.

'What is it?' I whispered.

'Gelignite,' he replied quietly.

I went quite cold when I realized just how close I had come to killing myself and probably Jack McIntyre when we made our own nitroglycerine.

At the end of 1937, I had completed my Leaving Certificate at night school, but I realized that trade work was not for me. I needed more to keep my mind occupied – I longed for higher mathematics, science, chemistry and physics. With this in view, I returned to Tatura in 1938 to study for Leaving Honours (Matriculation) by correspondence with Taylors College. I would become a science teacher.

Early 1939 saw me back in Melbourne when I completed Maths IV at Taylors, tutored there and took laboratory classes at University High. It was while doing these lab classes that I met Bill Dwyer who was to become a life-long friend. Like me, Bill came from a modest background but was determined to become a dentist. In about June 1939, I joined the Education Department as a student teacher and was sent to various schools around Melbourne. I also sat for my University Entrance Examination.

Back home there was unusual activity around the mansion at Dhurringile Estate, adjoining our farm. As the political situation in Europe was uneasy, speculation heightened that we were preparing for war. A secure fence was erected around the perimeter, electricity was quickly brought to the area, spotlights and alarms were installed. All of this was happening right on our doorstep. My father predicted that the mansion would probably be turned into some sort of prison.

As many had feared, the unrest in Europe soon exploded into war. I happened to be at the farm on Sunday, 3 September 1939, the day that war was declared, and I returned to Melbourne in a state of excitement for what adventures lay ahead. My parents later related that, on the following Monday, a trainload of 'enemy aliens' was unloaded at Tatura station and marched out to Durringhile estate. The deserted mansion also became home for captured German officers. As more enemy aliens were rounded up, six additional camps were hastily erected to serve as prisons for thousands of internees and prisoners of war in the Tatura, Murchison, Rushworth, and Graytown area. Dhurringile was staffed by World War I officers and my father, to his great delight, was made an honorary member of their mess.

In late November 1939 I enlisted in the Militia, now known as Army Reserve, but in May the following year I decided to join the AIF. I took myself along to one of the recruiting offices, a converted ticket box at Flinders Street Station. The Officer in Charge was about my father's age. I knew I was under age and certainly looked very young but thought I could bluff my way through.

'Name?'

'Wells, sir.'

'Age?'

'Twenty-one, sir.'

'Oh, Wells, is it? Not related to Lieutenant Dick Wells by any chance are you?'

'Yes sir, he's my father,' I replied proudly. He eyed me shrewdly.

'Twenty-one eh? Well now, if my calculations are right, Dick Wells can't have a twenty-one-year-old son. Last time I saw him was at the end of 1918 and he was going back home. He didn't have a son then so you can't be 21 yet.'

'Well, I'm not quite 21,' I admitted.

'Sorry son, you'll have to get your father's signature on these papers.'

The next weekend I caught the train to Toolamba. My parents met me at the station and I think they already knew what was on my mind as we discussed the war and its implications.

'Of course, they'll want me back,' my father predicted. 'They'll need men with experience, not you young blokes.'

He cheerfully anticipated renewing his army career while I ran the farm. He duly signed my application forms and was bitterly disappointed when I was accepted and he was rejected. As a dairy farmer he had been declared an essential industry and was obliged to stay at home. I learned later from my mother that he was in Tatura the next day proudly boasting that his son had joined up.

When I received my call-up papers, I reported to the Officer in Charge at the drill hall in South Melbourne. There was no messing about with aptitude tests, psychology or other frills.

'Now son, what do you do?'

'I'm a student teacher, sir.'

He raised his eyes in despair and asked without much hope –

'Got any hobbies?'

'Well, I'm a licensed radio operator and interested in telegraphy and radio communications.'

'Right-oh. Signals Corps.' And I was packed off to the South Melbourne Signals Depot. For once the army got it right.

I soon joined Australian Corps of Signals at the Royal Melbourne Showground, transferred to Caulfield Racecourse and then, from March to June 1940, undertook basic training at the Seymour Army Camp, just 75 kilometres from Tatura. Initial training remains hazy but my Morse skills were sharpened. I loved the orderly and logical way that the army functioned and found a lot of mental stimulation with line laying and operational radio training.

When my initial training was completed at Seymour we sat for our examinations. The list of names of those who had passed was posted and I was dismayed to see that my name was not on the list. I had failed. What would my father say? That day I was called into the CO's office.

'Now Wells, I suppose you are wondering why your name was not listed as having passed.'

'Yes, sir.'

'Well, we have decided to send you to Corps of Signals OCTU at Casula in New South Wales.'

'Yes, sir. What is OCTU?'

'Officer Cadet Training Unit. I'm sure you'll do well.'

'Thank you, sir.'

I was given permission for weekend leave before heading for Casula so I hitchhiked straight for home. I remember arriving at the peace and security of the farm. Dad was out straining fences and I walked across the paddocks to where he was working.

'Hullo, Dad.'

'Good day, son. What are you doing home?'

'They've given me leave before I'm sent up to Casula to OCTU.'

Dad didn't look up from his work. 'Must be hard up for officers,' he said. 'Here, hand me that strainer.'

I was deflated and hurt. I had felt so proud and was sure that he would be proud of me, too. I tried to hide my disappointment but a few days later Mum told me that again he was in town boasting that I had been selected for officer training. I found that many of my friends had enlisted – Roy Barker, John Stewart and his father Galloway, Reverend Charles Patmore and Dr Lyell Andrews.

OCTU at Casula was on the outskirts of Sydney. I arrived there in August 1940. The officer in charge was Captain Stan Hill. Training, carried out by Army Instruction Corps' officers, who had served in WWI and were known as bulldogs, was far more intense than basic training.

Stan Hill was a shrewd officer who I came to admire greatly. I found the three months' training intensive, arduous and immensely satisfying. In November 1940, I was posted to Bathurst for signals training, was promoted to 2nd Lieutenant and became Officer in Charge of G Section, 8 Division Signals, with about 20 men under my care. The CO at Bathurst was Lieutenant Colonel James Hervey Thyer. I suppose most officers maintain a vivid impression of their first CO and even now I have a clear picture of Thyer as I first saw him. Of slight build, he was always meticulously self-contained. The feature I remember most were his eyes – I very seldom saw them betray any emotion. His lips might move but his face and eyes always remained expressionless. He rarely smiled then or at any other time during his life. He ruled the Sigs autocratically and tolerated not the slightest delay or deviation in having his orders carried out. He always addressed us by surname and I don't recall even his superior officers addressing him by his first name. I remember once remarking to a fellow officer at Church Parade that it was strange that all the officers in the unit were Anglican. We had no Roman Catholics, Jews, or what might be called deviant Protestants.

'Good heavens,' he replied. 'You don't think the old man would tolerate any foreigners in his unit? You wouldn't have got a guernsey if you hadn't been an Anglican.'

If Thyer was unemotional, he never could be accused of being unfair. I particularly recall an exercise at Bathurst when my section had to supply communications to his headquarters. Everything went wrong from the start. The linesmen were slower than I anticipated, the dispatch rider got bogged in a creek and total disaster was never far away. At last we managed to get the lines through just in time to complete the exercise, and with relief I informed Thyer we were through.

'And where is my telephone, Wells?'

'We haven't had time to rig it up, sir,' and I launched into an explanation of all the difficulties I had encountered.

'You realize, of course,' he interrupted coldly, 'that in a real-life situation this would be a serious omission. Please make sure in future that my instructions are carried out.'

I was deflated and hurt, but later in the mess he came over to me, put a hand on my shoulder and said, 'Never mind, Wells. You really did have a bad day. Let me buy you a drink.'

We discussed the day's events in a detached way. I realized that as long as one kept trying he bore no resentment. Later, in Malaya, I was thankful for his meticulous training and his determination to instill self-discipline and integrity in his men. When I was promoted to 1st Lieutenant we held a rowdy party in our quarters. Sherry was ordered and we drank it by the beer glass full. Sometime during the evening, someone managed to spill some on the door and, when a pillow burst, the feathers stuck to the door.

'Let's get some water and wash them off,' someone suggested.

A bucket of cold water was produced and several of us prepared to heave it at the door. One! Two! Three! On the count of three, the door opened and Thyer, attired in full mess kit received the full charge of water. He stared into the suddenly silent room. An officer ventured an apology but the CO simply said 'Gentlemen let us say no more about this episode. Just clean up this room and pay for the dry cleaning of my mess kit and that will be the end of it.'

We felt we had been let off lightly.

It was while I was at Bathurst that I married Ellen Ethel Ashby, whom I had got to know before I left home to work in Melbourne; her father was a bank manager in Tatura. On Ellen's gaining work in the city we had met on several occasions and arranged, before I left for Casula, that we would be married as soon as we turned 21. We corresponded regularly after I was posted to New South Wales and decided to marry without the knowledge or consent of our families. I turned 21 on 1 January 1941 and Ellen travelled up by train from Melbourne for the ceremony at Bathurst Cathedral.

By now I was familiar with working conditions in my unit and expected to be sent to the Middle East. One day in March 1941, Thyer called me into his office.

'Wells, I'm posting you to 2/15 Field Regiment at Holsworthy.'

'Sir, I thought I would be posted overseas with this unit. I haven't done regimental signals.'

He studied me blandly from the toes of my shoes to the top of my head.

'You have a week to learn them. Thank you, Wells. That's all.' It was the shortest interview I have ever had.

The gap between unit and regimental work was enormous and after a week of intensive training I was posted to the artillery regiment. If the jump from a unit to a regiment was enormous so was the difference in style of my new CO, Lieutenant Colonel John O'Neill – a blaspheming, beer-drinking, piano-playing, overwhelming Irishman.

'Wells, you little bastard! Nice to meet you,' and a numbing handshake accompanied by a slap on the back almost sent me reeling.

The few weeks spent at Bathurst were some of the most satisfying I had experienced. All the theory I had learned was put into practice on a grand scale to an appreciative audience. But it was at Bathurst that my career almost came to an end. One morning, I sent the members of my platoon onto the firing range to retrieve some communication equipment left behind from an exercise the previous day. They had just departed when I heard the sound of artillery fire. I almost turned to jelly but managed to commandeer a vehicle and driver. As we arrived at the firing line, I bellowed, 'Cease fire! Cease fire!' Thank God the firing stopped instantly.

'What bloody idiot ordered the cease fire?' the CO's voice yelled.

'Me, sir,' and I hastily explained the situation. I had failed to read routine orders for the day.

'Bloody Sigs. Messing things up. You could have had your men killed.'

I was already ashamedly aware of that fact and resolved to be more vigilant in future.

In June 1941 we were given final leave and I went home to farewell my wife and parents. On the last few days of my leave, Dad came down to Melbourne and took me to the Naval and Military Club for a meal with Paddy O'Byrne. Winning a lucky number prize during the evening gave me enough money to pay for a sleeping compartment on the return train trip to Sydney.

After arriving at the harbour it was with greatly mixed feelings that we embarked on a troopship, SS *Katoomba* for – we knew not where. We were full of optimism, keen to put our training into action and to send the enemy packing. We were proud to be part of the AIF, to show our families and our nation that we could fight as well as our fathers had, just 20 years before. Although we may not have expressed our fears of death or injury, they were certainly there. Leaving behind families and loved ones was a great hardship, especially for those who, like me, had married in haste before departing.

Katoomba eventually docked at Fremantle where the residents gave us a very warm welcome. We were transferred to *Sibajak* and with two other ships sailed with a naval escort. Our destination had not been revealed. We assumed that it would be the Middle East but as the days went by and we continued northward in increasing humidity, we realized we were bound for Asia, probably Singapore.

It was on board that I met several young signals officers including Doug Lush, Ben Barnett and Ken Trumble, who became lifelong colleagues and friends.

One of the loneliest things to experience is a funeral at sea. When one of the sailors died, the ship's engines were stopped, the padre delivered a short service and the committal took place in absolute silence. After the noise and din of shipboard life it was quite eerie; then the engines restarted and we slowly sailed away.

Each day and night it became hotter and more humid but troops were kept busy with drill, exercises and lectures. We finally arrived in Keppel Harbour, Singapore, in time for the midday deluge and I ordered my men to put their coats on to disembark.

'What bloody fool ordered these men to put their coats on? Do you want to kill them?'

The words were shouted by Lieutenant Colonel 'Gus' Kappe, whom I later came to know very well. I had a lot to learn. We marched off smartly. We soon became accustomed to the heat and rain. As it was put, probably apocryphally, by one of the men when writing home, 'There are two seasons here – the wet and the dry. In the dry season it pours every day; in the wet it rains all the bloody time.'

Our war had begun. We would soon teach the Japanese how to fight.

Rod's ship SS *Sibajak* at Fremantle.

CHAPTER 5

MALAYA

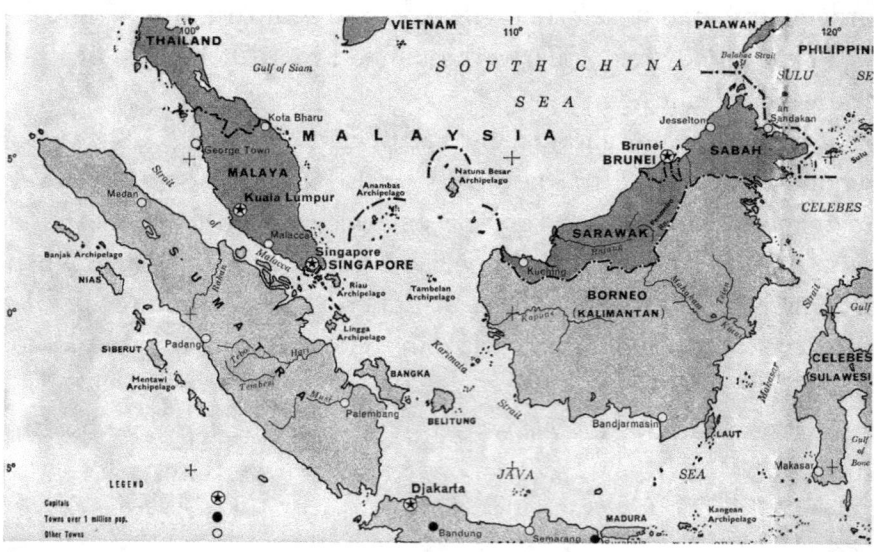

On our arrival at Singapore in August, 2/15 Field Regiment was transported by truck from Keppel Harbour to a camp near Nee Soon village in the centre of the island. The Japanese had not yet made any hostile move towards Britain and her far-eastern colonies, although this was undoubtedly their intention. For the past few years, their aim had been to take over the whole of the Far East and, since Germany had declared war in Europe, their ultimate aim was to sweep through South-east Asia and meet up

Clifford Pier, Keppel Harbour, Singapore, where Rod disembarked from the ship, 1941.

with the German army in India. In the name of their Emperor, Japanese forces had fought their way into China, had fomented war in Indo-China, and continued their way south. Their next objective was to capture Burma, Malaya and Singapore. Britain, stretched to the limit by the war in Europe, sent what forces it could spare, but was relying heavily on Australian and Indian troops to defend Malaya, if and when the Japanese attacked.

In September, the artillery regiment was transferred north to Tampin in Malaya, where divisional headquarters had been established at Kuala Lumpur, the country's largest city. Although based at Tampin, I also spent some time organizing communications for 4 Anti-tank Regiment in Malacca where, at 2/10 Australian General Hospital (AGH), I met up with Lyell Andrews, my mentor from Murchison. The conditions of our meeting were a huge contrast to the quiet companionable times we had spent conducting experiments during my boyhood.

Rod Wells, Malaya, 1941.

In October 1941, I was ordered to Jemaluang on the east coast of Johor state to open a signals' centre. From here I made frequent trips to Mersing, further north, and to Tampin, where the gunners were still based, about 270 kilometres to the north-west in the state of Negeri Sembilan.

As well as providing communications for the 2/15th, I was keen to undertake trials on air-to-ground communications for gunnery observation. With the large artillery guns positioned up to eight kilometres from their targets, the Forward Observation Officer relayed instructions to the gunners by telephone, using surface cables that could be cut by enemy action. An observation plane, relaying instructions from the air, would be far more effective and efficient. However, the air force, though out of its infancy, was still in its adolescence and inter-service ground-to-air radio-controlled communications were almost non-existent. High Frequency Radio was the only military radio system used at the time and was sourced by fitting to our vehicles some horizontal V aerials made from local parts. These increased the range of our equipment, designed for use in European terrain, to enable it to be used in jungle conditions. It was one of the first instances of using existing equipment to send signals from ground vehicles to artillery observation aircraft. Later I supervised the first use of ground to air radio-controlled communications for gunner observation.

The problems encountered in providing communications were many, and I enjoyed the challenge of solving the technical and practical details. However, while our training had been thorough, nothing had prepared us for the tropical humidity, daily torrential downpours and the desperate constraints of time under which we were working. On a lighter side, we had also not been trained to deal with wild elephants, which took great delight in uprooting the telegraph poles we had so carefully erected.

During this period I had an unexpected trip to Rangoon, in Burma, which was alive with Allied troops and civilians. The situation was so similar that we could have been in Malaya. We had dinner in the elegant dining room of the historic Strand Hotel, listening to the chatter of other diners. The strains of a Strauss waltz, played by a Burmese orchestra, kept time with the 24 ceiling fans revolving overhead. It was bright, bustling with army officers, and comforting, very much like Raffles in Singapore.

The task of 8 Division was to defend the state of Johor, and in early December we were all placed on first degree of readiness, with the 2/15th brought from Tampin to take up battle stations in the

Kluang-Mersing-Jemaluang area. It was at Jemaluang early on the morning of 8 December 1941 that, as duty signals officer, I received a signal from Kota Bharu that the Japanese had landed on Malaya's north-east coast and at Patani, over the Thai border.

The Japanese advanced down the peninsula far more quickly than we expected. Penang, then Ipoh fell, and by 21 December Kuala Lumpur was under air attack. Enemy ground forces were still a considerable distance from Jemaluang but, as a precautionary measure, we evacuated all civilians from the village on 23 December and set fire to it, along with the signals centre, to deny it to the enemy. We set up another signals centre, 18 kilometres away.

Two days later, it was Christmas – the last Christmas many of our troops would celebrate. While the officers, as was customary, were serving the troops their dinner, I fell into conversation with my Signals CO, Gus Kappe.

'Surely we don't need to worry,' I said optimistically, 'because reinforcements will come and we'll beat the Japs in the end.'

'Don't be so sure,' he replied.

He then told me of an exercise for the defence of Singapore, in which he had taken part at the Staff College in Quetta, India, in 1937. It was always anticipated that any attack on Singapore would come from the sea, hence the huge fortifications along the coastline and the construction of a massive naval base. Malaya, covered in thick, mountainous jungle was considered to be far too inhospitable for an overland attack and it was also considered there would be little chance of air raids from the north, as the nearest airbase from which the Japanese could operate was Saigon in Indochina, largely under the control of our ally, France. However, during the 1930s the situation had changed when the Japanese, seeking to enlarge their land mass and increase resources, had fomented a war in China. French Indochina, following the fall of France, was administered by the puppet Vichy French government, and therefore, effectively in the hands of the Imperial Japanese

Army or IJA which had, in December 1941, forced Thailand to enter into a treaty, making Malaya ripe for the taking.

The results of the Quetta exercise concluded that, if there were such a landing in Malaya, we would need something like 572 first line aircraft to defend the country against invasion. I looked at Kappe and said, 'That means that we've got what, about 100 now?' He replied, 'Probably. If we're lucky.' He went on to add that Singapore could possibly hang on for eight or ten weeks. If we didn't get aircraft sometime in January, it would be all over. Britain and its allies were fully occupied with saving Europe from total Nazi invasion and were unable to send reinforcements. We were facing an unwinnable situation with few resources left against a formidable enemy.

In spite of this gloomy prognosis, my optimism persisted. The old man could be a bit of a pessimist and psychologically optimism knows no bounds: something miraculous would happen. I still then believed in miracles and I think this belief later helped me more than it hindered me.

It is hard to describe my feelings at this time. I absolutely enjoyed the experience of putting all of my skills and training into practice; I embraced the camaraderie and discipline of army life and my role as lieutenant in charge of my troop of men. However, with the Japanese steadily advancing down through Malaya, things were obviously not going well for the Allies. After Christmas, from our temporary post outside Jemaluang, I was sent to Johor Bahru to co-ordinate post and telegraph lines as the Postal, Telephone and Telegraph Liaison Officer.

It had become evident that Allied troop movements and positions were being passed on to the enemy and, in January 1942, I was assigned to discover the source. After some investigations it was established that the signals were being transmitted from two or three locations. The residence of the Sultan's son was suspected of being the main centre, and my further investigations proved that this was so, but no action was taken due to the delicate political balance of the situation. Interference with the Sultan's family could result in disloyalty from the Royal Johor Military Force and we needed all the help we could get.

With the Japanese invasion of Malaya, it was impossible to carry out further ground-to-air radio trials; our utmost efforts had to focus on the immediate threat of the rapidly advancing enemy forces. Despite this I still enjoyed the challenge of putting my skills and training to effective use. As land battles and bombings increased we had to constantly relocate our signals' centre, salvage what equipment we could and set up the next forward operational post while the fighting troops valiantly tried to stall the enemy's progress.

The old method of supplying communications overland was time consuming, expensive and vulnerable to sabotage. Telegraph poles were destroyed, wires cut and repairs difficult to carry out in wartime conditions. Wireless Telegraphy (WT – coded messages sent in Morse code) was quicker, cost-effective and more secure, though with its own problems of messages being intercepted by the enemy and de-coded. Some commanders wrongly believed that wireless would not work in jungle conditions and were convinced that the Japanese could locate their positions, so they abandoned the use of WT transmissions.

The effect of this became evident on 14 January while I was in Johor Bahru. 8 Division finally went into action when our infantry laid an ambush at Gemencheh Bridge, against enemy troops pedalling from Tampin on bicycles. After allowing some to cross the bridge and enter a cutting, the engineers blew the bridge. Trapped either in the cutting, or bunched up on the far side of the river, the cyclists were mown down in a hail of bullets and grenade attacks. However, the ambush was only partially successful. After the bridge was blown, a battery of our gunners, positioned about seven kilometres away, waited for the command to open fire on hundreds of Japanese troops trapped on the river bank, which would have had devastating results. However the cyclists allowed to pass through the cutting had spotted the signal wire running from the Forward Observation Officer. They had severed it, and all communication to the rear, rendering the guns impotent. The surviving Japanese quickly regrouped, erected a makeshift bridge and continued with their relentless advance. I have often wondered what the outcome may have been if the artillery fire had been directed from an observation aircraft, rather than relying on seven kilometres of vulnerable field cable.

The failure to use WT put an extra strain on the signallers to maintain landlines and the despatch rider service almost collapsed under the extra work. It was not only the wish to overcome the enemy but also a matter of pride in our Corps and its past achievements that spurred us on almost beyond endurance to maintain field communications. Despite concerted efforts by Australian, British and Indian fighting men, by mid-January 1942, the IJA had advanced down through Malaya and we were being pushed inexorably to Johor Bahru.

While the gunners at Gemas had been readying themselves for the attack that never took place, over in the west another artillery battery from the 2/15th was preparing to engage an enemy force. Moving south along the coast 10,000 Japanese troops were attempting to outflank the main Allied army, now retreating down the main trunk road. Although the vastly outnumbered artillery and two Australian infantry battalions fought desperately, losing the battery commander, Major William Julius, whom I knew, and hundreds of men in the process, they too were forced to retreat, along with truckloads of wounded. Pursued by the crack troops of the Japanese Imperial Guards, who constantly outflanked them, the beleaguered column engaged in hand-to-hand fighting in a do-or-die effort to reach a bridge spanning a river at the village of Parit Sulong, their only line of retreat. After hours fending off enemy troops time and again, they reached their goal, only to find that the British guarding the bridge had decamped, and it was in enemy hands.

It was now that two of our signalers displayed outstanding initiative. After keeping their 109 wireless set going in unimaginably difficult conditions, their signals truck was destroyed along with most of the equipment and the code books. With the column trapped at the bridge and in urgent need of reinforcements, morphine for the wounded, and food for those still able to fight, they managed to cobble a few bits and pieces together and tap out a message in Morse code, by using the ends of two copper wires, just enough to make the necessary spark.

When the message arrived at Divisional Headquarters in clear language, General Bennett and Lieutenant Colonel Thyer realized that something drastic had happened to the code books. Wanting to let the commanding officer, Lieutenant Colonel Anderson, know that supplies were on the way, but mindful that the Japanese were most likely monitoring wireless traffic, they were in a dilemma about how best to convey the message. Thyer, who had never been known to smile, let alone crack a joke, hit upon a perfect solution – a message in the Australian vernacular that would be completely unintelligible to the Japanese: 'Look up at sparrow fart'.

Next morning, at the crack of dawn, as promised, the much-needed drugs and food were dropped by air. However, there were no reinforcements to be had, forcing the able-bodied to find a gap in the perimeter and try to make their way to Allied lines. The wounded, left in trucks and ambulances at the bridge under the supposed protection of a Red Cross flag, were subsequently massacred. The signallers received gallantry awards for their devotion to duty, and the infantry commander, a Victoria Cross, the only one awarded to an Australian in the Malayan Campaign.

While in Johor Bahru I met up with Galloway Stewart, Tatura solicitor and father of my friends John and Jim. He too was based in Johor Bahru with his ammunition transport unit. Gall, a World War I veteran, had enlisted, hoping to spare his sons from serving. Sadly, John, who joined the RAAF, was killed in action over Europe.

We discussed the current situation. I was optimistic but Gall was more realistic.

'We can't last much longer, son. Supplies are running out and troops up country are fighting a losing battle.'

In the next few days, as disastrous news came in from the battlefield, I realised he was right. The fighting troops were exhausted and dirty; food, ammunition and medical supplies were very low. At the end of January, General Percival decided full evacuation to Singapore would commence and had to be achieved as smoothly as possible in the circumstances; transports, thousands of troops, tons of equipment and wounded – all had to cross the causeway for a final desperate stand against the enemy. This was to be completed by the night of 31 January. That this was eventually achieved was in large measure due to the outstanding efforts of AIF Signals and units of our Royal Signals' counterparts in maintaining communications to our commanders. Later, on 7 February, a message was sent to Lieutenant Colonel Gus Kappe, Commander Signals 8 Australian Division, from Colonel Thyer, congratulating the unit on their efficiency, devotion to duty, and zeal which far exceeded his expectations.

Keeping up the pressure, the Japanese forced the main Allied army towards Johor Bahru. One of my last tasks would be to destroy the telephone exchange, should the town need to be abandoned. Orders were that, if destruction were warranted, I would receive the signal 'Sigma, Joto, Raffles'. Subscribers were to be informed and the demolition completed in twelve hours. At about 8 pm, while snatching a brief rest, I drifted into sleep and dreamed that I was back on the farm. Madge had been teasing me and I filled up a bucket with water and threw it over her. Suddenly my father's hand was shaking my shoulder. It wasn't my father however, but a signalman who had roused me. I half woke in a daze. 'What is it?'

'A signal from HQ, sir,' he said quietly.

I expected some routine order but as I looked at the paper he was holding out my heart fell. The words jumped from the page 'Sigma, Joto, Raffles.' It was grim news indeed but there was work to be done, the telephone exchange had to be destroyed.

I began by ordering a car to the home of the Chief Justice, who was first on the list of subscribers to be notified. His protests were no doubt reasonable, but orders were orders. Worse followed. Realizing that he and his family would have to evacuate he asked me to destroy their family pet, a beautiful cream Labrador. As I looked into its trusting eyes and fired my revolver, I saw only Buster.

After this episode I knew that if we were to telephone all the subscribers the job would never be done, so we disconnected the plugs at the exchange and laid the charges. It was destroyed according to plan and to such a degree that the Japanese were unable to use it during their occupation. We then retreated across the causeway to Singapore Island, where I was placed in command of a small section in the Singapore Botanic Gardens, just opposite the AIF's Tanglin Barracks and Headquarters.

By the end of the month, heavy fighting in Johor had taken more casualties and all our surviving troops were on the island. An event that I witnessed, on the last day of January as the Allies crossed the Straits of Johor, has gone down in history. I was working near the causeway when I thought I heard the sound of bagpipes. Looking up I saw about two dozen Argyll and Sutherland Highlanders marching towards me, tattered, exhausted and blood-stained, playing their pipes proudly and fearlessly.

The British now faced a dilemma. The 800-metre-long causeway, linking Singapore to Malaya by road and rail, had to be blown up in order to hinder the Japanese advance. However, they did not wish to destroy it completely as restoration would be too big a job after the war. The Royal Engineers responsible were ordered to demolish just 22 metres – quite close to the Malayan shoreline. It barely slowed the advancing enemy troops, who simply waded across at low tide and breached the gap within 24 hours, allowing their tanks and heavy equipment to cross. Even worse, when the causeway was blown, the pipe bringing Singapore's water supply from Malaya was also cut.

Within nine days the Japanese were on the island. Nothing had stopped them, not even flooding the Straights with aviation fuel and setting it alight as they swarmed across in boats and landing craft. While we could never hope to stem the relentless tide, we did manage to inflict death and heavy casualties. But it was not enough.

Even my optimism was now beginning to wane. As well as military casualties, thousands of civilians a day were being killed and injured; our supplies were running low and our supply and ammunition dumps captured. Shelling was constant, rest almost impossible, and showering difficult due to the failing water supply.

The British spirit of courage, some may say foolhardiness, was exemplified by an incident that occurred a few days before Singapore fell. I had to report to a major at British Signals Headquarters, situated in a summer-house at the Botanic Gardens. As I approached, a Japanese sniper fired at me. I pulled down my tin hat, dodging my way to where the major was sitting at a table, covered with maps and charts.

'Good morning, Wells.' Bullets ricocheted through the summer-house dislodging pots and covering his maps with soil and debris.

'Bit of a nuisance, these Japs,' he muttered. I pulled my tin hat down more firmly.

'Now, where were we?' He continued to calmly discuss communications while pot plants shattered about us, occasionally murmuring, 'Cheeky Japs, bit of a menace, what!' but otherwise taking as little notice of them as if we were sitting in the security of an office.

On another occasion, on my way to see a British Army captain, my driver stopped the vehicle in open ground and I ordered him to take shelter under some nearby trees. I worked my way towards the captain's tent dodging sniper bullets en route. On arriving at his tent, I was informed that he was further along the track near a creek. When I eventually located him, he was seated on a box blissfully soaking his feet in a bowl of Condy's crystals while shrapnel and bullets whizzed around him. Incredibly, in the midst of the turmoil, I noticed that the box was labelled 'SPC Peaches'. It was a moment of sanity to have this reminder of the Shepparton Preserving Company and of our orchardist neighbours who sent their fruit there. Unfortunately, when I returned to my vehicle my driver had been struck and killed by a bullet.

Every soldier has his share of close encounters with death. Before I left home my parents, thinking I would be sent to Europe, had given me a down-filled sleeping bag. Although too hot for sleeping in, it made a soft mattress for sleeping on. In the last week of fighting I was woken from an exhausted sleep by the sound of heavy shelling. Inclined to stay where I was, I realized that it was my duty to check on the troops under my care. I spent a few minutes going from soldier to soldier speaking to them and reassuring them. When I returned, my sleeping bag was a total mass of feathers, ripped neatly apart up the middle by a piece of shrapnel.

The heavy concentration of Allied troops holding the area was too concerned with dodging Japanese dive bombers and running for slit trenches to realise that the days of freedom and fighting were rapidly coming to an end. No doubt senior officers were more realistic. We had been forced to abandon our fuel, ammunition and supply dumps, the Japanese were in control of the water supply, medical and food supplies were running low and hundreds of civilians and military personnel were being killed every day.

My previous optimism of defeating the Japanese turned sour as bombardments continued ceaselessly, day and night. I realised that surrender was inevitable.

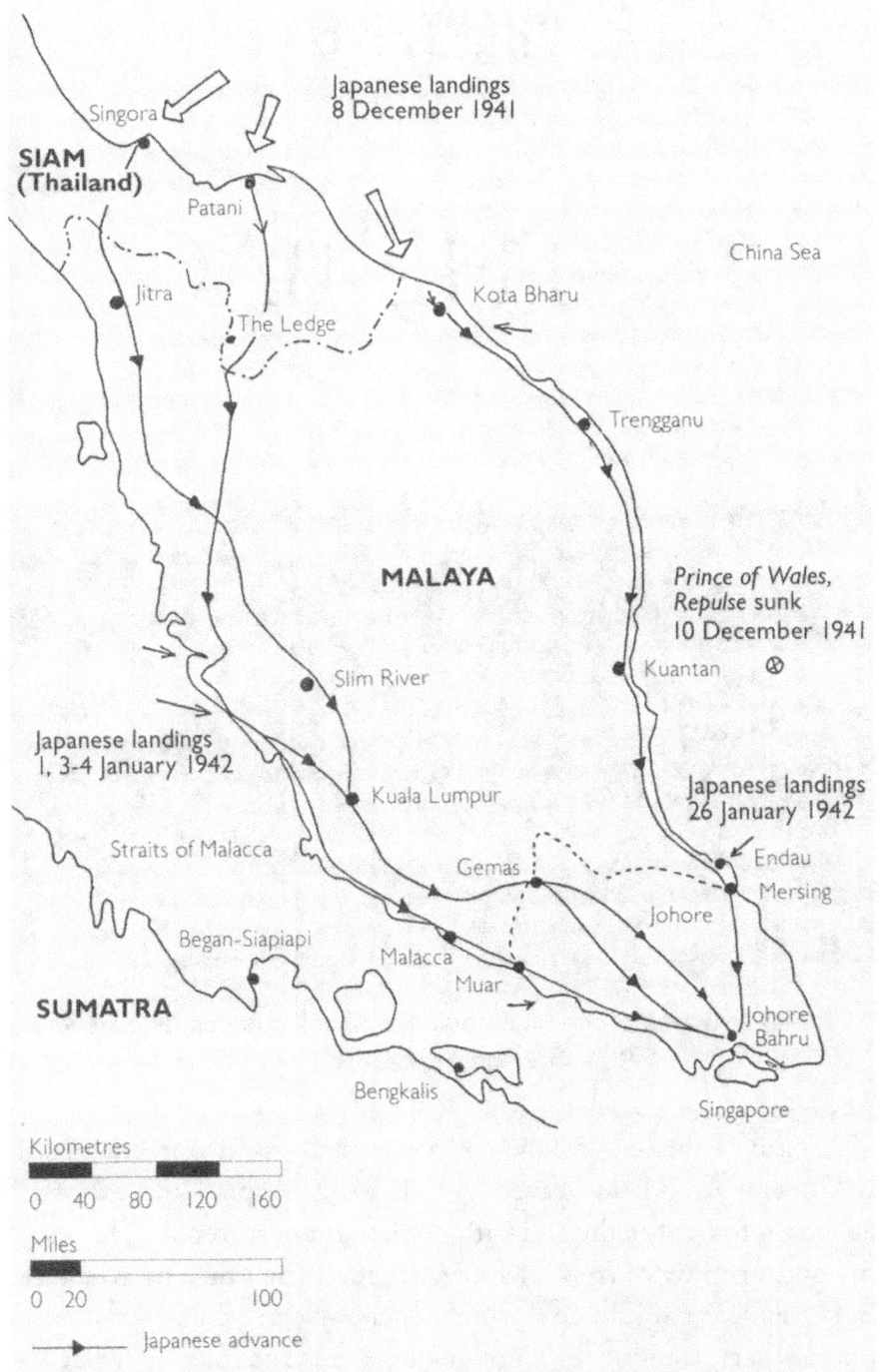

CHAPTER 6

IN THE BAG

The destruction of the oil reserves at Kranji cast a shadow over Singapore city, February 1942.

In early February, following our retreat from the mainland, General Archibald Wavell had visited Singapore and exhorted all troops to fight to the end with no thought of surrender. However, my optimism was such that I never thought that my end would be in surrender, it would always be somebody else's end. In any case, our military training had not included instructions on what we might face if captured by an enemy. We knew about conditions laid down by the Geneva Convention, but in the event of being captured we anticipated it would be individually or in small groups. We had never expected to be taken as a whole army.

On 10 February, the Japanese commander, General Yamashita, in a letter dropped to the General Officer Commanding Malaya, British Lieutenant General Percival, had made it abundantly clear that the Allies should surrender. The fighting continued but on the afternoon of Sunday 15 February, the two opposing generals met for a parley at the Ford Factory at Bukit Timah, a hill in the middle of the island. It was a one-sided conference, with the Japanese not only holding the high ground, but all the cards. Yamashita demanded, and received, unconditional surrender. When we heard the news, late that afternoon, that fighting would cease at eight o'clock that night, we were in disbelief. The uncertainty of not knowing what would happen to us as prisoners was tempered by the relief that the fighting was over. A message from Percival, delivered to all troops, briefly gave the reasons for surrender:

It has been necessary to give up the struggle and I want the reasons explained to all ranks. The forward troops continue to hold their ground, but the essentials of war have run short. In a few days we shall have neither petrol nor food. Many types of ammunition have run short, and the water supply, on which the vast population and many of the fighting troops are dependent, threatens to fail.
This situation has been brought about, partly by being driven off our dumps, and partly by hostile air attack and military action. Without the sinews of war, we cannot carry on.
I thank all ranks for their efforts during the campaign.

(Signed) A E Percival Lieutenant General

Percival was in an invidious position. He was made the scapegoat for decisions, often made by others, which led to the surrender and which saw him wrongly blamed for the loss of Malaya. I felt very sorry for him.

Rest, let alone sleep, had been impossible for the past ten or twelve weeks. The roar and scream of incessant shelling and mortar fire had left us physically and mentally exhausted. Dust, smoke and the turmoil of civilian and military movement had become a normal part of our daily lives. We were helpless, exhausted, filthy and completely demoralised; we were defeated and filled with dread and anxiety.

Wartime blackout conditions were in force so on Sunday evening, when the lights came on, the sudden brightness was eerie and unpleasant. Our senior officers told us that in the morning our arms were to be surrendered. Despite orders to the contrary we did our best to render them useless and all cyphers, confidential or incriminating evidence were destroyed.

The first few hours of surrender were horrible. After three months of intense combat most of us just wanted to sleep. Many front line troops hadn't washed for about two weeks and in the intense humidity bodies were red raw with tinea, tropical ulcers and sores. All we could do was to lie down wherever we were and sleep.

It was only the next morning, after a night's rest without interruption from shell firing for the first time in weeks that we were overwhelmed by the desperate reality and complete horror of our situation. Nobody talked much and the faint hopes we may have held of being rescued or repatriated were finally lost. We were finished. Our optimism and fighting spirit had finally been extinguished like a spent candle in an unknown cave. We were in the hands of an enemy not known for its acts of mercy.

It would have been around lunchtime that we first saw our captors, when Japanese officers walked among the troops taking personal items and anything else of interest. I had my camera on me, a present from my parents. I removed the film, exposed it to the light, then replaced it in the camera; some Japanese would think he had a new roll of film. A very small act of defiance, which strangely gave me immense satisfaction. My watch, wallet, money and several other items all disappeared. No food was provided so we scrounged what we could.

We speculated as to what lay ahead: we would be repatriated; we would be imprisoned; we would be let loose on the island to fend for ourselves? It was all speculation. The reality turned out to be far beyond anything we could imagine.

Not much happened on the Monday. Percival and other top-ranking officers were in negotiations with the Japanese, trying to obtain the best conditions for the troops and for as many supplies as possible to be transported out to Changi, on the south-east coast of the island. It was not until Tuesday morning that we assembled for the long route march out to Changi military camp. From the air we would have been an impressive sight – 15,000 or so Australians plus more than 100,000 British and Commonwealth troops all laden with as much food, clothing, utensils and medical supplies as they could carry. A sick and weary sight, we certainly did not march, but trudged and straggled along as best we could, trying to keep together as a unit, all that day and through the night. It was totally dark with little traffic except for the odd Japanese staff car, which drove past with lights blazing, horn blaring and red staff flags fluttering.

Everywhere was devastation. Roads were littered with rubble, buildings demolished, drains and footpaths blocked by debris. Singapore's population had been swollen by a million refugees from upstate Malaya, who had fled south as the Japanese advanced through the country. People thronged the streets, moving they knew not where, dazed, frightened and panic stricken.

We had several halts and were dispirited and hungry when we arrived at the huge pre-war army camp at Changi the next morning. However, water was our most pressing problem – we had only our water bottles and, with the city water supply from the storage reservoir disrupted owing to burst and damaged mains, we had no hope of replenishing them; certainly the Japs were not expected to supply water carts.

Covering 160 hectares, the Changi complex had several barracks, capable of housing thousands of troops, with married quarters, parks, gardens and all the facilities of a large town. The Australians' new home was Selarang Barracks, formerly home to a battalion of Gordon Highlanders. Not far away was Changi Gaol, constructed in the late 1930s, in the style of a 19th century prison. Built to accommodate 600 prisoners, it would now serve as an internment camp for British civilians.

As most of our barracks had been damaged, we set to work creating a proper camp; our captors weren't about to expend their own labour force on projects that could be done by prisoners. To our surprise, no Japanese appeared at the camp for quite a number of days, so conditions were relatively pleasant.

A camp hospital was established in nearby Roberts Barracks, where the British prisoners were accommodated. A great deal of equipment and drugs were smuggled in, thanks to the ingenuity of Dr Glyn White, 8 Division's Deputy Assistant Director of Medical Services.

In the last days of fighting, White was running a makeshift hospital at St Andrew's Anglican Cathedral. Following the surrender, his task was to evacuate all Allied patients from various Singapore hospitals to designated POW camps.

On 18 February, the chief Japanese medical officer, Colonel Sekiguchi, gave him one week to transfer 12,000 patients and the use of five ambulances. White, always a shrewd, uncompromising and persistent operator, said that this would be impossible and demanded more vehicles. Sekiguchi told him that if he could assemble them, he would give the matter further consideration. By the next morning White had gathered together 20 3-tonne trucks, over 50 ambulances and a car for himself. He was very surprised when passes were issued for all the vehicles.

Orders had also been given that only 250 hospital beds could be taken and no medical supplies or equipment at all. Despite this, 4500 beds and 7000 mattresses were successfully transported with supplies and equipment hidden underneath, along with vital drugs, including sulphapyridine, Atabrin and quinine sulphate powder. Fortunately, Sekiguchi had by now moved on and White convinced his replacement, who seemed to know few details of the orders, that he had been allowed a week to move each of the British, Australian and Indian contingents. When the convoy set out for Changi it stretched for more than three kilometres.

For a week or so after our arrival at the barracks, we were established on a unit-by-unit basis but, as things settled down, AIF Headquarters Changi, as we called it, was set up. Senior officers were kept busy getting the camp organised, maintaining discipline and distributing food, which was of great concern as the only rations supplied by the Japanese was rice.

The medical officers insisted that it would require a lot of expertise and ingenuity to keep the troops healthy. Fresh meat, fruit and vegetables were initially in short supply until we could set up some sort of trading system with the local people. This took some time, as market gardens had ceased commercial production and the Japanese commandeered what was now available. So, various schemes were implemented. Besides vegetable gardens, which expanded until we had many hectares under cultivation, a poultry farm was established and the eggs sent to the hospital. Rice was also fermented to provide yeast for its vitamin B content. Because I had some knowledge of chemistry, I was appointed Unit Yeast Officer, surely a unique appointment in military terms. About 30 grams of rice per man was put into each unit yeast fund and it was my job to allow this to ferment to produce a rather vile tasting brew. It was estimated that about half a cup of this per week would keep us healthy, but we had no quantitative way of measuring it.

Civil and military engineers came into their own and, over the next three months a perimeter fence was erected and unit messes were set up for officers, non-commissioned officers and other ranks. Shower blocks, medical huts and cook houses were also established and the area began to resemble a normal military camp.

The engineers also rigged hessian screens around the latrines, set over holes bored into the ground, and devised a water system for showers so, although we had no running water, we were able to keep ourselves reasonably clean. At first there was very little dysentery but later, when it took hold, sprinkler bottles filled with disinfectant to clean our hands kept outbreaks under control.

Initially, for transporting food and supplies, we had only vehicle chassis on wheels, which we pushed ourselves. Later on, trucks were supplied, but without fuel. It took 20 men to push one.

At first, rice proved to be a problem for our cooks. Our previous experience with rice was in the form of puddings or, more recently, the well-cooked fluffy white rice of the Singaporean shop-houses. It now had to take the place of bread and potatoes so it was important to make the most of it. However, Japanese rice was different from Chinese rice. At first, all that the army cooks could produce was a sticky grey mess but, fortunately, when men who had been professional cooks in civilian life lent a hand, the quality improved dramatically. By adding sugar and condensed milk they even made a kind of rice custard.

As life became more settled, we became experts at improvisation and certainly the discipline of camp arrangements made life tolerable and predictable. Our initial despair at becoming prisoners subsided a little, as educational classes, and eventually Changi University, were established. Exercise routines were also implemented, concert parties staged a variety of performances and hospital and medical facilities were set up. The Japanese also provided books from libraries, allowing the creation of the Changi library. Somehow books from Singapore libraries filtered in. By chance I came across the textbook *Applied Physiology* by Samson Wright. I managed to absorb its contents, which came in handy later during my incarceration.

It may seem strange that Changi was run on the normal military lines but this was absolutely vital in order to maintain health, morale and discipline; it worked very efficiently to reduce the anxiety we all felt about our welfare, besides which it gave a structure to our lives and kept everyone busy. At first, discipline was slack but, according to military law, prisoners were still under discipline and, under its guidelines, a microcosm of new life began. We became almost like a closed country, cut off from the world and we turned to each other with the mutual aim of survival. The future was unknown and we feared for it but had no faith in its outcome.

In the early days at Changi, and throughout my entire imprisonment, the bonds between the troops forged during our military service came to the fore, and strengthened into what can only be described as brotherly love. When death came, there was always someone to hold a hand, wipe a brow or whisper a word of comfort. There was no need for competition; we were all equal in belongings and provisions. We also developed special sayings and words, which meant nothing to anyone outside our camp communities.

Since our surrender, all prisoners were under the control of Colonel Ichiji Sugita and his intelligence officers, but the actual camp commandant was Lieutenant Okasaki. He made it clear that we were not prisoners but captives – a subtle distinction that we failed to appreciate.

Pre-war photo of buildings in Selarang Barracks, Changi, where the Australians were imprisoned.

CHAPTER 7

SANDAKAN

Sandakan waterfront, municipal buildings and Jubilee Clock Tower, 1935.

In order to make use of the unexpected labour force at their disposal, the Japanese soon put their 'captives' to work. Working parties cleared huge amounts of debris, restored water pipes, loaded tons of supplies appropriated from British warehouses onto ships bound for Japan and, very reluctantly, built memorials to Japanese war dead. However, while conditions in the camp were not too bad, it was now far better to be out of Changi than in it. Those on work parties were not only allowed a daily ration of about 120 grams of meat, they also had the opportunity to scrounge – that is, steal extra food and anything useful that might come their way.

In May 1942, it was announced by the Japanese that work parties would be sent 'overseas' and that our officers were to make the selection, although they had no idea of where or why the prisoners were being transferred. The first draft, known as A Force, left in May. No details were given but we all hoped that they would be sent somewhere where food was a bit more plentiful.

One evening in June, after our evening rice meal, the Australian CO, Lieutenant Colonel 'Black Jack' Galleghan, announced that two thousand troops were to be selected for the next work party. The selectors chose officers, NCOs and men from a cross-section of units so that, if there were a chance to overcome the Japanese, a miniature army would be at the ready, with representatives from transport, gunners, artillery, signals, medical and catering personnel. However, with so many men out on working parties outside Changi, only 1500 were available for the draft. Of these, 150 were officers.

I volunteered for the first contingent of what became B Force. On 8 July, all 1500 of us, under the command of Lieutenant Colonel Alf Walsh of 2/10 Field Regiment, were marched to Keppel Harbour or, if more fortunate, made the journey in trucks. Our transport ship, *Yubi Maru* was not the smartest looking vessel and we wondered how we were all going to fit on board. We did not have long to find out.

Boarding the ship, we were hustled into three holds, previously used to transport pigs and coal. The floor of each hold was about six metres below the deck and would have been seven to eight metres square. With five hundred men in each hold we were crammed shoulder to shoulder in coal dust and pig manure. In the corners of each hold were machine guns or sentries with hand grenades or automatic rifles.

The heat was appalling. We were served 'limed rice', not rice with lime juice added to give it a bit of flavour, but rice that had been preserved in calcium sulphide to prevent weevil infestation. Normally, it was issued to coolies after being washed to remove the preservative. We had it dished up as an unpalatable mess: poorly cooked, unwashed, full of dead weevils and with the terrible stench of hydrogen sulphide, or rotten egg gas. We now knew our place in the Japanese pecking order – we were lower than the coolies.

It did not take long for dysentery to break out. I would say about a quarter of the prisoners suffered from it; not the usual type of dysentery when, if you were well fed, there was excretion of a certain amount of solid waste. This was watery, and the body's urge to rid itself of something undesirable was uncontrollable. Pains in the stomach and anus were relentless. There were two or three crudely built toilets above deck, accessed by ladders, but most of the chaps could not get there in time. In any case, the Japanese would not always allow them out on deck and sent them back into the hold, where they fouled the rungs of the ladders as well as the floor. Added to the pigs and coal we now had human waste, along with an increased stench, but amazingly we soon became immune to it. Flies and mosquitoes were another source of discomfort. However, despite the foul conditions, our spirits were high and we thought only of survival; we were optimistic enough to still believe that help would soon be at hand, that things would not be too bad and that we could live through this ordeal.

I don't know how rumors start in these circumstances, but it wasn't long before word circulated that we were being repatriated to a neutral island where a submarine would pick us up. I doubt that any of us took these rumours seriously but, in a way, they helped to cheer us up.

When we had been herded onto the ship, the Japanese tried to keep the officers in one area of the hold, separate from the men. I seemed to be with officers of my own unit. We knew each other very well – well enough to know how we would react in certain circumstances – allowing for changes in behaviour, individual characteristics, strengths and weaknesses. So, despite the conditions, there didn't seem to be much trouble or friction as we tried to keep up the morale of our men. In the crowded area, we did manage to shuffle around and kept an eye on them, taking care not to interfere with men of another unit, if their officers were there to enforce some sort of discipline. Although it was all a very distressing experience, we were still hopeful that it would not be for long and that we would survive. After all, the Japs could not keep us sailing around for more than a couple of days.

When people became ill it became a question of survival, not so much for ourselves, but for those who were our responsibility. We did have a few laughs and jokes, which helped lighten the suffering but, on the whole, it was pretty grim. We talked about our backgrounds, schooling, work and army life but a lot of us realized that this was the end of the sort of life we had known. Strangely, we did not talk much about loved ones at home because some of the men became very sentimental. Most were reluctant to contemplate the future. The past was a safer place. In trying to recall our feelings at that time, I am convinced that there was an attitude of upholding the ANZAC tradition, the realization of what it meant to be an Australian, that we would not let the side down and that our fathers, many of whom had been WWI soldiers, would be proud of us.

During our last few weeks at Changi, Thyer had addressed the officers and senior NCOs on the importance of maintaining the strictest discipline; that our lives as prisoners would be difficult and uncertain, that our survival depended on our ability to mentally and physically foster all our resources. I am sure it was this attitude, which we officers tried to instill in the troops that kept things under control on *Yubi Maru* and later in the camp.

We had anticipated being offloaded within a couple of days, but it was actually some ten days later, after much stopping and starting and staying in one place for two days while we re-fuelled that, on 18 July, we sensed the ship was slowing and we heard hatches being opened. The fresh air found us starved, filthy, and desperate to get out of our hell-hole. It was late afternoon when we began moving onto the deck and caught our first sight of Sandakan Harbour. The red cliffs on the seaward side of Berhala Island at the harbour entrance were an impressive sight. For a fleeting moment I imagined that we had come to a peaceful place, one that the Japanese had left undisturbed. These happy thoughts were immediately dispelled by the sight of Japanese soldiers on the shore and the white flag of Japan with its red sun, flying on buildings all over town.

When we finally set foot on land it was dark, but I made out hills with lights scattered randomly like stars to welcome us. It reminded me of a holiday I had spent at Daylesford with my father when I was a lad which, in 1942, was really not that very long ago. In darkness, we were marched up a hill to a large stone church, where the officers spent the night in an adjoining school building. It was certainly peaceful with no enemy activity, the constant noise of Singapore only a memory. The sentries did not worry us as they knew there was nowhere we could go. I went to sleep dreaming that I was back in Daylesford and that the dream was true.

In the morning we were ordered to march. We knew only that we were in Borneo and that the name of the town was Sandakan but, as our geography of Borneo was limited, we had no idea of our geographical position. Nevertheless, it was a huge relief to feel cool once more, to see green jungle and to smell fresh air. Although we were starving, it was good to be moving after the cramped and filthy conditions of the ship. Perhaps things will not be too tough here, we hoped – the camp was a long way from Japanese command; discipline might be more relaxed. These were my thoughts as we marched along the road, leading inland. Shortly, in a small clearing, a tiny atap-roofed (thatched) shophouse, commonly found in

Malaya, came into sight. The stall keeper proffered some bananas to the passing troops. One man broke rank and ran over to take some fruit but without warning or orders was shot at by a Japanese guard. Welcome to Sandakan.

Such was my first impression of this new home, Sandakan, the pre-war capital of British North Borneo. After a march of 13 kilometres, we reached our new abode, a collection of timber and atap huts, about half of them built by the British to house army personnel guarding an airfield, construction of which had been halted by Japanese occupation. For a few weeks the barracks had been used to confine Japanese internees, who were released by the IJA when invasion forces had arrived on 19 January. With the internees no longer in occupation, the facility had been hastily extended with the erection of a number of sub-standard huts to accommodate the large number of incoming prisoners.

Interior of officers' huts, 8 Mile POW Camp, Sandakan, by POW artist F Woodley, 1942-43.

Passing by a guard house, we entered the camp gates, where a huge old mengaris tree stood. Towering 60 or 70 metres into the air, it was to become quite a landmark in our lives. A heavily reinforced and electrified barbed-wire fence surrounded the camp perimeter, with a chain of wooden watch towers constructed at intervals. In the midday light, it didn't look too bad, but it did not take us long to discover that things were not as good as at Changi.

Our officers set about allocating men and officers to the huts. We officers slept on bamboo platforms, on rattan mats infested with bed bugs, with 12 or 18 prisoners in each hut. The rattan mats were very small with barely 30 centimetres of space between each and rats had the run of the place. Underneath the huts were two large tubs, or tongs, which we filled with water to wash ourselves but the water was far from clean. The rations were worse than at Changi – the rice was plentiful but was full of weevils and boiled without salt until it was mushy and tasteless. There was no protein and very little fruit or vegetables. However, we just had to make the most of it and set about improving our lot as best we could.

Soon after our arrival at the camp, we were assembled under the big tree to be addressed by the commandant, Lieutenant Susumi Hoshijima, a civil engineer and graduate of Osaka University. Although he spoke very good English, he always used an interpreter whom he frequently corrected. It would have been beneath his dignity to address us in English or to address us in Japanese and then do his own interpreting. Hoshijima was very tall, indeed the tallest Japanese I have ever met. As I later found out, he was, incongruously, a fan of author and humourist, P G Wodehouse.

He began arrogantly –

'I am absolutely convinced that even if this war goes on for 150 years, Japan will never surrender. It well may take that long,' he continued, 'to conquer the rest of the Asian Co-Prosperity sphere and then with our allies, the Germans and Italians, we will conquer the rest of the world. But let there be no misunderstanding – this will happen. You will dismiss any thoughts of going home in victory.'

He finally told us that we were there to build an aerodrome.

Lieutenant Colonel Walsh then informed him that, under the provisions of the Geneva Convention, prisoners of war were not to be used in the construction of military facilities. Hoshijima's reply was that, as the aerodrome would also be used for civilian aircraft, it was automatically exempted from the provisions of the Geneva Convention.

At around this time, in an attempt to improve morale as well as the food supply, negotiations with the Japanese resulted in officers – who were not required to work on the airfield – being allowed to establish a vegetable garden on about half a hectare of land out towards the airstrip, well outside the camp wire. We desperately needed medical supplies, extra rations, and outside news and the vegetable patch created a perfect opportunity to make contact with the locals.

Lieutenant Norman Sligo had been appointed the B Force Intelligence Officer. However, after his death from dysentery at the end of August, six weeks after our arrival, Captain Lionel Matthews, whom I had known from my training days at Casula and Bathurst, was appointed in Sligo's place. Lionel was generally known as 'The Duke' because of his very strong resemblance to Prince Henry, Duke of Gloucester and brother of King George VI.

Lionel was over six feet tall; with his athletic build and military moustache he was an imposing figure with a personality to match. He was a natural leader, extremely brave and inspired fierce loyalty, confidence and optimism in his men. For his actions in maintaining communications under fire at a battle near Gemas in Malaya, and later on Singapore Island, he was awarded the Military Cross. Since our arrival at Sandakan, Lionel and I, as fellow signals officers, had become quite close.

Determined to set up contacts outside the camp to try to improve the lot of the prisoners, Lionel managed to become leader of the gardening group. This gave him opportunities to contact local people, who belonged to an underground movement already operating in the town. Through a local man by the name of Dick Majinal, who worked at the Agricultural Farm adjoining the camp, Lionel established contact with an Australian doctor, James Taylor, the Principal Medical Officer, and Gerald Mavor, Superintendent of the Sandakan Light and Power Company. Both these men and their families had been in the Colonial Service for some years before the war. The Japanese allowed them to go about their duties under 'simple confinement', which meant that they were not confined to the prison camp, but were nonetheless under strict Japanese scrutiny.

Many local civilians, especially the Chinese, were sympathetic to the British and the prisoners. Sergeant Abin, a Dusun in charge of the nearby Eight Mile Police Post, helped plan many of the contacts and supply routes. Ojagar Singh, a tall Sikh police officer along with the Funk brothers, Alex, Paddy and Johnny, and many others were willing to help wherever possible.

Johnny and Paddy Funk, c 1941.

To belong to the underground movement was a hugely risky undertaking. Apart from the rigid regime of the Japanese, it was difficult to know who was trustworthy. Could we trust every Asian who smiled at us and whispered that he would help? On the whole, the Chinese were loyal to the British, but some Malays were pro-Japanese – we could never be sure and the risk of betrayal was high. And while most of the prisoners were in favour of the work of the underground and were very supportive, not everyone had the same mind set. Some were apathetic, content not to know what was going on. A few others, however, were openly opposed to being exposed to the extra risks and dangers, and resented our activities.

The camp electricity relied on a large boiler, which drove a steam engine, attached to an alternator, to create a little power station. Copper wires ran from the alternator on bush poles to reach the camp. Lighting to the huts was turned off at 10 pm but the perimeter lights burned all night. In order to keep the boiler going day and night, the Japanese sent out wood-gathering parties. Initially, none of our officers was allocated to them.

This was a deliberate ploy on the part of the Japanese to keep the officers and men apart and to stir up resentment amongst the troops. Why should they be out working all day while the officers sat around in camp? I decided to make it my business to join one of these wood parties to see what was going on, hopefully to make some local contacts and to act as a buffer between the guards and the workers. It was no use telling the men to stop working, but I could encourage them to work more slowly and to put as little effort as possible into sawing the wood, just keep moving the hand saw. I didn't believe in disobedience unless it accomplished something worthwhile. If a worker stopped work, he was belted and made to do it anyway.

As soon as I succeeded in being assigned to a wood party, I set about fostering good relations with the guards. One spoke reasonable English and we managed to collect our wood without incurring too many beatings. However, one day the guard belted me unmercifully for some trivial reason. A few days later, when we were out working, he left me in charge while he enjoyed a sleep, telling me not to wake him. Shortly afterwards, a Japanese staff car came along the road and stopped near us. An officer asked where the guard was. I indicated that he was along the track somewhere. Next thing there was an almighty row as the guard was bashed and yelled at for sleeping on duty. He later asked,

'Why you no wake me?'

'Well,' I said, 'you said not to disturb you; I just obeyed your orders.'

It was quite soon after our arrival that the rank and file began work on airfield construction. They were advised by our senior officers to work as slowly as possible without incurring beatings and to engage in small acts of sabotage that would be undetected. It was about this time that we had a visit from Major Tatsugi Suga, commander of all Borneo prisoners, who arrived from POW Headquarters at Kuching, in Sarawak, to address us. It was incongruous to see him wearing World War I Allied ribbons on his chest and strange to recall that Japan had been our ally in that conflict. After his visit, pressure was increased on the workers at the airfield to speed up construction.

One morning, in early September 1942, we were woken by shouts and furious activity as the Japanese conducted a search of our quarters. No work parties were sent out that day and we were all assembled on the parade ground, under the big tree. We formed up with our senior officers in the front row, junior officers behind them, with a gap separating them from the lines of NCOs and other ranks. Things were tense. A large contingent of guards surrounded the assembly. Some, mounted on trucks, trained machine guns on us.

Hoshijima mounted a dais and addressed us. We must behave ourselves and work diligently for the IJA without any sense of hostility, he said. In other words, all the things we had been trained not to do. The crunch was that each and every one of us must sign a document acknowledging that it was illegal to escape and that, should anyone do so, we wished the culprit to be brought to trial and shot. In stunned silence, we watched the soldiers ready their guns, while Hoshijima invited us to come up and sign the document.

Lieutenant Colonel Walsh was first to mount the dais. He read the document aloud, put it down and then declared in a loud clear voice –

'I, for one, will not, repeat not, sign this document.'

There was an ominous clicking as safety catches on weapons were released and we all thought, 'This is the end.' I think it was at this point that Hoshijima realized that, if his men opened fire, the prisoners at the rear would rise up. Furthermore, his instructions were to finish the aerodrome quickly and that would not be possible if too many of us were slaughtered. Hoshijima barked an order.

Walsh was roped with his hands behind his back and led to a newly-erected post where the machine guns were trained on him. The interpreter then told us that we must all sign or else Walsh would be killed. This announcement was followed by a short consultation between Hoshijima and the interpreter. It was probably for only half a minute or so but, with tension rising on both sides, it seemed interminable. The impasse was broken when Major John Workman, our 2IC, suggested, after some tense negotiations, that if it was understood we had signed this document under duress, and the wording were altered to state that it had been signed under the direction of the IJA, then we would sign it. Until this time, Alf Walsh had not been very popular commander with the troops and a number of the officers but, after this episode, he was deeply respected and admired for his courage.

About 1500 signatures went on the document. Had they cared to peruse it, the Japanese may well have wondered why there were so many Ned Kellys, Bob Menzies and Mae Wests in the AIF.

To make sure we all understood the 'no escape' agreement, Major Suga also came up from Kuching to address us on the issues of misunderstanding and the penalties for escaping.

Despite this incident, life went on as usual, with work parties on the airstrip continuing to toil from sunrise until sundown. However, discipline on the wood-gathering parties was a little more relaxed. This allowed greater opportunities for passing messages and smuggling in supplies, and is how I made an invaluable contact.

Chan Ah Ping was the Chinese engineer in charge of the power station. I became quite close to him, as close as I could under such circumstances, and worked my way into a more or less permanent place on the wood party without raising any suspicions. Eventually, the Japanese expected me to come out in the mornings with them. It was only on odd occasions, such as a dysentery attack, that I managed to get a day's rest and someone else would take the wood party.

Meanwhile, as airfield construction progressed, it soon became clear that the Japanese had a deadline to meet, and life became much harsher for the workers there. There was plenty to eat – a ration of 750 grams of rice per man per day for labourers, most of which could be traded with locals working at the airstrip for other food. However, medical supplies were always in short supply and the guards at the airstrip could be brutal, inflicting group punishment for the slightest misdemeanor. Men were bashed for working too slowly, hit with wooden swords or pieces of wood for disobeying orders. Prisoners of war were slaves, enemies of Japan, and treated accordingly. As part of the dehumanizing process, and to reinforce our lowly status as commodities, on arrival we had all been issued with a POW number. Mine was 667. Rus Ewin, who slept alongside me, was assigned 666.

On 27 October, Alf Walsh and his most senior officers were sent to the main POW camp in Kuching. By separating the most senior officers from the men, the Japanese hoped to break down discipline and make it difficult for prisoners to organize escapes and carry out acts of sabotage.

Six months later, in April 1943, 200 British prisoners, previously engaged in airfield construction at Jesselton, on British North Borneo's west coast, arrived at Sandakan, where they were housed in a new camp near the airport; in a fortnight another 500 joined them. We also learned in April that 500 Australian prisoners, known as E Force, had arrived from Singapore and were in a temporary camp on Berhala Island. In June, they were transferred to a compound a short distance from our camp, known as Number 3 Camp. The total number of prisoners at Sandakan, both Australian and British, now stood at around 2,700. With the rise in the camp population, the Japanese decided to introduce new POW numbers, starting with B Force compound, then E and then the British, issued according to rank and alphabetically. Mine was now 124.

For the first year, conditions at Sandakan were endurable, despite harsh treatment meted out at the aerodrome by a specially designated 'basher gang', brought in to speed up the work in October 1942. A small wooden cage was also constructed as a disciplinary measure. Prisoners were sentenced to it for hours and days on end, without food and only very small amounts of water provided in the tropical heat. However, in April 1943, brutality increased with the arrival of young Formosan conscripts. Dubbed 'kitchi' guards because of their small stature, they were particularly vicious, delighting in inflicting pain on prisoners by deliberately bashing ulcerated shins and generally throwing their weight around.

CHAPTER 8

THE UNDERGROUND

Ojagah Singh with his children: Anup is 2nd from right.

Initially the reason for the camp becoming involved in the underground movement was to smuggle in medical supplies via Dr Taylor and the hospital. However, when Dr Taylor began exchanging foreign money held in the camp for local currency, a fund was established to make purchases. The black-market economy that developed then allowed more medical supplies to be obtained. These were left in safe places for collection. The underground organisation was later expanded to arrange an escape route to the Philippines, and for Lionel to make contact with guerrilla forces, who arranged for arms and ammunition to be smuggled in and secreted at Mile 15, about 12 kilometers west of the camp, should an opportunity arise to overthrow the Japanese. The cache consisted of two machine guns, 27 rifles and about 2500 rounds of ammunition. Added to this were the firearms of the constabulary, now under the command of Lionel, who had been appointed Police Chief by the former chief, Major A Rice-Oxley, before he was transferred to the Kuching Camp. The underground also provided radio parts for the construction of a receiver, in the hope of making contact with the outside world.

It is hard for us now to imagine a world where there is not instant access to information and still harder to understand that, after several weeks at Sandakan without news of any kind, the whole camp had a real craving for contact with the outside world. In order of priority, what we most longed for was news of home, medical supplies and food. The Japanese, of course, were telling us that all was finished in England and Europe, that Sydney was all but under Japanese control and that the Allies were fighting a lost cause. I took stock of the situation. By August 1942, I had advised Lionel that with some equipment smuggled in from outside and by improvising and making some of my own components, it would be possible to make a wireless receiver.

Because of my expertise with radio and communications, my enthusiasm to escape, my utmost loyalty and integrity, and my ability to improvise, Lionel appointed me second in command of the camp's underground movement. Prior to the war, British North Borneo was a British protectorate, run by a Chartered Company and with its own European systems of law and order, medical and civic services, including a police force. Known as the British North Borneo Constabulary, it employed Dusuns and other indigenous tribespeople, along with Malays, Indians and Chinese, all under the command of a small nucleus of British senior officers – a valuable source of contacts for the underground movement. Detective Ernesto Lagan, Matusup bin Gungau, Felix Azcona and Heng Joo Meng were all members of the town underground. The three Funk brothers were from a prominent and highly respected Sandakan family. Their father was a magistrate.

By offering their help, all these people and many others ran huge risks to themselves and their families. And all were invaluable to the underground. Inevitably, the larger the network became, the greater the risks of discovery and betrayal, particularly as there was a paid Japanese informant, doing menial tasks in the camp.

Several dropping off places for medical supplies, money and other items were established at certain points around the camp, usually in trees, at the police post, in drains or in piles of wood. Dr Taylor, Gerald Mavor and their local staff were vital in establishing an effective chain of operations for this purpose. Mavor was exceptionally helpful in making various items for the radio at the power station and smuggling them into the camp. Ojagar Singh and Sergeant Abin, along with many others, passed messages into, and out of, the camp. Heng, who had previously lived in Singapore and spoke English, supplied radio parts and maps and charts of local jungle tracks, Japanese guard posts, signals stations and the storage dump. He also made contact with the guerrilla groups and gave basic advice on how to survive in the jungle. Ernesto Lagan, a trusted associate of Taylor and Felix Azcona, a Filipino whose father ran a radio shop in Sandakan, was also in contact with guerrilla groups in the nearby Philippines. Alex Funk somehow managed to obtain a .38 revolver for Lionel, along with five rounds of ammunition, which was smuggled into the camp and hidden.

Ingenious ways were found to conceal illicit items and messages in the camp, but a simple slip of security, an unguarded remark or a search by the Japanese – and these were sudden, frequent and thorough – could jeopardize the whole operation with dire consequences for all. However, as many prisoners felt it was their duty to try to escape, these risks had to be faced and minimized.

My task was to build a radio. It must be remembered that, in 1942, there were no transistors, printed circuit boards or orbiting satellites to transmit radio signals. There was just the ionosphere and naturally occurring radio waves. It was here that my boyhood experiments, my knowledge of mathematics, chemistry, physics and radio signals were of critical importance to the success or failure of the project. However, perhaps my greatest strength was my ability to improvise and my absolute determination to perfect any project I undertook, even under circumstances as difficult as these.

I decided that a regenerative receiver would best suit our needs, mainly because it was simpler to build from scratch and, since components were scarce or non-existent, the simpler the better. This type of receiver is very sensitive and, as the high frequency spectrum was seldom used in that part of the world during the war, I hoped that we would pick up BBC short-wave broadcasts – a possibility that was confirmed by the Japanese, who sent for Gordon Weynton, a fellow signals officer, to repair their radio set one night. Spending as much time as he could in fiddling with it and repairing it, he managed to switch to the short-wave band, tuned into the BBC and heard the news that Prince George, Duke of Kent, had been killed in a military aircraft crash on 25 August 1942.

A skilled ham radio operator before the war, Gordon was an excellent practical wireless man, and together we set about designing a wireless set. The more equipment we could produce in the camp, the less risk of discovery. The major requirement was a power source to operate the receiver, while both high and low voltages were required for the single valve. Apart from a few dry (battery) cells, which did not last long, the only reliable power was the camp's 110-volt alternating current or AC supply. In order to use this, some way had to be found to convert alternating current into direct current (DC), to make the valve work. For the technically minded, this was achieved by using a home-made rectifier and smoothing choke. The 110-volt supply was not really high enough for the valve (more about that later) and it was also necessary to separately drop the voltage to energize the filament of the valve.

To operate a radio, several things are needed. Firstly, an antenna to pick up the signals. These signals are then rectified by the detector and the variable capacitor tuned into the desired frequency. The valve, acting as both detector and oscillator, amplifies the signal and feeds it to the headphones, which convert the electrical impulses to sound. Essentials for the job were a valve, headphones, condenser, variable capacitor and a rectifier. None of these items, apart from the rectifier and capacitor, could be made in the camp.

Other major items needed were resistors, a tuning coil to enable the receiver to be tuned to selected frequencies and low-voltage batteries to power the filament of the valve. How does one make these items to create a working receiver in a heavily guarded prison camp? By improvising, experimenting, by taking huge risks and by being highly inventive.

The underground's Matusup managed to provide a crystal detector and a headphone. Certainly, it was only one headphone, not a set, but one was better than none at all. Tied to the listener's head with a piece of string or rag, it worked reasonably well. With the help of Sergeant Alfie Stevens and Private Eric Davis, who worked in the engine room of the camp's small power plant, we managed to smuggle in, via Gerald Mavor, one valve and a variable capacitor. As Eric had permission to work outside the camp he was able to bring in various parts for the radio.

These, and other items, were left by Mavor at a prearranged hiding place for collection by Sergeant Abin, who was stationed most of the time at the police post near the camp. With a nod or a wink as we set out on wood gathering parties, Abin would indicate to us that there was an item to be collected. Over the next few days we would contrive to retrieve it from its hiding place, usually a certain tree or log, without being seen by the Japanese.

Once we had the vital components, Gordon and I began work. As he was older than most of the prisoners, Gordon was often assigned to menial camp duties, and used this time to scrounge a few more parts from around the camp and do the wiring.

Two or three fixed capacitors were required. One particular capacitor of about 0.01 microfarad was necessary. But how does one make such an item under these conditions? Very simply, by taking some aluminium foil from the tea chests in which the Japanese supplied the rice rations. Using a known equation for calculating capacity, I built up a 'sandwich' of small pieces of foil and layers of oil-soaked paper.

For the resistors we found that by using the impurities from wood and bark, particularly from cinnamon trees, rubbing some damp string in the burned bark and allowing it to dry out, resistance was produced. After some trial and error, I found that two centimetres of string provided one megohm resistance.

The first rectifier was made by oxidizing a small piece of aluminium foil with boric acid and sodium borate, smuggled in from the hospital along with test tubes and other items. This was then connected to two electrodes, one made from aluminium and the other from a zinc salt and aluminium; the zinc was obtained from pieces of zinc sheeting stolen from the aerodrome site. However, the problem with this rectifier was that it caused reverse voltage. I determined that a second rectifier cell and some sort of smoothing circuit was necessary, as the electrolyte was boiling after about 15 minutes of operation.

The new rectifier was made by first acquiring a piece of steel fishplate from the rail line, used to transport skips of earth at the aerodrome. Dropping this off at the power station, I asked Ah Ping, under my breath, to cut it into three pieces. These were used as the core. We then 'borrowed' about 15 metres of wire from the outside of beehives that the Japanese kept. To insulate the wire, we stretched it out and ran it through some palm oil thickened with a little flour, which was then heated to bind it to the wire. The treated wire was then wound around the fishplate core in layers, each layer insulated from the other by paper soaked in hot coconut oil, to which tree resin was added. This completed our rectifier. The other component of the smoothing circuit, a larger capacitor, was made using the aluminium foil technique.

Gathering parts, smuggling messages and making contacts was at all times an incredibly risky and dangerous business. The perimeter of the camp was protected by a heavily reinforced barbed-wire fence, heavily patrolled at night and floodlit. It was my custom to crawl out under the wire after dark to retrieve parts, collect cinnamon bark, messages and other items. I always wore just a pair of shorts, as I was keeping what was left of my 'shirt' for what I called 'special occasions'. One day, I was warned by a fellow officer that my back showed many cuts and scratches from the barbed wire and that I should wear my shirt in future.

Heeding the warning, I wore it on my next nocturnal excursion. I successfully collected the parts left at a rendezvous and was wriggling back under the wire when the shirt caught on a barb. Unaware of this I kept on crawling until the fabric tore free, vibrating the wire. As the sound of the pinging noise reverberated, a searchlight came on. I froze. I don't think my heart was even beating. When a burst of machine gun fire opened up and came within a couple of centimetres of my fingers I thought, 'the next one will get me.' It didn't. Miraculously the firing stopped. I didn't move – I couldn't.

After what seemed an interminable time the light went off and I wriggled back to the hut. I couldn't stand, my knees were jelly. My mates crept out to rescue me and I was very nervous for the next few days. I was lucky. I think that the Japanese assumed someone was going out of the camp, rather than back into it, or else had taken the noise for an animal caught in the wire.

One of the miracles of the receiver was that it was made entirely without the usual tools of trade – small screwdrivers, pliers, clips, screws and solder and a soldering iron. Since the only tool someone managed to smuggle in was a sledge hammer, we had to be inventive. In place of solder, wires were twisted together, or sometimes wrapped in paper or cardboard soaked in coconut oil. Wires were also used to hold the actual wireless components in place on a piece of wood about 30 centimetres square and the whole set lifted very gently.

While assembling the receiver, and after it was finished, we wrapped it in oiled paper and lowered it on two thin pieces of rope into a latrine, on the assumption that no self-respecting Japanese would put his head into a latrine. Prisoners, of course, were banned from using that particular latrine.

To have a working wireless set was of enormous importance to our morale. The Japanese, as part of their propaganda warfare, had told us that Europe was finished, England was under Japanese control and Australia would soon follow. We were desperate to know the truth, especially about Europe and Australia.

At last, in October, about ten weeks after our arrival at the camp, it was time to trial the receiver. Realizing that the camp's 110-volt supply was not high enough in voltage to operate the valve, I made contact with Ah Ping, and asked him to increase the voltage output from the engine room each night at about 9 pm. As a nationalist Chinese, Ah Ping was eager for news from his homeland. In those days, Chungking was the capital of China, and I believed that he would be able to pick up news from there once the receiver was operating. In exchange for providing extra power, Ah Ping would have the latest news from home, though I am not sure how I was going to translate it. Ah Ping agreed to play his role, provided the wood parties could supply extra fuel for the boiler, and thus more power to the steam engine driving the alternator.

On the appointed night Ah Ping was asked to be ready at 10 o'clock. To our absolute dismay, at the agreed time all the perimeter lights flared to maximum brightness. Ah Ping had stoked about another tonne of wood into the boiler and opened up the steam cocks.

The set, however, worked and it was with great trepidation that I carefully tuned in to try to pick up a broadcast. This had to be done with the utmost secrecy and meticulous care, as I had no idea of the exact frequencies or times of transmissions. It was a matter of trial and error, with some good luck thrown in.

The regenerative type of receiver was sensitive enough to give the user an idea of when he was near a station. Using a penknife, I had drilled a hole into a wooden skewer, which was then glued into the shaft of the capacitor with some flour. Because the set was in a very sensitive state of oscillation, it was impossible to get my hands close to it, so another stick was fixed about 15 centimetres along the skewer. By putting a couple of marks on the stick, I knew exactly where to tune in.

At first, I picked up a broadcast in Chinese, probably coming from Chungking. Then, after some fine-tuning and much anxiety, for the second time in my life I was intensely excited and relieved to hear the chimes of Big Ben and the beautiful measured tones of a BBC announcer. Big Ben did not, however, precede the much longed-for news. For almost three quarters of an hour, and at enormous risk, Gordon and I listened to a broadcast on growing hops in Kent, until it faded. The next morning, the CO asked me what the news was.

'We've got some good news, but I can't talk here. Come this way.'

So, he came along and asked me, 'What's this news you're talking about?'

When I said that I hadn't actually heard a news bulletin he became very angry and asked me what the hell I meant. I said, 'If British primary producing experts are able to spare the time to talk for three quarters of an hour about growing hops in Kent, Britain must still be alive and floating with their thumbs up, and as far as I'm concerned that's the best news I could hear.'

The next day, still nervous about the flaring lights of the previous evening, I went to see Ah Ping and explained:

'Gently, gently, catchee monkey, you know, a little bit of wood on at 9 o'clock, a little bit more at 10 and gradually work it up to about 300 rpm on the main fly wheel. Leave it there for about half an hour and then gradually bring it down.'

From that time on, Ah Ping would gradually increase the power output, and then bring it down. One of the Japanese guards, who noticed that from 9 o'clock onwards the lights would gradually brighten, and then reduce in intensity at about midnight, said:

'Ah Ping very loyal citizen, because when sun go down and get dark, we want lot of light to watch prisoners. After night go on and prisoners locked up, he let light go down, we save many wood.'

Listening to broadcasts and taking notes in total darkness was another obstacle to be overcome. We could not risk even the smallest light, despite having lookouts, or 'cockatoos' as the Australians called them. In the pitch darkness the wireless operator would attach the headphone, ready to take down the news but ever on the alert for possible interruption by the Japanese. As we could not see where to write on the paper, we devised a method using touch alone.

During the day we drew lines on the back of naval message forms, scrounged at Changi. On the left hand side of the pad, we made a small notch, to indicate the start of each line. On the right-hand side we made a nick and left the tiny piece of paper sticking up at the end, to indicate where the paper ended. To take down the news, we used a form of shorthand, using a stub of pencil, or whatever we could find, trying to keep our writing in a more or less straight line. For instance, if 500 bombers had attacked Hamburg I wrote down 500BHam. When I came to the end of a line I felt the tiny piece of paper sticking up and went on to the next line.

Gordon, who had been an accountant at the Castlemaine Woollen Mills before the war, had very even handwriting and was good at journalism, so he wrote up the notes in an unabbreviated form for selected officers. These notes were then destroyed and news disseminated to the men as coming from an 'unknown source'. What they did not know, they could not reveal.

The news we received was mainly about the European war, but at least it was news. We heard about the bombing of Dresden, odd bits of news about the Middle East, Russia, casualties, troop movements and bombings. The receiver, of course, was not always reliable and, when new parts had to be made or improved, we could not tune in. It was after a short blackout period that I heard a very excited American voice exclaiming:

'The war is over in North Africa, Rommel is knocked to pieces, he's out of the Middle East, the Germans are finished in the desert,' or words to that effect. That was it. Just three or four sentences from the Voice of America, no other detail.

So, we tuned in again at 12.30 am, this time to the BBC, hoping that Ah Ping hadn't reduced the voltage too much. The BBC was a little faint, but it suddenly became quite clear, lifting in volume. Big Ben chimed and there it was, a voice in the wilderness, calling. We listened excitedly as the broadcaster calmly described all of the 8th Army movements in North Africa, what each regiment had done, troop deployment, casualties and so on. Had we access to a tracing board, we could have mapped out where everything was happening.

After about 15 or 20 minutes, still in a very measured voice, the announcer said, 'It must be considered that as all resistance in North Africa has been overcome, the Allied victory is assured.' We were elated. The announcer had been describing the battle of El Alamein, which took place on 23 October.

After successfully developing the receiver, I decided to build a transmitter. I managed to smuggle into the camp two 6L6G valves to make a push-pull amplifier for the radio frequency output. I made the other components – capacitors from foil, paper and coconut oil; resistors from burning coconut husk onto some wood, providing a resistance of one or two megohms. I knew that the transmitter would work reasonably well with simple parts and designed it for CW (Continuous Wave) Morse code operation.

The idea was not to use the transmitter on a day-to-day basis. If I had my way I would have tried to broadcast our position, situation etc, but Lionel vetoed that idea as being too risky. The transmitter was to be used only if we learned that the Allies were close by. However, I did manage to send out two test transmissions, not knowing at the time whether or not they were successful. Years later, I learned that one of the messages had been picked up by an American signaller, monitoring wireless traffic.

While I was busy building the radio equipment there was a lot of other subversive activity by members of the underground movement. Sandalwood trading boats had become an important part of the organization. With their help, seven E Force prisoners, and one B Force prisoner who managed to join them, escaped from Berhala Island and reached the Philippines, where they joined the Philippine Liberation Army. The trading boats were also used to smuggle in additional medical supplies as well as the arms and ammunition organised by Lionel. It was later estimated that our underground was one of the largest to operate in Japanese occupied territory in World War II.

So, for twelve months from July 1942 until 22 July 1943, we clandestinely and successfully operated the radio receiver until disaster, which had been constantly on our minds, hit like a South China Sea typhoon.

CHAPTER 9

ARREST AND INTERROGATION

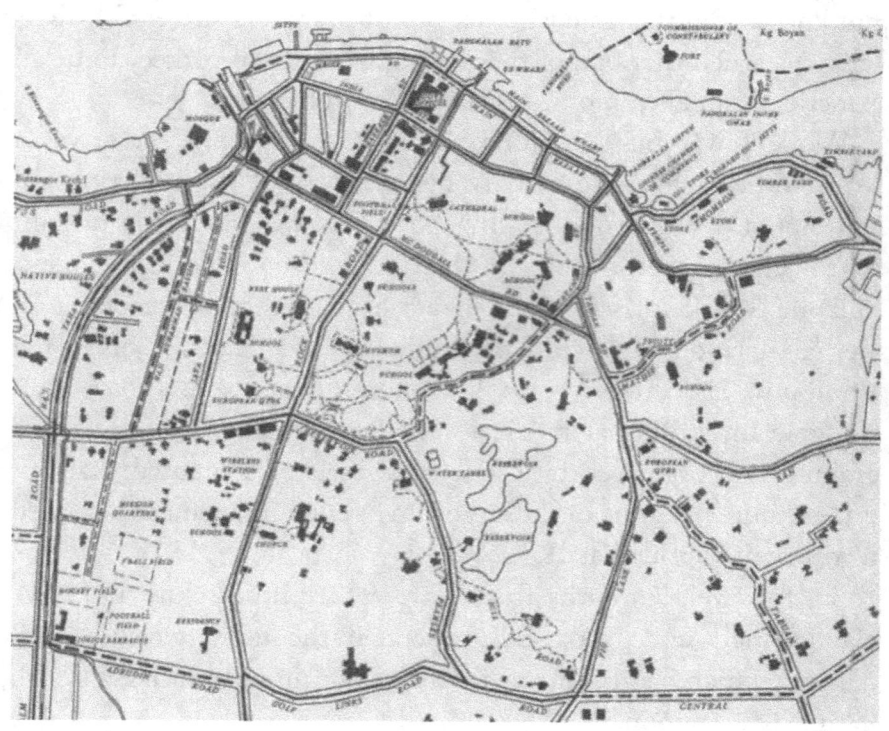

Kuching, 1945.

As a result of a Chinese member of the underground refusing to pay hush money to two local men, who learned of his activities, he was betrayed to the spy planted at the camp, Jackie Lo Ah Fuh. He, in turn, informed the Kempeitai, military police similar to the German Gestapo, who were much feared for their brutal and ruthless treatment of prisoners. Experts in interrogation and torture, they were more powerful than the IJA and answered to no one. On 18, 19 and 20 July, Heng, Matusup, Dr Taylor, his assistant Dr Hugh Wands, Paddy Funk, Detective Ernesto Lagan and several others, were arrested and taken away for interrogation.

On the 22nd, the Japanese swooped on the camp. Everything was in an uproar as we were turned out of the huts, our belongings torn apart and thoroughly searched. As a result, Lionel and several others were arrested and removed from the camp. Fortunately, one of the officers, who was confined to the hut with illness at the time of the search, managed to hide Lionel's .38 revolver and the five rounds of ammunition in the bottom of a cupboard. As soon as he was able Rus Ewin arranged for them to be smuggled to Abin's house, where they were hidden in the chimney, along with Ewin's diary and some nominal rolls. However, during their search, the Japanese had found the news summaries that were hidden in my socks, ready to pass onto Abin for delivery to Dr Taylor. The next two days and nights were not very happy for me, especially as I had given reports on camp conditions to Abin for safe keeping. I later learned that a Japanese staff car, on its way out to search Abin's home, was delayed when it hit a buffalo. Abin had been arrested on 23 July. Fortunately his wife, sensing that something was wrong, burned all incriminating notes, hidden behind a rock in the chimney, before the Kempeitai arrived.

Returning with a work party from the airstrip the next day, I was horrified to see Hoshijima waiting at the lower entrance to the camp and that the entire compound was surrounded by Japanese troops and Kempeitai. I thought Hoshijima was going to address everybody. Then he called out those two words that I'll never forget – 'Lieutenant Wells.' I went to jelly at the knees. A couple of fellow officers helped support me and tried to cheer me up. Hoshijima signalled me to come towards him and confronted me with the fact that we had a radio set. I said no, we didn't. With that he drew back his fist. I thought he was going to strike me on the jaw as he had done on two or three past occasions. Instead, he grabbed the sweat rag that I was wearing around my neck and screwed it around until he just about choked me. He persisted to rage and shout at me.

'This radio, I know you have one. If you don't provide it, I will shoot you with my own pistol!'

I decided that if I had to produce something I might as well hand over the transmitter; this would mean that the prisoners who were left would be able at least to get some news from the receiver. So, after leading Hoshijima around the camp for some time pretending to look for the radio, I dug up the transmitter. Hoshijima then hauled me up on the back of the vehicle and spoke in English to the prisoners.

'You all look at this man, you will never see him again,' and then led me off, bound by rope from head to foot.

Everyone was allowed to go back to camp after that. Flanked by two guards I was taken away in a vehicle to Sandakan to be interrogated and charged. On the way I had a sort of dying wish that somehow or other the receiver would be preserved and, unbeknown to me, it was, at least temporarily. The team members operating the radio were initially shaken but, about a week or so after my arrest, they started to use it again and continued to use it until 30 August when Gordon, brutally interrogated about the existence of another radio, was forced to admit to its existence, resulting in its recovery and the arrest of its custodians.

I was immediately taken to the Kempeitai headquarters at Sandakan, a substantial European-style house opposite the sawmills on the outskirts of Sandakan township. The house looked innocent enough, perched on stilts like a Queenslander with wide verandas and wooden shutters. Four cells had been created in the sub-floor area. I was placed in one for three weeks in solitary confinement, well apart from the other prisoners who had been there for some days. Washing was permitted only when the Japanese guards gave approval for the latrine buckets to be emptied – this varied from once a day to twice a week. No clothing other than shorts and singlet was allowed. Rations, consisting of a small teacup of cooked rice with about a cubic centimetre of either salt fish or rock salt, were distributed by two Chinese, twice a day at irregular times. Later, an equivalent amount of vegetable replaced the fish. Local prisoners were permitted to have food brought in to them and, although it was forbidden by the Japanese, they sometimes managed to smuggle some to us. Water was also strictly rationed. The light burned in my cell day and night, a form of torture widely used by the Kempeitai.

Gordon, who was kept in the cage at the camp for a couple of weeks following his arrest, subsequently joined us at Kempeitai headquarters. After my release from solitary confinement at the end of July, I was confined with Lionel, Gordon, Gerald Mavor and the dozen or so local people who had previously been arrested. Worst of all were the constant cries and groans from prisoners being interrogated and tortured.

So began a period of unbelievable torment. We were forced to sit cross-legged from 7.30 am to 9.30 pm. We had to constantly face the front of the cell and refrain from looking at other prisoners. While asleep at night we were compelled to lie in such a way as to prevent communication. A light burned continually to enable constant surveillance by the guards, who inflicted their own punishments where and when they saw fit.

Our day would begin in the most terrifying way, when we heard footsteps above, the scraping of chairs and the sound of voices as the

Kempeitai got down to business. Soon the chairs would be pushed back, footsteps would clatter down the stairs, guards would appear, point to one of us and escort us upstairs. We lived in constant terror of what would happen each day. At first it was mainly interrogation, without too much punishment. We would be taken into a room and forced to kneel, filthy and stinking with weeks of beard growth, in front of the interrogating officer and a civilian interpreter, Miura, seated behind a desk. Sporting crewcuts, both men were showered, shaved, immaculately dressed and smoking large American cigarettes in ivory holders, which seemed to be some sort of status symbol.

On the wall behind the desk hung a board with Japanese writing, hieroglyphics and various symbols. There were different lines and colours, which changed from time to time as information was gathered. I studied this assiduously to see if I could discern a pattern, as it was obviously an intercommunication pattern of who was known to whom. If prisoners gave an answer, inconsistent with their current information, they were whacked over the head or neck or shoulders with the sharp edge of a piece of wood while the interrogator screamed 'Think! Think! Think!'

It was not any particular piece of evidence or information that caused the collapse of the entire underground. By gathering lots of small pieces, and plotting and linking them, a picture emerged to provide enough information to confirm Japanese suspicions. Also, too many people had become involved; the larger the organization, the greater the risk of discovery. Even Lionel did not know the names of all of those who were helping; the web just spread beyond a manageable limit.

One time during my solitary confinement under the house, which I think was around 14 August, I was asked if I was hungry and of course I said I was. They brought in a container of uncooked rice and ordered me to swallow it. When I refused, two of their bullies, including a particularly nasty piece of work known as The Bulldog, held my hands behind my back and opened my mouth, forcing in the rice with a spoon and tapping my head until I had swallowed what seemed to be three or four cupsful. Then they brought in a garden hose, pushed it down my throat and turned it on. When at last water started to flood out of my mouth, they threw me back in the cell. I knew what would happen next. About four hours later I was wracked with excruciating pains in my intestines as the rice began to swell. After about 36 hours, part of my bowel was forced out through the rectum. It bled for a while but, with no medical attention available, I managed to push it all back inside by hand and the pain gradually eased. On another occasion, my tormentors forced water down my throat and then jumped on my swollen stomach. That was almost as bad as the rice treatment.

The most severe of the tortures took place in August 1943, and it was during this time that my mother, who was staying in Melbourne with my father at the O'Byrnes' house, suddenly woke up in great distress when she heard me calling to her. She had reason to remember this episode as it took place on her birthday, 16 August. This would have been when, after one interrogation, the interpreter lost his temper and I was suspended by handcuffs to a rail on the verandah. My knees were about a centimetre from the ground with my feet turned back so that the instep and toes rested on the ground. They then placed a thick piece of wood about 10 centimetres square across the back of my knees. As a form of racking and stretching, two guards see-sawed on it, tearing the flesh behind my knees and on my insteps, and applying such pressure that I could hear the joints in my feet cracking. I passed out and was revived with a bucket of water.

On another occasion, my interrogator decided on a different technique. He had me tied up as before, to the veranda beam. I braced myself for the wooden beam behind my knees but instead he produced a small piece of wood like a skewer. He pushed it into my left ear and hit it with a small hammer. The sound was horrible but excruciating pain soon took over as the skewer was driven through my eardrum and into my middle ear. I passed out. After being revived with a bucket of water I was thrown back under the house. The ear bled for a couple of days and I was terrified of infection as there was no means of even rinsing it out with clean water or antiseptic. The Japanese certainly could not be expected to give any medical help. After a couple of days, a little pus came out but eventually it healed. I have never been able to hear with the left ear since. Once again, at home on the farm something inexplicable happened. A photo of me, which sat on the kitchen mantelpiece, suddenly fell, smashing onto the hearth. My mother had a strong feeling that something terrible had happened to me and cried out to my father, 'My son's being hurt.'

During one interrogation, I noticed on the table a letter from my mother. Now we had not had any news from home since just before Singapore fell; we could not write to our families and had no way of finding out whether or not they knew of our fate. I was asked if I would like to read the letter. When I answered yes, the interrogator struck a match and burned it in front of me. Not all tortures were physical.

We were also subjected to floggings with riding whips and beltings with wooden swords. I suppose anyone who has undergone such treatment finds it difficult to describe the intensity, the viciousness and persistence of interrogations. It goes on relentlessly, day after day, randomly, fiendishly and brutally. I was fighting two overwhelming battles simultaneously. The first was to survive the physical torture; the second, not to divulge information. I decided that it was a matter of closing my mind to physical torture.

The strange thing about the Japanese is that prisoners of the IJA, as we had been at Changi and the Sandakan Camp, could be bashed to death by any guard or soldier and the authorities would not worry too much. However, once in the hands of the Kempeitai, a prisoner, although only a number, had to be accounted for. They were fanatical about numbers, rules and routines; if you died it messed up the paperwork. Prisoners could be belted to within a hair's breadth of life but the Kempeitai generally stopped short of actually killing. However, if they wanted information, they were determined to get it. So, I got through the physical torture as best I could.

Withholding information was a more difficult matter. While conscious, control was possible; but if semi-conscious, as I seemed to be a lot of the time, I did not have full control over what I was saying. I wanted to live, I had confidence that we would win this war and I wanted to get through it. I would never intentionally betray my colleagues, so it was imperative to control the information the Japanese demanded without revealing the essentials. After the war, I wanted to be able to look my friends in the face and say that I had done my utmost not to reveal information. I just had to steel myself as best I could to withstand the physical and mental attacks. Of course, if anyone gave everything away, he would not have been treated any more leniently and would have been doubly despised by the Japanese as a traitor.

We did have one triumph over the Japanese. When we were brought up from under the house, we were seated in a room under close guard while each of us was taken out and interrogated and then returned to the room. We were ordered to sit cross-legged with our arms across our chests; talking was strictly forbidden. One day, as Lionel, Gordon and I sat apart on the floor in a triangular formation I noticed that Lionel, who had just been brought back from interrogation, was tapping the fingers of one hand on his back. I suddenly realised that he was tapping out Morse code. He slowly communicated what questions he had been asked and the answers he had given. It may not have helped us much but at least with this information we could give consistent answers. While engaged in our silent communication we would try to hold the eye of the sentry so as to distract him from our hand movements. This was visual Morse – a short tap for a dot and a longer tap for a dash. It takes much longer than the usual audible signals but we had plenty of time. The feeling that we were communicating under the noses of the sentries gave a much-needed lift to our morale.

Only one sentry made a comment about our behaviour. When being relieved, he indicated to the next guard, by tapping his head, that Lionel was to be watched as he seemed to be going a bit mad. Thank goodness they were just ordinary soldiers and had not been trained in Morse code or signalling.

There was a brighter moment when I was escorted to the toilet and managed to snatch a bun, filled with bean curd, from a tray that had been left in the passageway. Bolting it down while in the toilet probably didn't do my digestive system much good but, after what it had already been through, it probably didn't matter.

So, we got through each day as best we could. We tried to remain optimistic, but I think that Lionel, and certainly I, did not to expect to survive. And then, suddenly, on 25 October we were taken from the house, transported to Sandakan Harbour and placed on a coastal type boat. On board were about 18 of us, including Lionel Matthews, Gerald Mavor and Gordon Weynton, plus several other Australian military prisoners, some European civilians, and the unfortunate local people who had been so loyal to the underground. At least we had fresh air, in fact plenty of it, as a tropical storm hit us shortly after we sailed and lasted for some days. Being handcuffed to the rails in gale-force winds was another form of torture but the Japanese were oblivious to our pleas for help and the sea spray did help to cleanse our wounds. At first, we travelled north-west, then almost due south until some days later we finally arrived at Kuching Harbour. Someone remarked, 'It's Melbourne Cup Day,' so it would have been 2 November 1943.

We were escorted across planks from one ship to another and then finally onto the quayside, where an enclosed truck was waiting to transport us to Kuching POW Camp, situated at Batu Lintang, outside the town, where those not undergoing trial were sent to various compounds. We were then driven to the Kempeitai Military

Prison in town. An outside staircase led to the first floor where our officers and senior NCOs were separated from the men. We entered a large room, its barred windows making the interior light and airy. Part of it had been divided into eight cells, with wire walls, four of which held up to 20 prisoners. Six or eight prisoners were herded into each of the rest of the cells. A bucket in the corner was the only sanitation. The arrangement of the cage-like cells within the room meant that only one guard was needed to patrol the perimeter corridor. There we sat, cross-legged and at attention from 7 in the morning until 10.30 at night, looking straight ahead. Any attempt to relax tired muscles invited a beating with rattan canes, wooden swords and even fists. Talking was strictly prohibited but we managed snatched whispers of conversation and tapped out Morse code.

The next move was to Kuching Civil Prison which, despite all of the confinement we had undergone, was our first real gaol with real cells. It had been built in 1882 when Kuching, now the capital of Sarawak, was under the control of Rajah Brooke, a colonial soldier and adventurer, who was given Sarawak by its then owner, the Sultan of Brunei, as a reward for ridding the area of pirates.

Although the gaol itself was kept reasonably clean by trusted native prisoners, our cells were infested with bedbugs and vermin, which made sleeping difficult, and we were required to exercise twice a day, in spite of the inadequate rations. Just 200 grams of raw rice and a small helping of vegetables, or what passed for vegetables, split into two meals at 2 pm and 8 pm, with a measly piece of rank-smelling fish once a week. Two cups of water had to be shared among five of us, per day. Dr Taylor was allowed to administer limited medical treatment under supervision of the guard, but no hospital admissions were permitted, with the exception of Gerald Mavor, who needed treatment for a double hernia soon after our arrival. Five days after an operation by a Japanese doctor he was sent back to the cells and compelled to sit for most of the day like the other prisoners. Within a few weeks the hernia reappeared.

One of the worst cases of medical neglect concerned Sapper Ted Keating who, at the time of his arrest at Sandakan, was suffering with a huge leg ulcer. Dr Taylor was permitted to provide only limited medical attention but finally, after his repeated efforts, Keating had been admitted to Sandakan hospital for six days prior to sailing for Kuching. On the voyage he contracted dysentery, which became worse during the voyage. By the time we arrived at Kuching beriberi had developed and Keating's condition was critical. Depriving themselves of much needed food, all the other ranks in his cell contributed small portions of their meagre rations to keep him alive.

Taylor made frequent appeals for his admission to hospital, but in vain. He would eventually die at 0745 hours on 11 February 1944, having received no medical attention from the Japanese, apart from a few vitamin tablets two or three days prior to his death. He was buried in the Christian cemetery behind St Joseph's Roman Catholic Cathedral. At the funeral service, the Japanese stated that they respected the dead. However, his treatment by the Japanese, and that of thousands of other prisoners, typified how little they respected the living.

In the meantime, although the major part of our interrogation had been conducted in Sandakan, we discovered that there was still more to come. Over the next couple of months we were taken to St Teresa's Convent, next to the cathedral, where the Kempeitai had set up a court room. The interrogations were spasmodic and of a minor nature, mostly going over old ground and, while I received an occasional crack over the head, there was no torture of the kind meted out in Sandakan.

In the latter part of December 1943, I was interrogated, for the first time, by Captain Watanabe. It lasted two hours and was based on statements prepared by the Kempeitai at Sandakan, alleging that Lionel and I had possessed a wireless and had planned an armed uprising at the Sandakan Camp, by far the most serious charge and one that we had to deny. We replied that we had a wireless but claimed that the other allegation was quite unfounded. Altogether I was interrogated seven times by Watanabe, prior to my official 'trial', each session lasting two or three hours. He also interrogated Lionel several times, and Sergeant Stevens and Corporals MacMillan and Roffey once each. On each occasion, a Japanese civilian, Sugama Yoshiro, acted as interpreter.

During one of these sessions, in the middle of February 1944, Lionel and I protested to Watanabe, through an interpreter, that on our arrest at Sandakan we had been told that we would face a court martial and that we had not been told at any time what were the charges against us. We wanted to know what we were being charged with. We also asked for a defending officer for our forthcoming trial. He replied:

'You will be tried in accordance with Japanese Military Law.'

I asked, 'What about the Hague Convention?'

He replied, 'We are not interested in the Hague Convention.'

The Sandakan evidence was gone over again and, although we received the odd whack with a wooden sword, there was no serious torture. This went on until Christmas and then spasmodically until the end of February.

Meantime, the trials had started, with the first one held on 3 February. Dr Taylor and Gerald Mavor, among the first to appear, were each sentenced to 15 years' gaol. On 26 February, Gordon was tried and found guilty of spreading rumours and violating POW regulations. He received a gaol sentence of ten years. There were now only five Australians – Lionel, Sergeant Stevens, Corporal Roffey, Corporal McMillan and me – and the remaining Sandakan civilians to be tried, including the eight major suspects. The next day some of the Chinese prisoners told me that four Chinese employed in the gaol cookhouse had informed them that, on the instructions of the Japanese, they had that day dug eight graves at the rear of the cathedral. This did not sound good.

We had received no formal notification of the date of our trial. The only warning we received was on the evening of 28 February when a sentry told me that we were to wear our 'Number One' clothes in the morning as we were to go to 'The Big Room'. What our 'Number One' clothes might be was a moot point! That night, Lionel and I were escorted to Suga's office. Now promoted to colonel, he gave us some bananas, papaya and other edibles, which did not seem to be a good omen. He also had an old copy of the Tokyo daily newspaper, *Tokyo Ichinichi* with a photograph of Lionel and me on the front page. Although we could not read Japanese, it obviously indicated that these two bastards were enemies of the Emperor, his empire and his people, and had committed terrible crimes against them. We now knew that we would be punished severely. I later learned that no one was brought to trial by the Kempeitai unless a guilty finding was assured. The colonel regretted, he said ingratiatingly, having to deal with us in this way but he had no option. He added that even if Japan lost this war, within 50 years they would have economic control over all the region, including Australia. We were then escorted back to the cells.

St Teresa's School, Kuching, 1980.

The next day, the five of us still awaiting trial were taken by vehicle a short distance from the gaol to St Teresa's School for our official court martial. As we arrived we were acknowledged with very sympathetic looks and bowed heads from the Dutch nuns who ran the convent. A few minutes before we were marched into the courtroom, Colonel Suga handed Lionel two letters from his wife. I noticed that the envelopes bore a 'Sandakan' postmark approximately twelve months old. So far as I am aware no other POW under arrest in Borneo received any mail.

We were led, ironically, into the science room where the trial was to be held. Armed guards stood behind us as, once again, we faced the judges, just as we had faced the Kempeitai at the headquarters at Sandakan. The court was assembled, with the President of the Court, a lieutenant colonel, in full uniform: polished leggings, boots and white gloves. We were led into the court and stood at the foot of the judge's area. We were still emaciated, filthy and fearful; the five of them sat sleek and confident behind a table on a

It was on this pathway in 1944, between a store room (right) and the Kempeitai courtroom (left) that Rod and Lionel Matthews said their final farewell.

raised dais at one end of the room, probably the teacher's platform. In the middle was the presiding officer, to his right sat a major, then a captain. To the president's left was Captain Watanabe and then an officer who appeared to be a clerk of some sort. Sugama was the interpreter. Major Suga, as the officer in charge of all the Borneo camps, was also present, though he took no part in the proceedings. The trial began with our names being called out, to which we answered. Lionel then said to the court, 'We have no defending officer.' His remark was not interpreted and was ignored by the court.

The proceedings continued with Watanabe reading in Japanese from some papers, presumably the charges against us. I heard our names mentioned but understood nothing else. We were still not allowed legal representation. The next time Watanabe questioned us, at least we were given a brief interpretation – it concerned the alleged radio, alleged espionage on our part and the alleged formation of Sandakan POWs to take part in an armed insurrection. The Kempeitai obviously knew of Lionel's involvement, but it was an admission that none of us dared to make. Twice Lionel answered 'no' to questions by Watanabe concerning the espionage and the planned insurrection. On each occasion the interpreter Sugama answered 'Sou desu' which is Japanese for 'This is so'. Each time Sugama did this I corrected him but, except for the guard behind me calling out 'Kora', which means something like 'shut up', no notice was taken of either Lionel or me.

At no time during the proceedings were we asked to plea, or if we had anything to say. Nothing was interpreted for us, apart from direct questions, put via the interpreter. It was obvious that the verdict had been pre-determined and that we were presumed guilty before the trial had even begun. What we said in court was irrelevant.

There was one heart-stopping moment. As the evidence against us was presented, the court suddenly produced the transmitter, which I had handed over in lieu of the receiver and had expected never to see again. To my horror the two 6L6G valves stood out like sore thumbs and were a dead giveaway that this was indeed a transmitter. Their technical expert examined it carefully. A receiver in the camp would have been bad enough, but the revelation of a transmitter would certainly seal my fate. To my astonished relief he identified it as a receiver. It gave me some sort of grim satisfaction to know that I had outwitted their 'expert'.

The whole proceedings took just over half an hour. We were pronounced guilty with a recommended sentence of capital punishment. At about 10 am we were led away for sentencing at a later date. On our return to our cells, Lionel was taken away with the eight civilian prisoners to another part of the gaol.

The cell door clanged shut. I stumbled onto the platform and sat hunched on its bare boards. My head sank between my knees. So, this is the end, I thought. Death is certain now. By this time tomorrow, I will be dead. It was too late for the miracle I had always believed in.

The following day, 1 March, the final batch of Sandakan civilians appeared before the court. All but the eight major suspects, who were to be sentenced the following day, were given various terms of imprisonment. Apostol received 10 years, Dick Majinal 7, Paddy Funk 6, and Johnny Funk and Chan Ah Ping, 4.

Early the next day, 2 March, the remaining eight civilian prisoners were taken to the court for a final sentencing, leaving just us five – Matthews, Stevens, Roffey, MacMillan and myself, to await the final verdict. Because of the seriousness of the charges against us, Lionel and I had no doubt as to what this would be. At about 9 o'clock we were escorted barefoot and handcuffed through the streets of Kuching to the school, where we were held in a store room for about 15 minutes before being taken across a walkway to the courtroom. When we entered the room, we found the eight local people were absolutely distraught, crying and pleading for mercy. One of them passed his hand across his throat, wordlessly indicating their fate. These eight loyal and courageous civilians were Ojagar Singh, Sergeant Abin, Ernesto Lagan, Heng Joo Ming, Wong Moo Sing, Alex Funk, Felix Azcona and Matusup bin Gungau.

The court officials were the same as on the previous occasion. The president and his officers were immaculate in full uniform – polished boots and leggings, white gloves and gleaming leather belts. Again, we were made to stand in front of the tribunal, emaciated, disease-ridden and filthy.

The president rose impressively and read out our sentences in strangled English:

'Captain Matthews – death by firing squad.'

I heard him whisper, 'Oh God.'

'Lieutenant Wells – twelve years penal servitude and solitary confinement.'

At first, I could not grasp what was said. My mind was in turmoil; relief mingled with guilt that I had escaped while the bravest man I had ever known was to lose his life. He would never see his son David grow up; he would never return to his devoted wife Lorna. It was almost too much to grasp. I could not believe my ears. I thought I was dreaming. I don't know how I felt. I don't think I felt anything. It may seem strange but in the tumult of my emotions I somehow did not want to be separated from Lionel. Wherever he went I felt I should go too. But there it was.

I prayed that I might somehow survive and have the chance to meet Lionel's family and let them know what he had done for his men, his king and his country. Outside the courtroom, Lionel and I were allowed some parting words. He gave me messages of love for Lorna and David, believing that I would survive to meet them. He told me to keep my spirits up and, with a final firm handshake, was taken away flanked by six armed guards from the Judicial Department. As I, and the remaining seven prisoners, began the march, under escort, back to the gaol, I heard a volley of shots in the distance. I felt weak, shaken and desolate and cried like a child.

Suga later confirmed that, before his execution, Lionel removed his blindfold and called out, 'My King and God forever! My God and King forever!' At about 2 pm that same day, a Japanese sentry at Kuching Gaol told me in a mixture of Japanese, Malay and English that Captain Matthews had been shot through the head and that the Asian civilians had also been executed.

I later found out that at the camp at Kuching that night, a bloodstained wooden coffin arrived for burial. As it took place, a piper, who had been allowed to bring his pipes into the camp, played *The Flowers of the Forest*, an ancient Scottish lament.

Lionel Matthews, 1940.

CHAPTER 10

OUTRAM ROAD

Entrance to Outram Road Gaol. A cell block is visible on the right.

A couple of days after the executions, we were taken down to the docks, where each of us was nailed into a small crate, swung by a crane about 15 metres above the wharf and dumped into the bowels of a ship. Once the vessel was underway, the crates were opened and we found ourselves in a contained area of the hold. To our surprise, on the other side of the hold were six or eight Japanese comfort women, being transported to Singapore. Although treated as chattels by the IJA, they were better fed than us and had the run of the ship.

We were in total darkness and had no way of telling the time, but it was probably after about three days that we were off-loaded at Keppel Harbour in Singapore, herded into a godown (a type of shed or warehouse), put onto a truck and, as far as we could tell, driven along Outram Road towards Pearl's Hill. We had no idea that Outram Road Gaol, a colonial era prison condemned by the Colonial Office in the 1920s as being unfit for human habitation but still used for remand prisoners, had been put back into circulation by the Japanese to house prisoners of the Kempeitai.

The gaol was a forbidding sight. High brick walls were topped by jagged glass set in concrete and surrounded by barbed wire, reminiscent of Melbourne's Pentridge Prison. We passed through a huge wooden door, which was wound open by hand. Inside were three or four colossal cell bays. I thought, 'this is the end. Once I'm in here, I'll never get out.'

The prison had been divided into civil and military sections by a wooden wall. The civil section was under the control of a Japanese Civil Administration who controlled the prisoners through Indian and Malay ex-warders. The military section was further divided into two sub-divisions, one for Japanese and the other for all 'foreign' military personnel.

I was divested of what little clothes I had and was issued with a very small pair of shorts with a numbered patch; the number printed on it became my new number – 641. The first big shock on entering the gaol itself was the sight of prisoners walking slowly around wearing just a lap-lap or nothing at all. I could see where their leg bones met their pelvic joints; from behind, I could see their genitals hanging between their legs. All were covered in scabies and sores. They were dejected, walking skeletons with blank faces and absolutely no will to live. They walked because sitting down with no flesh on their bones was just too painful. If anyone could get a word out of them, they would whisper, 'I'll be dead soon. Can't last long.' I realised it would not be long before I, too, looked like these men. Sandakan Camp was like home compared with this silent and brutal place.

My new abode presented a grim sight. The solid wooden cell door, reinforced by iron bars, opened to reveal its contents – two wooden planks for sleeping, a wooden block for a pillow and, in the corner, a wooden latrine bucket. A small barred window was set high in one wall. The cell would have been about two metres wide and 2.5 metres long. No blankets were provided but later on, during the monsoon season, a filthy thin cotton sheet appeared. The rules and regulations were not explained or published in English, only Japanese, so had to be learned by bitter experience. The main points of the rules were: (1) talking and communication between prisoners by any means including laughing or smiling was strictly forbidden. (2) Between the hours of reveille (7.30 am) and turn-in (9.30 pm) prisoners were required to sit to attention with legs crossed, hands placed upon the knees and heads turned rigidly to the front. Leaning against the wall or sitting on anything else other than the bare wooden bed boards was not allowed. (3) All movements, such as washing, eating and exercising, were regimented by orders in Japanese. The only voluntary movement permitted by a prisoner was the use of the latrine bucket while in the cell.

The military section of Outram Road Gaol was under the administration of guards whose rank badges had a white background, as opposed to the fighting troops who had a star on a red background. The guards, or warders, were special personnel, mainly active ex-servicemen trained for the administration of Japanese military justice. All Japanese military personnel and native recruits, found guilty of committing crimes against IJA regulations, came under the control of the military police, along with Allied prisoners and civilians. Inmates were no longer prisoners of war but convicted criminals of the worst type.

The military section of the gaol was subdivided into two sections, one for Japanese and the other for 'foreign' personnel. Although the same regulations were applicable to both sections, in practice there was a great difference. The regulations were slightly more strictly enforced on the Japanese prisoners, but our treatment was infinitely worse than theirs. Japanese prisoners received better rations, new clothing, books, soap, beds, blankets and pillows. They also had proper showers. Their cells were cleaned and disinfected daily and they worked in the regular gaol workshops at more interesting, less tedious work.

Administration of the gaol was by the officer in charge through an NCO orderly and guard, who were changed daily. From November 1944 the guards were replaced by Japanese 'good conduct' prisoners. In order to impress the gaol officials with their efficiency, and in an endeavour to obtain early release, these 'trusties' enforced the regulations with brutal severity.

A glass observation hole cut into the door allowed the guards, who wore soft slippers, to creep along the darkened corridors and watch us at any time. At night the cells were lit and I was not to experience darkness for 13 months.

I have often been asked how I managed to survive the horrors of my imprisonment.

When I was arrested and interrogated at Sandakan I decided that I would have to forget about my body and concentrate totally on my mental and spiritual survival. It was a waste of time and energy to think about food, or rather the lack of it; no use dwelling on the tortures inflicted by the Japanese. So, I disciplined my mind to be always resistant to brain-washing and interrogation, torture and deprivations. I strove to maintain a part of me that could never be manipulated by others, challenged by brutality or coerced by any person other than myself.

That inner core would be reachable only by me, no matter how hard others might try to breach the barriers. It would be the one thing, and indeed the only thing, that the Japanese could not take from me. I would have to fight against almost insurmountable odds to ensure my mental survival. My body would have to survive as best it could.

I do not remember much about my first night at Outram Road Gaol. I felt stunned, almost in a trance, probably because of what I had recently been through and by the thought that this gaol would probably be my final resting place. On top of all this, I was still getting used to hearing with just my right ear. Yet I remained optimistic that I could survive. I began some mental exercises by keeping track of the date. Saying the date to myself every morning gave me something to focus on each day. I became the unofficial timekeeper and, during the brief snatches of whispered conversation we were able to have, I was sometimes asked 'What's the date today?' When, 13 months later I was sent back to Changi, I had the day and date exactly right. The importance of this exercise was that it kept me in touch with reality.

On a typical day, we were woken at 7.30 am and called to attention for roll call. The roll was actually a book in which cards were fixed, like an album, containing details of each prisoner's number, name and cell number. If a prisoner were moved around the gaol, the cards could be moved around in the book.

At roll call each number was called out in Japanese. Failure to answer immediately incurred a blow across the back with a sword in its scabbard, producing a large welt. We then sat cross-legged for the next half hour or so until breakfast arrived.

Rations for our section of the gaol were cooked by Japanese prisoners who took far less care in the preparation of food for foreign prisoners. For the first two months I was at Outram, our meals were fairly distributed by five POW orderlies under the supervision of Penrod Dean, an Australian lieutenant who had tried to escape from

Changi Camp. He and his mate, the first Australians to be sent to Outram Road, had been sentenced in May 1942 to imprisonment for two years. The increased freedom enjoyed by Dean, who was due for release on 18 May, enabled him to assist foreign prisoners, especially the sick, until his sentence terminated, when Japanese mess orderlies took over and fair distribution ceased.

When breakfast did arrive a small bowl was put into a slot in the cell door, measuring about 7 x by 12 centimetres. We were not permitted to touch the bowl until all the food had been distributed. By this time the sloppy, overcooked rice was cold. About ten seconds after the order to eat was given, we were ordered to stop. If caught eating after that, we were punished. Lunch was a similar, very slightly larger meal, which we were given a few seconds longer to eat. On rare occasions we received a tiny lump of salted fish. It is estimated that we existed on about 60 grams of uncooked rice a day. The evening meal was a repetition of breakfast and lunch, with the addition of a small bowl of brownish coloured water, which passed for tea – cold of course. That was the only liquid we were allowed; no water was supplied. Twice during my 13 months at Outram Road, I received half a banana. Turn-in was at 9.30 pm, although, naturally, there were no 'lights out'.

Discipline was strict and retribution swift. Occasionally we were ordered to do simple stretching exercises in the cell. Ablutions were allowed about once a week and shorts were changed about once a fortnight but it was all carried out at irregular intervals. However, the changeover of shorts followed a strictly enforced ritual.

We were ordered to stand and all the cell doors were opened while extra guards stood by. We were then ordered to drop our shorts and stand to attention, before descending the two or three steps from the cell into the corridor. Sometimes we had to come out with the shorts, in which case we knew they were going to be exchanged for 'washed' ones; if ordered out of the cell without the shorts, it meant living in the same ones for the next few weeks.

The fresh shorts were barely cleaner than the previous issue and I worried that they still held diseases from their former owners. As well as the usual complaints, syphilis flourished in some prisoners. Soap and hot water had been nowhere near these garments and they stood up by themselves from bodily secretions, something I tried not to think about.

Ablutions were also strictly supervised. We would be ordered from our cells and marched naked out of the prison block, single file, into the courtyard. Small buckets, probably holding four litres or so of water, lined the courtyard. It was a grim day when there were not enough buckets to go round. We stood to attention behind the buckets until the order was given to start washing. There was no soap – occasionally just a tiny piece of rag, about 10 centimetres square, with which to wash, in the few seconds allowed before the order to cease washing was given. Although some of us had toothbrushes, we were permitted to use them only once or twice during my term of imprisonment.

On rare occasions we were ordered to do more vigorous exercises before we washed. Numbers would be called out in Japanese – one, two, three, four, etc., with a guard wielding a wooden sword following behind each of us. A crack across the back made sure we did exactly what we were supposed to do. With our limited knowledge of Japanese we strove as best we could to avoid unnecessary punishment. At the end of the washing session we returned to our cells, standing naked just inside the door with arms raised and legs apart. We were then physically searched. 'Clean' shorts were distributed, and we picked them up as we walked in. Orders were then given to put them on and the cell doors were banged shut. On good days this activity would take no more than five minutes.

Every two months or so a Japanese prisoner-cum-barber arrived with a pair of shears to give us a rough haircut. The shears were as big as horse clippers and caused nicks on the face and head. He was on a stop-start time of about 20 seconds per haircut, which was overseen by the warder. Later on, when we were put on hemp duty, I managed to keep a small strand to use as a sort of dental floss. Although my teeth became loose, they remained in reasonably good order and, at the end of my imprisonment, there were no caries to be attended to.

Sometimes we would vomit up segments of tapeworms or pull them whole out of our mouths, a demoralising event because we realised the tapeworms were getting what little nourishment should have been ours. And whatever ended up in the latrine bucket remained there until it was emptied on the next round.

Anyone who has had an infestation of scabies mites will never forget the intense itching as they burrow under the skin, lay their eggs and leave their droppings. With not even water to regularly clean ourselves, and no disinfectants, our bodies soon became red from scratching and were covered in pus-filled sores. At first, I tried to resist the urge to scratch because it only made things worse – more open skin, more sores, more chance of infection. But, after a couple of hours, the strain would become unbearable and I would mentally break. For half an hour or so I would almost tear myself to pieces. The relief was great but, with my limited energy, I was left absolutely exhausted. Of course, by going through this cycle I was spreading the mites across my body; mentally it was something I could not control.

Bedbugs were another constant source of intense discomfort. They ran uncontrolled over the concrete floor, not even bothering to hide. In the morning we could see the red lines on our bodies where they had come up through the gap between the planks to suck our blood; they, too, caused intense itching, pain and swelling.

As well as insect invasion, we suffered from a number of complaints caused by lack of nutrition – scurvy, beriberi, pellagra, failing eyesight, dehydration, malaria, swollen and bleeding gums, loose teeth, constant infections, ulcers and also mental conditions, brought on by our confinement and uncertainty about the future.

From minute to minute our survival depended on chance, on the whim of our captors, on our own diminishing abilities to keep going. We were physical, mental and emotional skeletons. Nevertheless, I tried to remain optimistic that we would soon be rescued from this loathsome place.

Constipation was also a huge problem, probably due to the lack of food and roughage, and it put an unnecessary strain on the body when trying to expel a motion. I think for the last three or four months in Outram Road I did not move my bowels. I have sometimes been asked whether or not we thought about sex. I would say that after about twelve months of captivity our sex drive was almost non-existent; survival was uppermost in our minds. Erections were a waste of precious energy.

In the intervals between meals, I re-lived my boyhood life on the farm, walked through the paddocks, saw the dew-covered spider webs that festooned them on autumn mornings. I recalled the chores I had to carry out, playing football and cricket, riding Codger the horse around the farm, swimming in the irrigation channel, bird nesting with my school friends, schooling with the convent nuns, my scientific experiments, hobbies, scouting days, family and friends. I pictured what the family would be doing at certain times of the day. Each evening, as I heard a flock of birds settling for the night, I imagined there must be a tree nearby though I could not actually see it. This brought on fanciful thoughts that the birds might fly to Australia and over the farm. All were fantasies; all seemed real. This form of day dreaming was a way of relaxing. We had no outside news and seemed to be in a strange new world – unknown, alien and closed to all except ourselves – it was as if we were in a strange country. We were forbidden to talk; no reading or writing materials were provided – daydreaming was our escape and only comfort. However, I soon realised that I needed more to keep my mind active and, in between meals, and later work, I set about this in as orderly a fashion as possible.

To begin, I started going over all my physics, maths and chemistry laws, equations and formulae; the periodic table of elements, astronomy, optics, biology, engineering, photography, radio communications, atomic physics and anatomy – anything and everything that I had ever read or learned was revised in fine detail. Prior to my enlistment I had studied an introduction to infinitesimal calculus – a form of higher mathematics dealing with physical properties used in many areas of engineering, dynamics, heat, light, optics etc. By extending the basics in my head, I had, by the time of my release, successfully reached the fifth and final level of differential calculus.

Being a signals officer, I was proficient in Morse code and it was surprising that, despite the thickness of the walls, we managed to communicate by tapping out messages. This was obviously an extremely hazardous undertaking but we were desperate for news. Talking was the worst crime you could commit as a prisoner, and Morse code was marginally less risky.

Although most prisoners had been sentenced to solitary confinement, the gaol soon became so crowded that I occasionally had company. I was very fortunate that, for some two or three months, my cell mate was a British public servant, Robert Scott. Prior to the war he had been stationed in Tokyo and, when war broke out, was posted to Singapore with the British Ministry of Information, which was closely allied to the secret service organisation MI6. He was a graduate in law and humanities from Oxford University and had been called to the bar. He was about 15 years older than I and inspired me tremendously.

We whispered and mumbled together and became expert at looking out for sentries. He quoted lengthy legal passages, remembered important legal cases and problems; he recited passages from the Bible and Shakespeare and *Paradise Lost* from end to end, and opened my mind to all sorts of exciting things. It was a refreshing addition to my scientific background. Rob Scott had a wonderful command of the English language and urged me to seek further studies after the war in whatever field I chose and not let the POW experience define my post-war life. His philosophy had a huge influence on me at the time and for the rest of my days.

Billy Young, on enlistment, aged 15.

Billy Young was another cellmate. Aged only 18, he had been tried at Kuching and sent to Outram Road in mid-1943 for attempting to escape from Sandakan, and was initially very suspicious of me. He was instinctively resentful of officers and the discipline they represented. After we had gradually established some form of communication, I overcame Billy's hostility and set about informing his uneducated but very sharp mind. Optimistically, I even began instructing him on the mysteries of atomic physics, as much to keep my own mind active as to enlighten his. I urged him to get an education, to make the most of himself and take every opportunity after the war to rise above his POW experiences. It kept both of us sane and, in the end, we became good friends.

Another prisoner I came to know at Outram Road, and later at Changi, was a Royal Signals officer, Eric Lomax. He had come under the jurisdiction of the Kempeitai and was sent down to Outram Road from the Thai-Burma Railway. Having a cell mate, and I had several over the time I was imprisoned, was a morale booster and, on the whole a plus, but it was not without its difficulties. In such a confined space with very little time away from each other, our nerves constantly on edge and our health was in a fragile state, the smallest things became major problems. The way someone scratched himself, snored, coughed, his 'conversation', such as we could have, any minor mannerisms were magnified sometimes almost beyond endurance. The worst of these problems concerned food. Unless nipped in the bud, it could become a major source of ill feeling.

Accordingly we needed to come to an agreement, before the food arrived, as to who would take the left or right hand bowl from the slot, because if one bowl appeared to have a few more grains of rice than the other, it caused huge resentment. One cellmate suggested that, because he was bigger than I, he should always have the bigger-looking serve. Such dissention over a few grains of mushy rice! To preserve harmony in the cell it was best to have a pre-arranged agreement as to who took which bowl, the left or the right.

Not all of my cellmates were as mentally stimulating as Rob Scott and Billy Young and that was also an irritant. Mental sparring kept us active. To have a person with you who had no mental communication, and to have to put up with their physical foibles as well, was sometimes a definite minus. Some could only focus on their truck driving or wharf labouring and picture the food they were missing. Unless I had someone whom I found mentally to be on a similar plateau, I preferred to be alone.

Strangely, time did not seem to drag. I kept focusing my mind on a wide range of subjects. When I became fatigued with the mental calculations, I would occasionally drift off into physical things like food or my health or recall events from my life so far. This imaginative state did not matter and my mind would gradually take up some other theme. For instance, that wall is not quite perpendicular, it slopes a little to the left and if it were straight, how much further over would it move? Trivial things like that kept me busy and if I could not arrive at a solution it did not matter. It was a strange state to be in; it was as if I were in a self-inflicted quiescence. My main preoccupation was to use the available time for thinking. It was a pleasant feeling and I certainly did not hate it. I was in limbo. There were no responsibilities – no administrative tasks to attend to, no troops to keep an eye on, no one to think about except myself. I would have welcomed some menial tasks as a diversion, but this would have expended what precious little stamina I had. So, I had nothing to concentrate on except my survival.

In the first days after our arrival at Outram Road we were not let out of the cells except for the 20-second wash and a change into the so-called clean shorts. After two or three weeks we were set to work outside the cells, picking hemp. Prisoners employed on this duty sat in three rows on a thin layer of hessian in several sheds with dirt floors, on which were scattered large bales of tangled hemp ropes, delivered from a rope factory. The sheds were open-sided and poorly roofed, allowing rain to enter, but we were not permitted to break formation during downpours. Trusted prisoners were allowed to tear apart bundles and allocate them to the workers. Under extremely close supervision we untangled strands of hemp from the old ropes to make new ones. The ropes were too tough to break with our hands so we had to find the ends and undo the knots. If we left any of these knots untouched we were belted across the back with a sword in its scabbard. As an added incentive, if we didn't make a hundred new lengths of rope a day, by picking out 200 lengths of hemp for each and knotting them into hanks, there was no rice ration. Normally, this would have been the most mind-numbing job in the world, but to us it was a welcome change of routine. Occasionally, when we were on hemp duty, we might manage to snatch some hibiscus leaves or the odd slug or snail, which we hastily ate – raw. Raw or not, it nevertheless gave us some satisfaction to know that we had managed to do it under the noses of our captors.

Our health was always of great concern to us but there was not much we could do about it. The condition of the old prisoners was appalling and the new arrivals rapidly lost weight. The absence of fresh vegetables soon caused vitamin deficiency diseases and from early July 1944 our diet comprised solely of curried tapioca 'soup' and putrid rice. It has always amazed me that, while the Japanese were so fastidious about their own cleanliness, they were completely oblivious to the filthy conditions in which we lived. Not only that, they expected us to survive on subsistence food while undertaking hard manual labour.

Our bodies were infested with lice, scabies and bedbugs; tropical ulcers, tinea and sores that just would not heal, and we all had malaria, tapeworms and dysentery. Medical treatment was very poor. Occasionally a medical orderly would condescend to bandage bad sores and, at infrequent intervals, about five times during my incarceration, a doctor visited when extremely sick cases needed to be transferred to the Changi Prison hospital.

Kempeitai prisoners were numbered and accountable so, if anyone became too sick to work, he was transferred to Changi to 'recuperate'. If it appeared that a prisoner might die, the sentence was suspended, he was returned to Changi and the sentence restarted on returning to Outram Road. It may seem strange that we were sent to the Changi Camp hospital rather than to a Japanese military hospital, but the IJA did not waste resources on a prisoner who was probably going to die anyway. Besides, if the patient died at Changi, the Japanese could always blame our own medical people.

Several inmates became mentally unstable. Occasionally, I

heard a sickening thud as someone bashed his head on the cell wall and committed suicide. Despite all of the privations I never once, for a moment, thought of ending my life. I wanted to survive imprisonment and resume a normal life, return to my wife and have a career.

One of the tasks I decided to undertake to keep my mind active was to measure my pulse rate. To do this I needed a pendulum with a known oscillation period as a time reference. By holding a piece of hemp about 45 centimetres long between my buttocks, I managed to smuggle it into my cell, and hide it in a splinter of wood on the underside of one of my sleeping planks. To weigh down the pendulum, I smuggled in a stone using the same method and secreted it in a small hole in the corner of my cell.

These minor triumphs happened over many days but I still needed a reference to calculate the correct length of hemp to make a pendulum with an oscillation of one second. Then I had some luck. One day, when we were let out to wash, I noticed a heap of shorts lying on the corridor floor. A tape measure lay across them and happened to be positioned along the patch on which the number was stamped. It revealed that this patch was one and three-quarter inches (4.5 centimetres) long. By using the number patch on my own shorts, I realised that I now had a reference against which to measure the hemp for the pendulum, and set about calculating, as accurately as I could, the required length.

The maths and algebra were reasonably simple but, being unable to write things down, and with my sluggish brain function, the calculations became a major mental exercise. However, I persisted. When I was finally satisfied with my simple pendulum device, the next major problem was a juggling act to count two things at the same time – that is, to count 60 swings of the pendulum while counting my pulse beat. Having achieved this to the best of my ability, I calculated that my pulse rate was about three quarters of what it would normally be.

A lowered pulse rate was natural in our reduced circumstances and there was nothing I could do about it anyway, but the mental challenge and the extreme vigilance needed to accomplish this task kept me occupied over several weeks. Luckily, the stone and the hemp were never found.

As long-term prisoners we were considered by the Kempeitai to be the worst offenders of all and were treated, or rather mistreated, accordingly. Short-term military and civilian prisoners were put to work on menial jobs such as emptying the latrine buckets once a week. It doesn't sound much of an ambition, but it was one to which we aspired. On the rare occasions when I was allotted this task it provided a great change to the awful monotony of everyday routine, in fact a bit of stimulation!

As well as 'alien' military and civilian prisoners, Outram Road Gaol also housed Japanese military personnel who had fallen foul of the Kempeitai. Being Japanese, they had better rations and had longer to eat them. They were given lots of lovely cooked rice with black beans in it. The beans were full of protein and if swallowed whole they passed through the intestine and into the latrine buckets. I have seen our chaps so hungry that, if the opportunity came while they were on bucket-washing duty, they would grab a handful of beans from the bottom of the bucket when it was almost empty, wash the muck off and eat them while the guards weren't looking. I almost did it one day, but reason told me that I would be at even more risk of disease and that very little protein would be left in the beans anyway. I'm sure those who did it regularly realised this too. Desperation drove them to it.

A distraction of major significance was an episode concerning the commandant's pig. The Japanese kept several pigs at the gaol and it was discovered that one had a problem with its testicles. Someone must have informed the powers-that-be that I was a farmer, so I was chosen to castrate the animal. Although I had been brought up on a dairy farm and my talents ran more to science and engineering, I had no choice in the matter. Besides, it would be a welcome diversion from the boredom of daily life.

I was led from my cell to the pig's enclosure and presented with a knife. I made a big deal of requesting a stone on which to sharpen the knife, testing it and generally making the most of my time out of the cell, while one of the guards and a prisoner held down the unfortunate pig. The deed having been done I was then asked in broken English what should be done with the offending testicles.

Wanting to have a bit of fun, I said, 'Well, in Australia, these are considered to be the greatest delicacy and are usually eaten by important people for breakfast.' Sadly, I never had the satisfaction of knowing whether or not they were served up to the Commandant next morning, but I gained immense satisfaction from thinking they may have been.

On my arrival at Outram Road, I had wondered how penal servitude could be done in solitary confinement. However, the Japanese had a solution. For three months after October 1944 some of the prisoners were employed in monotonously polishing one Japanese water bottle per day or scrubbing and greasing boots. Occasionally parties were formed for gardening and other domestic gaol duties. This included a party of ten who spent four weeks gardening outside the gaol walls, chained together by the waist.

From February 1945 a special party of about 50 were employed on hard labour digging tunnels at Pasir Panjang and Buikit Timah, where many of the undernourished prisoners collapsed. Very occasionally those employed on manual labour were issued with slightly more rations and received an extra drink.

Towards the end of the war, we were set to work digging tunnels at Jurong, presumably to store ammunition against any Allied attack to re-take Singapore, although of course we did not know this at the time. Like the gardening detail, the work was performed in chain gangs A thick chain, about 15 metres long, was strung around our waists, padlocked at the back, with a metre or so left between each man, until six of us were chained together. In our emaciated state the chain chafed the skin of our hip bones causing even more sores and discomfort. But at least we were out of our filthy cells.

Despite the rigid conditions under which we were kept, some news did manage to circulate among the prisoners. We had no idea how accurate it was, but I 'heard', via the Morse taps, that Gerald Mavor had died as a result of the inhuman treatment he had received.

Early in April 1945, after 13 months of imprisonment, I became too weak to work on the chain gang and realised that I could not go on for much longer. The ability to work was becoming increasingly difficult; my sight was going and my whole body showed signs of malnutrition. My swollen and painful joints, itchy skin, lack of concentration, bleeding and tender gums, and shortness of breath were the result of months of starvation and torture. All of us were in the same state, yet the Japanese still expected us to put in a full day's work, which at that time was digging fox holes for a last Japanese stand against the Allied invasion they feared was coming. I just could not lift the baskets of earth and, despite my heavily calloused feet, trying to walk over rough stony ground with my load caused excruciating pain. I was trembling more and more each day and was being bashed by a particularly vicious guard.

'I can't go on,' I thought.

I had to get to Changi, so I had to convince the Kempeitai that I was sicker than I appeared. If my timing were too soon, I would be forced to continue working and would never survive. If my timing were too late, I would die anyway. Several prisoners, including Eric Lomax, who deliberately injured himself, had tried this manoeuvre and succeeded; others had tried and failed. I was gambling with my life.

One day, after being hit with a basket full of earth I decided the time had come. I was down in a hole and dropped my basket of soil to the ground, knowing I would be beaten. For a couple of minutes, I was kicked and bashed. I didn't move. I kept my eyes closed and thought, 'This is it. There's no point of return now, you've made your decision, it can't be changed.'

They left me in the sun all afternoon. I steeled myself not to move or open my eyes.

When evening came and it was time to return to the gaol, they bellowed at me to get up and walk. A couple of fellow prisoners were ordered to pick me up and carry me to the transport vehicle, which was a huge imposition in their weakened state.

'You know I'm conscious,' I whispered.

'Yes. Keep it going chum. You've got to go through with it now.'

'Yes,' I whispered back.

On reaching Outram Road, I was unloaded from the vehicle and thrown back into the cell. There was no food that night.

In the morning I was ordered to get up to work. I said I couldn't and was left in the cell. Lunch was a sip of water. I had to continue the charade. If I responded now, they would realise I was faking and would give me hell. By the next day I was barely conscious. When the guards came, they shouted 'DOCTOR' and told me to get up and walk

'I can't walk,' I muttered.

'No walk, no doctor.'

I stayed put. To walk now would be fatal.

At last they stretchered me off to see their doctor. He felt my pulse, put his stethoscope to my heart and shook his head. I could only imagine how slow my heartbeats must have been. Neither knee reacted when he tried a reflex test. He sent me back to the cell, where I went through a most trying time, wondering what, if anything, would happen. I lay quite still, trying not to think about the huge gamble I had taken. Eventually, footsteps approached. I held my breath and then heard the most beautiful words:

'Six four one, Changi.'

I almost jumped and shouted, 'Three cheers,' but just stopped myself in time from making a disastrous move. As I lay there, the guard kicked me and shouted at me to get up and walk.

'No walk. No walk. Stretcher. Stretcher,' I muttered.

If I got up and walked now, I would never get out. Eventually the guards carried me out on a stretcher, threw me into the back of a utility and off we went – out through the gates of Outram Road Gaol.

CHAPTER 11

BACK TO CHANGI

From May 1944 - September 1945, Changi Gaol was used as a POW Camp.

We rattled off towards Changi. The guard and driver were ordinary IJA soldiers, not Kempeitai. I could not believe the relief it gave me to be out of the hands of those fiends from hell. The guard chattered away in Japanese, offered me a cigarette, smiled and lit it for me. This was the only semblance of any civility I ever had from the Japanese. The cigarette was foul but somehow reassuring. I was no longer serving a sentence. The guard had no axe to grind with me, as all he had to do was to deliver me safely to Changi POW Camp. When we stopped in front of the entrance, I still insisted that I couldn't walk in case they decided to take me back to Outram Road. So, between the driver and the guard I was off-loaded from the vehicle and dumped outside the gates.

Changi inmates were always on the lookout for new arrivals from Outram Road and, as the vehicle drove away, it was only a matter of seconds before a couple of our people came out. I was overjoyed to see that one of them was Dr Glyn White, whom I knew from our time in Malaya. He had spent his imprisonment in Changi where, after setting up the hospital with the items smuggled into the camp, he did a heroic job of providing medical help and reassurance to the patients under his care.

He picked me up in his arms and carried me into the camp hospital. I estimate that when I arrived at Outram Road Gaol in March 1944, I would have weighed about six stone (38 kilograms). 13 months later, Glyn White, a paediatrician prior to the war, picked me up in his arms like a small child. Many years later he recalled:

'There was Rod Wells ... Rod was unrecognisable. You could count the surface anatomy of every bone he had in his body, he was so emaciated, almost too weak to talk. I was only about seven stone (44 kilograms) myself, but Rod, it was just like picking up a weeny little baby. I can still feel how he just relaxed as soon as I got him into my arms. It was a very, very emotional episode. He was almost too weak to speak but you could see the smile under his whiskers.'

One of the POW hospital huts, erected in the grounds of Changi Gaol, September 1945.

Somehow a set of scales was produced – I weighed 43 pounds (20 kilograms).

The important difference between Outram Road and Changi was that Australians ran the latter, with Japanese guards confined to patrolling the perimeter. Other than the usual restrictions on movement outside the camp, things were pretty much administered along military lines by our own officers. I could not have believed how much difference this would make. It sent my spirits soaring. For the first time in more than three years there was hope. Previously my future was an unknown quantity, full of fear and with death an imminent possibility; now, in all probability, I would survive. Once hope took hold it transformed my whole being.

I was admitted to the camp hospital straight away. Although the medical staff thought it crude compared to a normal AGH, the relief of being with my own people was overwhelming. The whole place seemed like a holiday camp to me, after the horrors of Outram

Road. Everyone at Changi looked healthy and reasonably well fed, compared to the emaciated state of the prisoners at Outram Road.

It was incredible how quickly the news spread, 'Rod Wells is here.' Gus Kappe came to see me, followed by various other people I knew – signals colleagues, hospital staff, orderlies – all greeting me with warmth, goodwill and sincerity, which I had not experienced for more than two years. Medical supplies were limited but that night I was given tablets of some sort and a little sweet rice. Someone managed to produce a hibiscus leaf cigarette; it was pretty awful but in the circumstances much appreciated. After years of starvation and malnutrition my stomach had shrunk so it was imperative that food was introduced gradually and, over the next few days, I relished even the smallest amounts that were rationed out. Somehow a drum of quinine powder had been obtained for the hospital and I was given daily doses, wrapped in toilet paper, which did little to disguise its extremely bitter taste. I was also advised by medical staff that, because my testicles had atrophied, I would probably be rendered sterile. Although the testicles subsequently recovered, this diagnosis proved to be correct.

The day after I arrived, a bath was produced, a large drum of some sort, filled with warm water and sulphur disinfectant. It was so beautiful to lie in this mixture using soap that some prisoners had managed to manufacture. I had not had the luxury of even a decent wash for over two years. The water was kept warm for an hour or so, allowing me to have a good soak. As my skin softened, I began to scratch myself and heavy layers of skin began to peel off the soles of my feet, leaving them as soft and tender as a baby's, so soft and tender that I was unable to walk. So I was carried back to bed where Dr White gave me an enema to try and get my bowels functioning. It was three months since I had had a motion and clearing the bowel set me on the way to recovery – and to talking.

It was many years since I had been able to talk free of constant fear. Fear of giving away the underground, fear of divulging information under interrogation and torture, fear of betraying my mates and at all times fear of being bashed for simply talking. What a bore I must have been. Unable to sleep for two or three days and nights, I just talked ceaselessly with no control over myself.

The Japanese still had ultimate control of the Changi Camp but, after Outram Road, it seemed to me to be an almost free and easy way of life. However, there were some regulations. All officers were compelled to wear single star pips on the left breast pockets of our shirts or whatever we had to wear. This pip did not indicate our actual rank. It was to show the Japanese that we were officers and every time we came across a Japanese soldier, we had to bow from the waist or receive a bashing. Not being anxious to be bashed unnecessarily, we found this directive more or less easy to comply with.

I soon learned that there were one or two radio sets in the camp and I was anxious for news. I got the rundown on the Normandy landings, which had taken place on 6 June 1944, the subsequent campaign and the happenings in South-east Asia. News also filtered through of the German surrender on 6 May 1945 so things were looking optimistic. Early in July, we learned that British Prime Minister Winston Churchill had been defeated in the general election by Labour Party leader Clement Attlee. Things were changing in the outside world. I just had to remain hopeful that I would not be returned to Outram Road. At random intervals, Japanese doctors would arrive to see if the Kempeitai prisoners were fit to be returned to resume their sentences of penal servitude. Our medical people realised that if I were recalled I would never survive. If our lookouts thought a Japanese doctor was arriving to carry out an inspection, word quickly circulated and I was given some mixture, which presumably relaxed me, or lowered my blood pressure so that my reflex reactions were dulled and I was declared unfit for work.

It would have been towards the end of July that the atmosphere at Changi began to lighten. We had no definite news, but the IJA guards seemed to be a bit less inclined to ill treat us; if we failed to show deference to them, the usual punishments were not inflicted. Japanese orders were that Changi hospital patients were not to mix with the other prisoners but we gradually began to mingle with our mates in the camp, returning to the hospital to sleep. One evening, at about sunset, I was outside a hut, half dreaming of my return home, when a platoon of Japanese guards marched past. Normally I would have been compelled to bow to them. I thought, 'I shouldn't have to do this. The war's probably all over.' As I was about to bow from the waist, the guard commander gave the order, 'Eyes right!'; gave a butt salute with his rifle and took his guard past me, with all eyes to the right.

Shortly afterwards, one of the lads came in and whispered that a big bomb, called an atomic bomb, had been dropped on Japan. I later learned it was dropped on 6 August 1945. Having some physics background, I suspected that it must have been a nuclear fission bomb of some sort. I tried to imagine the magnitude of it and the devastation it would have caused. There was no immediate reaction from the Japanese guards but we did manage to get a copy of *The Shonan Times*, a propaganda newspaper published in English by the Japanese throughout the occupation. Amazingly, they admitted that a bomb had been dropped, adding that the anti-Axis forces had the audacity to demand a Japanese surrender.

The bomb did not worry them in the least, they claimed. In fact they would be asking for a surrender from the Allied Forces. They had rejected the terms of the Potsdam Declaration, as drawn up by America's President Truman, Prime Minister Attlee of Great Britain and China's Chiang Kai-shek on 27 July. They would fight on for their Emperor.

As we found out later, despite a warning that another bomb would be activated if they continued to fight, the Japanese kept up their campaign until 9 August when a second bomb was dropped on Nagasaki. On 15 August, Emperor Hirohito delivered his surrender speech in what was known as the Jewel Voice Broadcast. It was the first time his subjects had ever heard him speak.

Sometime after the dropping of the Nagasaki bomb, the Allied Commander of Changi, Lieutenant Colonel Edward Barclay Holmes, and 'Black Jack' Galleghan, his AIF counterpart, sought permission from the Japanese to have a radio receiver. The Japanese officer dealing with this request answered that, if the prisoners had a radio set, they could use it. Almost immediately an amplifier miraculously appeared and was strung up on a tree with the volume turned up to full bore. We now knew that all the rumours of victory were true. The next piece of momentous news was on 2 September, when the Japanese signed the Instrument of Surrender with General MacArthur on board the battleship USS *Missouri* in Tokyo Bay – an event that none of us would ever forget.

Before any Allied troops arrived to release us, our senior officers held a parade in the prison grounds to show the Japanese who was really in control. This was, and remains, one of the most sentimental moments of my life.

A band of sorts was somehow gathered together, instruments appearing magically from within the camp. With our two commanders in charge, and the Japanese watching from the sidelines, the Rising Sun flag was lowered slowly and surely from the mast. Then, out of the hoard of stuff hidden in the prison, a colossal Union Jack appeared – the same flag that had been lowered in surrender on that fateful day in February, more than three years before. It was now slowly raised to the masthead while the band played *God Save the King*. Not even the hardest soldier remained dry-eyed. The Union Jack fluttered at last over Changi.

CHAPTER 12

WAR ENDS

The day of liberation, September 1945, Changi POW Camp.

In the four months spent at Changi before the end of the war, I gained a little weight as better food was available. Hibiscus leaves boiled into a soup and properly cooked rice with a little condensed milk may not have been classified as a normal diet but, after the subsistence rations of Outram Road, they were a luxury.

The hospital was a place of complete rest and mental relaxation; the communication and fellowship with my comrades, their care so lovingly given, made Changi seem like Heaven. It was a rest home; it was marvellous. By the time Japan surrendered, my eyesight, though not good, had improved, along with my weight, about four stone (25 kilograms).

We learned that hostilities had ceased on the afternoon following the parade at Changi, when we saw a single aircraft circle over the gaol, coming lower with each pass until it was only about 150 metres above us. The bomb bay opened, and an Australian Royal Air Force airman waved as he bundled out packages of leaflets.

At last it was official – the war was over. Instructions in Japanese, Malay, Chinese, Tamil and Hindustani ordered the Japanese to move to an area at Jurong, where they were to lay down their arms at a designated area. POWs and the populace were instructed not to molest or hinder the Japanese. We were also informed that, at dawn the next day, a commander, medical officer and two medical orderlies would arrive with medical supplies. The relief and excitement was electric. Hope was rekindled and morale rose. We hospital patients may have been emaciated and dishevelled but this uplifting of our spirits was a wonderful tonic.

Next morning, everyone was up early with eyes glued skywards. Sure enough, at dawn, an aircraft flew over and four or five men, dangling from white parachutes, drifted earthwards, followed by a large number of black parachutes with canisters of supplies. We subsequently learned that the commander and two medical officers, along with two medical orderlies, had landed safely. They soon got to work distributing the supplies with help from our own medical officers – everything had to be carefully rationed so that the sickest prisoners received priority treatment.

I noticed with great interest that, although the commanding officer wore only lieutenant's pips, he appeared to be of a much higher rank and was obviously a specially trained officer from

Admiral Lord Louis Mountbatten's staff. I suspect that dispatching a mere 'lieutenant' was a deliberate act to humiliate the Japanese, who would have expected to be confronted by a much more senior officer. To me, these relief troops looked like giants; they were immaculate, well-fed, muscular, alert and well disciplined.

On 4 September, two days after the official surrender, news spread rapidly that an Allied warship had arrived in Keppel Harbour. It was the Royal Navy's HMS *Sussex*, a heavy cruiser. On board, as we later found out, the Japanese discussed the terms of surrender with Lieutenant General Sir Philip Christison and General Sir Robert Mansergh, and signed the terms of re-occupation.

With great excitement we also learned that, on 12 September, Admiral Lord Louis Mountbatten would arrive at the Municipal Building in Singapore for a special ceremony, at which the Japanese would sign an instrument of surrender, officially ending Japanese occupation.

Sussex also brought troops and much-needed food and supplies, which were restricted initially to the hospital but gradually distributed to other prisoners. The cooks made up some jam tarts and we had mugs of hot water with Marmite, a rich source of vitamin B, which tasted better than any drink I could remember, even my favourite gin and tonic. We were warned not to accept too much food from the British troops as it would not be good for us. Inevitably some people took no heed and, having been starved for so long, were dead within 24 hours through over-eating. The Outram Road prisoners were much better disciplined, having survived much harsher conditions. It was easier for us to comply as we had learned to live with constant and extreme hunger and did not want to fall at the last hurdle.

In the week between 4 and 12 September, it was interesting to note a further and dramatic change of attitude in the Japanese. Despite all the cruel and atrocious acts they had perpetrated on us, as soon as the order came for their surrender there was a rapid turnabout in their behaviour. Whenever we saw a guard, he would immediately bow. We could have done anything to them, kicked them, bashed them and they would not have retaliated in any way. During the next few days it gave us great satisfaction to see hundreds of Japanese, on their hands and knees in long rows, cutting the grass on the main padang (field) with small hand scythes in preparation for the surrender ceremony. If a row got out of alignment, a big Sikh guard would inject his boot into the offending backsides as the watching crowd cheered.

On the morning of the 12th, the excitement was almost palpable as we prepared for the surrender parade. We wanted to make ourselves as presentable as possible and were keen to put on a good show at the padang, directly in front of the magnificent colonnaded Municipal Building. For four years or more, we had fought the elements relentlessly and endured this hot humid climate with its flies and mosquitoes and tropical downpours. Now, as we stood waiting on the padang in the midday sun I don't think any of us thought about the rain, the heat, the humidity or the flies.

Mountbatten and his staff were an impressive sight as they arrived, immaculately dressed and confident, to a cheering crowd. The Japanese representatives were booed as they were escorted into the building. At last, after an hour or so, Mountbatten emerged amid more cheering from the thousands of troops and civilians, gathered outside for this historic event. He told us 100,000 relief troops were currently disembarking and that General Seishiro Itagaki had signed the surrender document in the absence of Field Marshall Hisaichi Terauchi, Commanding Officer of the Southern Expeditionary Army Group, who had suffered a stroke in May.

Mountbatten stressed that this was not a negotiated surrender but a capitulation by the Japanese to superior forces. In our emaciated and brow-beaten state it was a cheering thought to be regarded as a 'superior force'. Mountbatten went on to thank all for their efforts and urged us not to take any nonsense from the Japanese should we encounter them. There were over 200,000 prisoners of war and civilians to be attended to and it was his job to see that orders for their release and sustenance were carried out as quickly and efficiently as possible. The pride and relief we felt is indescribable.

Our Allied forces and the local authorities faced a formidable task to restore order out of the chaos that was post-war Singapore. Apart from the thousands of our troops waiting to be repatriated, there was a huge civilian population to be returned to their homes, many from upstate Malaya. The Japanese, now at the bottom of the pecking order, would have to wait. It is estimated that, in September 1945, there were 77,000 Japanese troops on Singapore Island and another 26,000 scattered throughout Malaya.

Japanese who had committed atrocities were now rounded up to face trial as war criminals. I had the pleasure of identifying and assisting in the arrests of some of them and seeing them imprisoned in the same cells that I had formerly occupied. This was very satisfying work but I was anxious to get home to my wife, Ellen, and my family on the farm. I had not had any news of them throughout my imprisonment and did not know what information they had received regarding my survival. Rumour went around that a rehabilitation scheme for returned soldiers was to be set up to allow them to make up for time lost in their education and training. I desperately hoped that this would allow me to attend university to do a science degree.

Although evacuation priority was given to hospital cases, it was decided that prisoners from Outram Road needed more time to fatten up before returning home. While recuperating I spent a couple of weeks recording as much detail as I could recall of the names, times and places of the deaths of the prisoners at Sandakan, Kuching and Outram Road. I also wrote up a full report on the discovery of radio messages sent to the Japanese from the home of the Sultan's son, which I had confirmed just prior to our capture.

At last, word came through that we were ready to be sent home to Australia. I left Singapore with mixed emotions – there was the anticipation of reuniting with my wife, family and friends;

the prospect of studying at university; and the need to contact the families of those who had died in Malaya and Borneo, especially Lorna, Lionel's wife. Above all, I felt an intense sadness at leaving behind so many brave and loyal friends who had perished at the hands of the Japanese. Another whose loss I mourned was Lieutenant Colonel John O'Neill, CO of 2/15 Field Regiment, who was killed in Malaya in early November 1941, when the car he was driving skidded and overturned. I had first met him at Holsworthy and we had become very friendly. He was an inspiring leader with a huge personality who cared very much for the welfare of his men. Some years later, on one of my many return visits to Singapore, I sought out his grave at Kranji War Cemetery. We junior officers had always referred to him as 'the old man'; I was surprised to see that he was just 35 years old when he died.

Lt Col John O'Neill, 2/15 Field Regt, 1940. Inscribed on the back of the photo by Rod to his wife, 'Please keep this darling as a memory of a friend I always wish to remember.'

O'Neill died before the Japanese attacked Malaya on 8 December 1941, but something that has always puzzled me is that the Americans should have been aware of the enemy landings at Kota Bharu on the north east coast, at 00.30 hours Malayan time. As signals officer on duty that night at Jemaluang, I recall the signal, alerting us that Japanese forces had landed, came through at about 0100 hours on Monday 8 December. This would have been at 0700 hours on Sunday 7 December, Hawaii time. This signal, as well as being passed to Allied headquarters throughout the Pacific area, would have been relayed to US Command in the Philippines and thence to Hawaii. They should have had an hour to prepare for the attack on Pearl Harbour, which took place at 0753 hours, Hawaii time. It remained a mystery to me for years as to why this attack was not anticipated by US naval commanders. However, some historians in recent times have concluded that sending the aircraft carriers out to sea prior to the attack was not a stroke of luck. They argue that the high command knew, from intercepted and decoded signals, that an attack was planned but allowed it to go ahead, to protect the secret of the intercepts and to bring a reluctant America into the war.

Another controversy, surrounding the fall of Singapore, is that Singapore fell because the guns were facing the wrong way. The fact is that the guns could be, and were, turned on enemy positions in Malaya. However, as it had been anticipated that any attack would come from the sea, the ammunition was not high explosive, for use against personnel, but armour-piercing, designed for use against warships and requiring considerable impact to detonate it. The few shells that were fired inland whistled over the heads of our troops, only to fall harmlessly onto the soft earth of tropical Malaya.

Financial constraints were also a factor in the defence of the island. The Japanese aim was to sweep through East and Southeast Asia to India, forming a Greater East Asia Co-Prosperity Sphere by putting puppet governments in conquered countries. Accusations that Britain failed to send further troops, aircraft and support, to Malaya and Singapore, ignore the fact that, at the time, the European theatre was facing defeat from an enemy of vastly superior force. If Allied forces capitulated, and shipping lanes closed, there would have been no chance of victory. Every effort had to be put into the defence of Britain and Europe. If defeated, there would be no hope of stopping Japan. Put very simply, there were just not the resources to spare for Singapore.

In his book, *Why Singapore Fell*, written in 1944, Lieutenant General H Gordon Bennett gave several reasons why the tactics used by the Allies in the Malayan campaign were quite unsuitable for jungle warfare. His valid first-hand assessments, delivered on his return to Australia after his controversial escape on 15 February 1942, helped change the way in which jungle warfare was carried out. In his book, Bennett also revealed that he had planned his escape prior to capitulation. He justified this on several grounds. Firstly, army instructions advised that the first duty of a POW is to escape. Secondly, he did not implement his escape plans until after the surrender was signed and not before he had organised his men in preparation for the laying down of arms. He said, 'There was nothing I could do to help the unfortunate men. The moment the Japanese reached my headquarters I would have been taken away under escort.' Bennett also stated that he wished to escape to provide valuable information to army and government authorities in Australia concerning Japanese tactics and how to combat them. Despite this, I and many of my colleagues felt that he, and several other senior officers who also escaped, should have remained. One of the responsibilities drilled into officers is that at all times they must look after the wellbeing and welfare of their men. To me, it was as if a father had deserted his family in their hour of greatest need.

CHAPTER 13

HOMECOMING

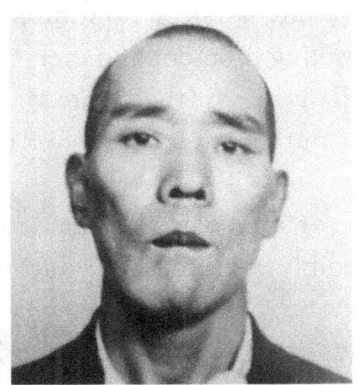

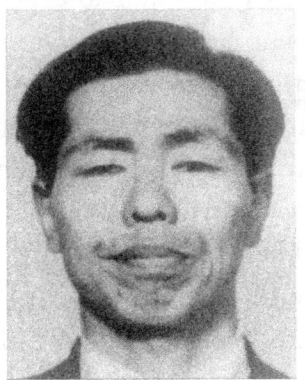

Japanese Judge Chief Sobei Egami.
Japanese Judge Junior Yoichi Tsutsui.
Japanese Judge Prosecutor Watanabe Haruo.

On 18 September, we embarked on the hospital ship *Manunda*, and headed for home. We were excited, but apprehensive, about being reunited with our families after such a long absence. There was much speculation about the meals we would enjoy, the places we would revisit and the reunions with our wives and girlfriends.

Our experiences had changed us and, although we were eager to return to civilian life, there were many doubts as to just how this would be achieved. At this time, I was still very much underweight, but I was beginning to feel more optimistic about the future. For years, and certainly during the 21 months spent in Kuching and Outram Road gaols, there had been no future. Striving for survival had taken up every waking moment and every last atom of strength and concentration. Planning for the future was something that we had lost, along with our freedom. Now we could start thinking about it again.

The calm discipline of shipboard life, the cleanliness and medical attention, were incredibly soothing after our inhumane treatment. Food, especially for the Outram Road survivors, was carefully rationed, as digestive systems were still sensitive. But after the fanatical discipline we had experienced, a few more days of careful eating was no hardship.

Instinctively I found my way to the radio operator's room and spent many happy hours chatting and catching up on outside news. I was there one day when his lunch arrived. He took one look at it and said, 'Oh no, not roast lamb again. Here, you have it.' I decided that I had been on light rations for long enough, that my stomach could take this mouth-watering offering and was about to tuck in when Matron caught up with me. 'No you don't,' she bellowed. I was hauled back to custard and jelly.

After a few days on board, the ship altered course and we were sent to Labuan Island, off the north-west coast of Borneo. I think the powers-that-be had decided that most of us still looked too emaciated and wretched to be seen by our families, so we were taken to 2/6 AGH at Labuan, to put on some condition.

I was frustrated by this delay. The authorities had notified me that, as soon as my health permitted, I would be asked to testify at a Japanese War Crimes Tribunal, which had been set up in Australia. During my time at Kuching Gaol and Outram Road I had heard nothing of the Sandakan prisoners, whom I had not seen since my arrest in July 1943. A few rumours about their fate were circulating in the last few days before I left Singapore and the news was not good. There appeared to be no survivors.

In Labuan I learned some details of what had happened. In August 1944, the Japanese High Command had issued orders that no prisoners were to survive. The following January, with the Sandakan airstrip bombed out of existence, making the labour force redundant, the local POW administration had no qualms in sending a batch of more than 400 prisoners on foot through the jungle to Ranau, about 250 kilometres away in the heart of British North Borneo. At the end of May, believing that Allied air attacks heralded an invasion, the Japanese withdrew many of their troops into the interior, taking more than 500 POWs, who could still walk, with them. As many had died in the interim period, about 300, who were too sick to leave, remained behind. A third march of about 60 left about a fortnight later. All but six, who managed to escape and were sheltered by local people, died either on the marches or at destination camps. No one left behind at Sandakan survived.[1]

I had to wait at Labuan until someone decided that I was ready to be viewed by my family in Australia. Luckily, a meeting at the hospital with Lieutenant Colonel George Parker, CO of 9 Division

---

1 A full and accurate account of the Borneo prisoners and the death marches can be found in Lynette Ramsay Silver's book, *Sandakan – A Conspiracy of Silence*.

Signals, whom I had known before the war, moved things along. A Catalina flying boat was due to leave in a few days for Darwin; if I could get kitted out, he would wangle me a place on it. The fact that I was in pyjamas didn't seem to bother the staff at Army Q-stores. I suppose they were used to personnel arriving in various forms of dress, or undress. They supplied me with jungle greens, which I hid under my bed for a few days, until I was alerted to be ready for a 1am departure.

I left Labuan unofficially, arriving undocumented in Darwin on 27 September, a place totally unknown to me and, in that era, to most Australians. They took one look at me and promptly put me into quarantine for a week. Although I had heard that Darwin had been bombed by the Japanese on 19 February 1942, I was shocked that there was still so much evidence of the raids. It brought home to me just how perilously close we had come to being invaded by a foreign power. Northern Australia had been subjected to almost 100 air raids on towns and air force bases in the Kimberley region and the Northern Territory, as well as three raids on Townsville on Queensland's east coast. Japanese submarine activity had been detected all along Australia's eastern seaboard and three miniature submarines had even entered Sydney Harbour. One had attacked, hitting a converted ferry used as accommodation for naval personnel, and killing a number of sailors as they slept. It was disturbing to hear of how close the Japanese had come, but I felt proud of being part of the forces that had eventually defeated a brutal enemy and allowed me to return to a free homeland.

The day after my admittance to Darwin Hospital, a lady from the Red Cross came around to greet new arrivals and asked if we would like to contact our families. It could take about eight hours to get a line through, she said. When she asked for the number, I immediately remembered it after all those years – Tatura 285. Later that morning, I was invited to lunch with the Chief Signals Officer of the Northern Territory. I was the first signals officer to return through Darwin and he was anxious for news of his comrades who had been sent to Malaya. I was surprised that the staff car sent to pick me up was driven by a female. We had encountered army nurses but women serving in active roles was something completely new.

'What do you do all day?' I asked her.

'Oh, a bit of driving and a bit of spine-bashing.'

'Spine-bashing, what's that?'

'You know – sleeping. Where've you been for the last five years?'

Where, indeed.

When I arrived at the colonel's office, in jungle greens and slouch hat – no officer's cap or rank badges – I was further surprised to see women actively engaged in signals duties. The colonel greeted me warmly.

'Have you put through a call to your parents yet?' he asked.

'Yes, I've booked a call through the Red Cross.'

'Red Cross be buggered. You're a bloody signals officer. Headquarters Melbourne,' he bellowed into the phone. 'Now what's the number? Priority emergency call to Northern Victoria, Tatura 285, please, operator.'

In about five seconds I was connected. Of course, as prisoners of the Kempeitai we had received no letters during our incarceration and there was no way of communicating with our families, even after our release. However, despite having had no personal contact, I had assumed that my family had been notified weeks ago that I was alive. They hadn't. As news gradually filtered back home, they had feared the worst. Names of survivors appeared in the newspapers only after definite confirmation that the person was alive and, so far, my name had not been among them. However, if a name did not appear it did not necessarily mean that the person was deceased, it just meant that the list was a work-in-progress, giving the authorities time to notify families of those who were definitely known to have perished. By an incredible coincidence, it was only that morning that the records, having worked their way from Singapore to Colombo, finally arrived in Melbourne, where the lists were immediately published.

Strangely, the very morning I had arrived in Darwin, Paddy O'Byrne had seen my name in the list of survivors in the Melbourne paper and phoned my parents. In those days, metropolitan newspapers did not arrive in Tatura until the afternoon train. Dad was in the milking shed when my mother took Paddy's call. She called out to him that I was alive, and promptly fainted. Dad, who had been having trouble with a lad who was helping with the milking, threw a bucket of milk over him and ran up to the house for an excited conversation with Paddy.

When I phoned a couple of hours later, I assumed that they had already known for a few weeks that I was alive. When my mother answered the phone and I said, 'Hello Mum, it's Rod,' she collapsed again and my father was almost as bad when he tried to speak. I told them I would probably be with them within a week. During that week my rations were gradually increased and the feeling of wellbeing that came with the improved diet encouraged me to believe that I would soon return to normal, both physically and mentally.

From Darwin, the Catalina took me to Sydney, where I arrived on 1 October 1945. Close friends of the family, who were in town and managed to get to the flying boat base at Rose Bay, were there to greet me. In Sydney, I boarded a train for Melbourne, along with four or five other ex-prisoners. It was on this trip that I realised some Australians believed our troops in Singapore had not fought hard enough and that this, in turn, led to resentment over wartime rationing measures. At Albury on the NSW border, where we changed trains, our POW group was treated to a special meal of poached eggs. Three or four RAAF officers walked in and abused the restaurant staff and everyone else about our special treatment.

'Who do these bloody soldiers think they are? They haven't had such a bad war. Half of them wouldn't know what a bloody war was.'

We didn't take too kindly to that and I said something like, 'You bastards wouldn't know what it's like to miss a decent feed. Have the blasted eggs if you want them.'

When they found out who we were they quickly left. It was a very tense moment, and one that was repeated several times over the next year or so.

It was a hugely joyful reunion at Spencer Street station when the train finally arrived on 3 October. My wife Ellen and my mother couldn't let go of me and the rest of the family were in tears. I learned that my sister Madge had married an Air Force officer, Flight Lieutenant Lex Goudie, and had a baby daughter, Anne, born in October 1944. My father's hair had turned grey and, although they tried to hide it, I'm sure the family was shocked by my appearance. By this time, I probably weighed about 32 kilograms and thought I looked pretty good but there was no hiding what I had been through. I assumed we would immediately head for home but my father had other ideas.

'You're not going home until we've been out to Heidelberg to have you checked out. We World War I chaps went straight home and later had a hard job to prove our illnesses were war-related.'

For the next two days the staff at Heidelberg Repatriation Hospital gave me a thorough going over, recording all my injuries and permanent damage. Thanks to Dad's advice all of my health issues have been looked after without question by the Department of Veterans' Affairs.

At last, on 5 October, I was discharged from Heidelberg and we set out on the 160-kilometre drive home. The countryside looked fresh and green in the spring sunshine. As we crossed the bridge over the Goulburn River at Seymour, late-blooming wattles were a blaze of golden colour, such a contrast to the never-ending green of the jungle that I had become so accustomed to seeing. The open plains of rural Victoria with stock grazing and crops ripening gave me a feeling of freedom and space I had not experienced for almost five years. At last I could relax.

Aunts, uncles, cousins, neighbours and old friends welcomed me warmly but both Wells grandparents had died and I was saddened to learn that one of my best mates, John Stewart, had been killed in action. It was incongruous to see Dhurringile Mansion still encircled by barbed wire and a large number of Nissen huts outside the surrounding towns, housing military prisoners, civilian internees, and enemy aliens, some of them Japanese. A kilometre or two from the farm was a prison camp, holding survivors of the German ship *Kormoran*, which had sunk off the West Australian coast after sinking HMAS *Sydney* in 1941. The convent nuns welcomed me back and told me that they had prayed for my safe return. For the nuns it was a triumph of faith in their God; for me it reinforced faith in myself. After my experiences, nothing could destroy or defeat me.

I had assumed that I would soon regain my strength and help with the wheat harvest. After a few days, I offered to help Dad with the hay-making but, after half an hour or so, was completely exhausted. However, as each day passed I gained strength and stamina. At the end of October, Ellen and I moved to the Melbourne suburb of Essendon and on 1 November I made my first appearance at the War Crimes Tribunal, set up in 1945 and presided over by Sir William Webb, Chief Justice of the Supreme Court of Queensland.

I began my longed-for studies at Melbourne University in March 1946. Prior to my enlistment in 1939, I had taken a university entrance examination in the hope of doing a science degree. In January 1946 I learned that, as a result of that exam, I had been accepted into Melbourne University and could do my course under the Returned Servicemen's Rehabilitation Scheme. Settling down to study did not come easily for us ex-servicemen during the first year. To begin with, our fellow students were all young people who had only recently left school. They were accustomed to study and did not have severe physical and mental challenges to overcome. Their knowledge, especially in my field of science, was up-to-date whereas ours was outmoded. We were unused to the discipline of academic life – for the past four or five years we had lived independent lives in both thought and action and found it hard to fit in. However, by second year uni, we began to catch up and by third year were forging ahead. We wanted to make up for lost time and the other incentive was that if we failed a year we would be unable to continue our course under the Rehab scheme – we would have to drop out or pay our own fees to finish.

While attending Melbourne university, I testified several times at the War Crimes Tribunal and was questioned minutely about the trial at Kuching. Much later, I was interviewed again and swore an affidavit at Shepparton, where I was teaching. I had thought that re-living these experiences would be harrowing but it helped to purge some of my deep feelings of hatred towards the Japanese. The court process, unlike our trial at Kuching, was thoroughly fair. On one occasion, when I was not totally sure of the identity of a suspect in a photo shown to me, my evidence was discounted.

As a result of trials held in Australia, New Guinea and Southeast Asia, between 1945 and 1951, many Japanese charged with war crimes were found guilty. Some were hanged, others shot and many received long prison sentences. Unfortunately, in the chaos that followed the Allied victory, many of the perpetrators escaped and have never been brought to justice. Both General Masao Baba, head of the Japanese 37th Army, based in Borneo, and Captain Hoshijima, CO of the Sandakan POW Camp, were found guilty of various war crimes and hanged. Hoshijima, defiant and arrogant to the end, bit the hand of the Australian provost escorting him to the gallows.

Each time I testified, I could still see in my mind's eye the cruel, unyielding faces of my tormentors. As a result of war crimes investigations, I learned the names of the five members of the Kempeitai present at my court martial. As Lionel and I had sat facing them, the Chief Judge, Lieutenant Colonel Sobei Egami was in the centre; to his right was Major Shuji Nishihara, acting chief judge and, on Egami's left, junior judge Captain Yoichi Tsutsui. On Egami's extreme left was prosecutor Captain Watanabe Haruo and on the extreme right sat the secretary Ishikawa Takeo. No punishment could have been too harsh for any of them.

The trial proceedings also helped explain, in some part, the reason for the miracle of my escaping the death penalty.

Kempeitai prisoners, unlike ordinary POWs, had to be strictly accounted for. Command Headquarters were in Saigon so, when the Kuching court found Lionel and me guilty, a message seeking permission to execute two Australian officers was sent to Saigon. When the reply was received, permission had been granted for one execution only. Because Lionel was the senior officer and the ringleader of the camp underground, his sentence was carried out. I heard after the war from British cryptanalysts intercepting Japanese signals that, when the reply arrived from Saigon, the Japanese decoding clerk made a transcription error, typing a 1 instead of 2. The miracle I had hoped for had happened but, with the loss of a gallant friend and colleague, I felt no triumph in the fact that I was still alive. I also realised the irony of my survival, despite the ordeals I had been through. Had I not been arrested by the Kempeitai and sentenced to Outram Road; had I been left at Sandakan when the bulk of the officers were moved to the Kuching Camp in October 1943, I would probably have perished on one of the death marches. I had a lot to be thankful for.

Lord Russell of Liverpool wrote a book, *The Knights of Bushido*, published in 1958. In reference to what became known as the 'Double Tenth Trial', held in Singapore in 1946, he quoted from the opening address by the prosecutor, Lieutenant Colonel Colin Sleeman:

> *'It is with no little diffidence and misgiving that I approach my description of the facts and events in this case. To give an accurate description of the misdeeds of these men it will be necessary for me*

to describe actions which plumb the very depths of human depravity and degradation. The keynote of the whole of this case can be epitomized by two words – unspeakable horror.

Horror, stark and naked, permeates every corner and angle of the case from beginning to end, devoid of relief or palliation. I have searched, I have searched diligently, amongst a vast mass of evidence to discover some redeeming feature, some mitigating factor in the conduct of these men which would elevate the story from the level of pure, horror and bestiality, and ennoble it, at least, upon the plane of tragedy. I confess that I have failed.'

These words perfectly describe the acts of the Kempeitai, perpetrated on so many thousands of service personnel and civilians throughout the war. There was no punishment great enough for the crimes they had committed.

My trials and tribulations were over, but rumours and accusations about my activities while involved in the underground circulated for years. It has been wrongly asserted by several prisoners that Hoshijima had found a notebook or diary in which I had recorded our activities, and that this was responsible for our arrest and that of our helpers, and for Lionel's death. Now, I may not have been a trained intelligence officer, but I did know enough to realise that keeping any records in the camp was hazardous in the extreme, which is why I sent them out of the camp with Abin. Yes, I compiled coded news summaries on scraps of paper for Dr Taylor, and this is what Hoshijima found, hidden in my spare socks, ready for delivery the next day. Any notes written to our helpers, and left for collection in the jungle, were destroyed immediately after being collected.

Over the years, I have verbally, and by correspondence, denied keeping a diary but, despite this, several authors have recorded scuttlebutt as fact. A small black notebook was indeed found, along with three maps and details of military installations and

Japanese dispositions, given to Lionel, but it did not belong to me. I did not even own a notebook. It was no good my protesting my innocence – by the time I returned to Australia, two years of gossiping and innuendo in the Kuching Camp by my fellow officers had turned rumour into firmly entrenched fact.

In the interval before I began university, I spent a lot of the time writing to the families of the men under my charge who had died in Malaya and Singapore. It was important to let them know as many details as possible – when and where their sons had died and how bravely they had fought for their country. I also compiled a detailed six-page report on the activities of B Force and the underground for the twelve-month period from July 1942-43. It is not very often that a junior officer tenders a report on a senior officer for a bravery but, during my first few weeks at home it was my great privilege to submit to the Army a report of Lionel's activities in Sandakan as part of a recommendation, also supported by Dr Taylor, Gordon Weynton and others, for a posthumous George Cross for gallantry. We were successful and the award was subsequently gazetted in December 1947. A George Cross is the non-combatant equivalent of the Victoria Cross, and Lionel Matthews remains the most distinguished and highly decorated member of the Royal Australian Corps of Signals.

Adjustment to civilian life was difficult. I could not bear to share anything with anybody. The knife and fork with which I ate my first meal became mine. I washed and put them away after each subsequent meal. I would look after myself; 'Please give me the raw rations and I'll cook them myself,' I wanted to cry out. I had to know that everything I was responsible for, or concerned with, was accounted for. Sleep came reasonably easily for the first few weeks I was home. There was a feeling almost of numbness, with none of the tension that I had been under for so long. It was strange to see only European faces – no Chinese, Malays, Indians or Japanese. Most of all, I missed the presence of my army colleagues and friends. I kept expecting to see them around the farm or in town. Then, about six months later, bad dreams began to bother me. I wasn't really home. I was back in Outram Road. The war had finished but it wasn't really over. Nobody knew where I was. I was back in Borneo and Singapore, suffering the same ill-treatment. It was very confusing and frightening but I suppose it was one way of getting rid of the bad memories.

Having enlisted in the AIF on 4 May 1940, I was officially discharged from the Army on 4 January 1946. The discharge papers stated that I had served for 2072 days. The majority of this time, from 15 February 1942 until 4 September 1945, was spent as a prisoner, and for a period of 21 months I was in Kuching and Outram Road Gaols, some of it in solitary confinement.

On reflection, I had not realised how my world had gradually contracted during my time as a POW. From the freedom of my boyhood, through army training, active service, imprisonment and solitary confinement, my world had become smaller and smaller. After my actual imprisonment I had turned inwards, my only aim to stay alive. I had been in a closed country, cut off from the world, totally reliant on my own resources. Now I found it hard to adjust to the larger world, to learn that I could rely on others.

I was on my way by tram to Victoria Barracks in St Kilda Road, to be discharged, when I was again upset by the lack of understanding by my fellow Australians. Still in uniform, I unexpectedly suffered a recurring malaria attack and began shaking. A woman passenger remarked to her friend, 'Well what do you expect? Drunken soldier! Now the war's over they can't even have a meal without getting drunk.' I refrained from remonstrating with her but felt she had no right to make such ill-informed comments. Many members of the public did not know the facts and neither did they want to know. Their wartime lives had been safe. They never gave a thought to those men who had fought and suffered so bravely to keep the country free.

One memorable trip I undertook, early in 1946, was to travel by train to Adelaide to see Lionel's widow, Lorna, and his son David, born in July 1938. I was very excited about meeting them, but apprehensive about the delicate task of telling them the circumstances of Lionel's war service and execution, while keeping back the more harrowing details of the horrors he had undergone. The Signals Association paid my train fare and it was an emotional meeting for Lorna and me, especially when I gave her an account of Lionel's death and his last words to her and David. I spared her as much as I could of the torture and interrogation, reassuring her that he was greatly admired and loved by all who had known him for his courage, loyalty and resourcefulness under the extreme conditions we had endured. Years later, David related to me how he remembered meeting a very old man walking with two elbow crutches and talking with a nervous stammer. I would have been just 26 years old.

In January 1946, Ellen and I were still living in Melbourne, but things were not well between us. I had left her as a healthy, mentally fit 21-year-old, and returned a nervous wreck, anxious, looking much older than my years, frail in health, chain smoking and unable to have a family. We parted by mutual consent but that did not stop me from feeling a rejected failure. Once again I just had to make the most of things. I felt that three and a half years of my life had been wasted. I had to make up for lost years and was determined to use my talents to the best of my ability and never squander a minute of whatever time was left to me.

I have sometimes been asked how I found Australia after so many years' absence. In some ways, unlike many servicemen, I was fortunate in being able to talk about my experiences. I tried to keep things general and not dwell on details of my torture and interrogation. Certainly, I kept the more gruesome facts from my mother, though my father had a fair insight into what I had been through. Two factors influenced returning servicemen from talking openly about their experiences. The first was that families had been told not to ask their loved ones too much about their time as prisoners of war, since it was all just too dreadful and going over the events would not be good for their return to civilian life. The second was that, if we did speak of the starvation and deprivations, we were told that things had been pretty tough back in Australia with food and petrol rationing!

At this stage, I felt no need to keep in touch with other POWs. Because of my experiences, I was a bit of a loner. With the exception of Gordon, I had not seen any members of my unit for three years. Like me, they were getting back to their civilian careers and going about their business. Many joined the RSL but my only visit to a club was disappointing – all they wanted to talk about was what hard times they had been through and how poor old so-and-so was. I just wanted to make up for lost time.

Somehow, the Australia I returned to was a disappointing place. I had assumed that during the war we would have had a composite government with no elections; that everyone would have concentrated heavily on the war effort. Yet elections, football matches and horse races were still held. In fact, life went on pretty much as usual. My muddled feeling was that if everyone at home had tried harder, the war would have been over sooner. What more they could have done was not clear to me and, as our contribution to the world war effort was small compared with other nations, it would probably have not made much difference anyway. But such were my thoughts. In October 1946, *The Bulletin*'s journalist Malcolm Ellis echoed these thoughts in his column 'The Serviceman'. Using the pseudonym 'Ek Dum', Ellis wrote:

> *Borneo was the POW grave. But so little has the disaster impressed itself on the minds of the public that a Sydney jockey's funeral created more interest and hysteria than the loss of all the tortured of Borneo.*

Over the years there has been controversy over the dropping of the atomic bombs on Hiroshima and Nagasaki and I have often been asked for my thoughts on this. In *The Knights of Bushido*, Lord Russell gives a comprehensive account of the political, military and social changes that took place in Japan during the 1930s. The government was virtually run by the army, which pursued a deliberate policy of expansion using murder, rape and plunder as it worked its way down through China to South-east Asia. The atrocities the IJA inflicted on military personnel and civilians are well documented.

In August 1945, prisoners in remote camps were made to dig their own graves and were to have been bayoneted or shot – orders were for not one person to survive. After the first bomb was dropped on Hiroshima the Japanese were warned that another would be dropped unless they surrendered unconditionally, which they refused to do. My answer, to those who say the bombing should never have happened, is that by these actions thousands of Allied prisoners' and civilians' lives were spared. Retribution was completely justified.

Towards the end of my second year of university I became publicly embroiled in what, at the time, was a major controversy, but which soon faded from public interest. One of the prisoners at Sandakan was Sergeant Macalister Blain, member of the House of Representatives for the Northern Territory. In Federal Parliament, in November 1947, NSW Labor MP, Mr Mulcahy, accused him of using his gold parliamentary pass to curry favour with the Japanese. I knew this was completely untrue and promptly wrote to Mac and the two Melbourne papers, *The Sun News-Pictorial* and *The Herald*, in which the allegations had been published. Things heated up, with the publication of allegations and cross-allegations, along with my letters of support and my photograph. The storm soon died down as more important matters took over the front pages and I was too involved with end-of-year exams to waste any more time on it. However, Prime Minister Chifley wrote to me suggesting that I should get on with my life and leave him to get on with his.

Getting on with life was a job we were left to do on our own. At no time after our homecoming were we given any debriefing, counselling or psychiatric help. In those days it just was not done. Although it was acknowledged that we had endured extreme conditions as soldiers and prisoners, the community regarded us as somewhat of a failure. It had somehow been our fault that we had been captured. Certainly I felt a bit of a loner; I still feel that, in spite of trying hard to the contrary, I am a bit odd compared with other people. I am looked on as being different. This may or may not be true and it is probably up to others to judge me, but this is one of the psychological issues I have been left with. I know I react differently in some ways from other people and still must account for everything. For instance, if I am doing some technical work and drop a screw, I must get down on my hands and knees to find it, even though I might have hundreds more screws on hand. Although I know that showering and washing use up lots of time and water, I feel obliged to soap up and rinse off several times before I feel really clean. Even when I am putting on clean clothes, I need to smell them to see if they are fresh. These sorts of things must drive people mad.

For the first 20 years or so of my post-war life, I would say I had a complete lack of confidence. This was particularly noticeable when I rejoined the army in 1951. I had a terrible time for the next eight or nine years, feeling nervous about addressing people because they would have had more experience than me, they would not have had a blank period in their lives of six years. This may sound silly but this is how my subconscious mind worked. Colleagues and superiors had the benefit of more training and life experience, denied to me during those lost years. I felt that I would be condemned or criticised, even punished, for doing things that were not right. This was a huge worry. In retrospect, it was probably a result of being punished by the Japanese for even the slightest breach of their rules, such as not even being able to talk freely. I was striving, not for perfection but mediocre performance, but worrying all the time that I might hurt or displease someone, that I had to step gently in case someone reacted badly. Now a man of confidence would not worry about something like that – he would go and carry out his plans boldly. My self-esteem was very low. There was a huge hole in my life, which made me feel inferior. To overcome this, I sometimes became aggressive in ways that would make people resent or dislike me more. I felt that I could not get the amount of contact or communication quite right. I was never criticised but, many years later, when I was finally being assessed by an army psychologist, he said, 'I haven't got you quite worked out yet,' whereas he had worked out everyone else.

I was helped to some extent by becoming a Freemason. Due to my father's involvement in his local lodge, I had an insight into the workings of this organisation with its emphasis on tolerance, brotherhood and charity. I was invited to join The Army Lodge, Melbourne, a Freemasons lodge for men with an army background, and was initiated in September 1946 while still a university student. Although my subsequent career and studies left little time for other than occasional visits to my 'mother' lodge, I always took the chance to visit other lodges, particularly in the United Kingdom where, in April 1961, I was initiated into Chiswick Lodge of Mark Masters & Royal Ark Mariners. During army postings in the 1950s and 60s, I visited a number of lodges throughout Britain. It was a great way of getting to know people and the feeling of brotherhood was very much like the camaraderie I had shared with fellow soldiers and prisoners.

There were some positive things to come out of my wartime experience. It reinforced my father's insistence on self-reliance and discipline – to think things through, to be able to remember things. I thought I was self-disciplined due to my upbringing and army training, but the Sandakan underground and Kempeitai experience forced me to exert even more self-control and become more self-aware. Getting to know men and human nature was a positive asset and it was an honour to have been associated with so many brave and loyal men. At the time, experiencing life in a foreign country was an absolute plus. The terrain, climate, religions, food, languages, customs and mixed races of Malaya were a revelation to me coming, as I did, from an English speaking, European-type background. In my subsequent career, Malaya, which later on became Malaysia, became my second home. But that was some years into the future.

CHAPTER 14

FRESH START

Rod Wells, 1-56 Australian Regular Army Field Officers' Course 1952.

At the end of 1948, I graduated from university with a Bachelor of Science degree, then for the next year undertook a Diploma of Education. At the beginning of the first school term in 1950, I found myself head science master at Shepparton High School, travelling from the farm at Dhurringile on the school bus each day. My appointment caused some resentment as, due to my qualifications, I had been promoted over several less-qualified staff, who had kept the science and maths departments running during wartime staff shortages.

The Army Cadet Unit at the school had become rather neglected so I took it upon myself to motivate the lads to join and became second-in-command. At the annual cadet camp, held at the Puckapunyal Army Base, not far from Shepparton, we were marching back one Sunday from Church Parade when I spotted my old CO, James Thyer, and Gus Kappe, in full uniform, walking towards us.

The cadets from Melbourne Grammar, Scotch College and Geelong Grammar marched on in smug ignorance. I ordered a salute and my unit responded magnificently. Out of 3000 cadets at the camp that year, Shepparton High School's squad was judged the most orderly and efficient in dress, bearing and discipline. I was put in charge of all camp communications and we received many favourable comments on our general conduct. It was a great morale booster for the boys, the school, and me.

Ellen and I finally divorced in May 1950 and, in January 1951, I married Linda King. After a year of teaching I was also ready for a change in my professional life. I found the routine dull and realised that in 20 years' time, on the first day of the last term of school, I would still be teaching 'An Introduction to Calculus'. I was very anxious, still had my severe stammer, and was ridiculed behind my back by the students for my nervous mannerisms. I also did not like the unionism that was becoming more evident in the teaching profession and besides, with one or two exceptions, most of the students were just not interested in learning.

It so happened that I was walking along Collins Street in Melbourne during the term holidays when I ran into an old brigadier friend. When he asked what I was doing, I replied that I was teaching, but looking for a change.

'Well,' he replied, 'if you re-enter the army, I can guarantee you a place at the Royal Military College of Science (RMCS) at Shrivenham in Wiltshire. We have never had an Australian signals officer attend the college and we are looking to send someone there.'

The lure of postgraduate study was just what I was looking for and, as an added bonus, I would be able to meet members of my mother's family. So, in 1951 I returned to the army as Senior Wireless Officer at Army Headquarters' Signal Regiment, Melbourne and, over the next two years, completed a degree in Electrical Engineering at Melbourne University. By the end of 1952, I had also passed the necessary examinations and been promoted to Major. Strangely, the curriculum had included the battle of El Alamein, which I first heard about on our clandestine radio at Sandakan and which, starved as we were for news, brought us some hope that Europe was holding out. Since that time, I had become a great admirer of General Bernard Montgomery and the tactics he used to crush his arch enemy, Field Marshal Rommel, so it was satisfying to study the campaign in detail. With my course completed, I was accepted into RMCS 7th Military Past Technical Staff Course.

In May 1953, Linda and I sailed for England on *Strathnaver*. It was the fresh beginning I had been looking for and so began the most satisfying period of my professional life. The few weeks on board ship were definitely a time of relaxation but the army, to my surprise, classified it as being on duty.

We happened to arrive in England in June 1953, a few days after the coronation of Queen Elizabeth II. As we sailed towards Southampton, we were treated to the most wonderful spectacle. Gathered on the Solent were hundreds of ships from the Royal Navy, Commonwealth and foreign countries, ready for a full Spithead Fleet Review by the newly crowned monarch. Naval bands rehearsed; the ships, outlined with lights at night, were decked in bunting; and crews immaculately dressed. It was an unexpected and rare sight, and one that I will never forget.

Set in the beautiful Wiltshire countryside near the village of Shrivenham, not far from the Vale of White Horse, RMCS was a revelation. The main part of the college, Beckett Hall, dates from 1831 and overlooks a lake and extensive grounds. Almost 500 fellow students from Commonwealth countries were undertaking postgraduate studies in a wide range of military and scientific subjects, making it, academically, extremely rewarding and paving the way for my future careers.

Atomic physics was a developing science and electronics was in its infancy. My fellow students and I made a remote-controlled bicycle, which we sent down the High Street of Shrivenham, much to the startled delight of the villagers. Our tutors were experts in their various fields and outside lecturers often visited, including, to my great joy, the now Field Marshall Sir Bernard Montgomery. He arrived by helicopter, which landed in the grounds, and we were warned that we had best do any coughing, sneezing or shuffling before the great man arrived. His speaking voice grated, he name-dropped shamelessly and informed us that he was on his way to meet a European leader. Altogether he was the cocksure commander I had expected him to be, but I still admired his abilities and achievements.

My mind was stretched and tested by the lectures, and the company of like-minded students was very stimulating. We lived on campus and could join in a huge range of extra-curricular activities, ranging from rugby to Gilbert & Sullivan, debating to gun clubs. Joining the photography club opened my eyes to new photographic equipment becoming available in England and Europe. During this time, I also undertook a course in nuclear physics at King's College, Cambridge. When I finally left RMCS in June 1954, I was seconded to the UK Ministry of Supply, where I was attached to the Signals Research and Development

Establishment (SRDE) and the Royal Radar Establishment (RRE), working on development projects.

It was at Shrivenham that I had another near-death experience, albeit of a slightly different kind. Each year, a Summer Ball was held to celebrate the end of our academic courses. Victor Silvester's Orchestra came from London, the mess hall was decked out, with service personnel in summer mess kit and ladies in their formal gowns creating an ever-changing and colourful kaleidoscope. During the evening, I noticed a fellow Royal Signals officer, Major Ludovic Rutherford, with his distinctive red hair, bending over a table. His breeches stretched tightly over his backside presented an irresistible target.

'Ludo, you old bastard,' I enthused while delivering a stinging flick with my fingers. Up rose the red head, up rose the shoulders, up rose the impressive rank badges of Major General Michael Gambier-Parry MC, Deputy Lieutenant of Wiltshire and a special guest at the ball. My body absolutely froze with shame and embarrassment. Across my mind flashed visions of being drummed out of the course and being sent home in disgrace.

Finally, I managed to stammer out, 'I'm terribly sorry, sir, I mistook you for someone else.'

To which he replied, 'I certainly hope you did,' then added, 'Aussie, I think you could do with a drink.'

He was absolutely charming and we had an amicable conversation. I concluded that it was just unfortunate that there happened to be two red-headed officers present and reflected, rather prematurely, that not all of my escapes from death necessarily happened on the battlefield or in a prison cell.

A visit to my parents on the farm during a period of leave proved me right. My father asked me to check out a noise coming from underneath his Austin Sheerline Saloon. This distinctive car, weighing about two tonnes, was fitted with four inbuilt jacks which I deployed to raise the whole vehicle. I slid under, resting my head on a couple of bricks, and began work. I realised I needed another tool, debating several times whether or not to slide out and get it, and eventually did so. As I emerged, the jacks gave way and the car settled silently and gracefully, crushing the bricks on which my head had just been resting. Another miracle of survival.

Back in England, I had also met up with my mother's family – several aunts, uncles and cousins, who made me very welcome. It was a shock, especially in London, to see the extent of wartime bomb sites. Things were still fairly austere and food rationing continued until July 1954. Heavy smogs and fogs were also something I could never get used to – and when the sun did appear it was a half-hearted effort.

At the end of 1955, I returned to Melbourne to the Design and Inspection Branch of the Department of Supply as Technical Staff Officer, responsible for the design and inspection of radar and telecommunications equipment for the Australian armed services.

It is strange how the past sometimes catches up with you. One of my duties with Supply was to inspect the Ordinance Factory at Maribyrnong where I had begun my electrical apprenticeship. I was astonished to discover that the foreman was Charlie Lovell, the leading hand whose wrath I had incurred as an apprentice so many years ago. He was equally astonished to see me carrying out the inspection.

Early in 1956, I was chosen to be the Australian Army's representative on the Scientific Response Team for the British Atomic Tests to be held at Maralinga in South Australia. This involved some trips back to the UK for further training until finally the tests got under way. My studies were about to be put to practical use. Life was suddenly very exciting.

CHAPTER 15

MARALINGA

Rod Wells, Maralinga, 1956.

'Wake up, Major Wells. We'll be stopping at Watson siding in ten minutes to let you off.'

I struggled out of a deep sleep, gathered up my kit and followed the guard to a nearby exit. The train slowed, barely stopping. I threw out my gear and stepped into mid-air, to land on the hard, central-Australian earth. The train glided off into the intense blackness. No lights showed from its carriages. The whisper of its engine faded into nothingness. I was eerily alone, almost literally in the middle of Australia with no sign of the promised transport.

I was about to join a group of scientists undertaking the most exciting experiments of modern times. How ironic that as a prisoner of war, whose life was saved by the dropping of the atomic bombs on Japan, I had been selected not only to witness nuclear testing in the Australian desert, but also to provide the telemetry equipment.

While I waited for someone to fetch me, I sat on my kitbag, musing on the previous three or four years of my life with only a canopy of brilliant stars and a chilling wind to keep me company. It was eerie but not frightening – I was more excited about what lay ahead in the next few months. At last, faintly at first, then growing brighter, the lights of a vehicle wove their way through the scrub towards me.

'Major Wells?' asked a cheery voice, 'Welcome aboard for Maralinga, sir.'

Nothing could have been less inviting than my first view of the base camp. In the faint morning light, rows of huts appeared, rising out of the hard, red dirt. Spinifex, a few stunted mulga trees and the endless gibber stones, hardly made an inviting scene, but I was not here for the scenery. Work soon began on setting up the equipment, installing the tower and preparing the test site, about 160 kilometres from the base. Hundreds of huge crates, all serially numbered, had to be unpacked, their contents sorted and assembled – it was a military operation on a large scale.

Dr William Penney, United Kingdom atomic physicist, was

in charge of the project, which was being undertaken by the UK Government and its Atomic Energy Authority. Dr Ernest Titterton, a British scientist working under Sir Mark Oliphant at the Australian National University, Canberra, was the senior scientist representing Australia. I was a member of the Electronic Target and Response Team (ET), which comprised four British members, one Canadian and myself. The other Australian Army officer assigned to the project was Major David Lloyd, a pharmacist, who was a member of the Health Physics Team. Although many other Australian military personnel were also present, they were employed as drivers, guards, orderlies etc, to provide our logistical backup. There was also an 'Indoctrinee' Force, a group of officers, mainly from Britain and Australia. Their task was to observe the tests and then enter ground zero to analyse and report on the impact of the explosion on military equipment. Because I was the first member of the scientific team to arrive, I did most of the preparation work on the test sites. We dug our own earthworks but later, when the indoctrinees arrived, they helped with construction.

The UK Ministry had put an enormous amount of planning into the tests. Every single item had to be transported to Maralinga – accommodation, generators, fuel, vehicles, heavy equipment, a solid metal tower for the device, hundreds of tonnes of cement for its base as well as refrigeration plants, food, water, decontamination huts, protective gear, monitoring equipment and ablution blocks. A whole village to accommodate thousands of personnel had to be constructed and serviced, to say nothing of the vast amount of highly specialised scientific equipment necessary for the success of the operation.

Between June 1956, when some minor tests were carried out, and September, when Operation Buffalo, the final test, was to take place, I returned once or twice to the UK for further training and briefing. Buffalo was scheduled for late September and the last few weeks were spent in refining procedures, re-checking equipment, learning how to fit our protective gear and how to perform post-operational decontamination routines. By mid-September, all the teams were well prepared and we waited impatiently for suitable weather conditions. After one or two false starts, we were advised on 26 September that, provided current weather conditions held, the nuclear device would be exploded the next morning.

It was an early start for all on site. Over the previous few weeks, dozens of observers had arrived from the defence forces, government departments and scientific organisations to witness this historic event. Those of us permitted into the forward area removed all of our clothes in special caravans, before proceeding naked over a wooden walkway to the next zone. Here we put on our protective white gear – underwear, suit, boots, head covering, respirator and gloves. Like an army of white robots, we assembled at the specified area, facing away from the blast site.

The countdown began.

A brilliant light blotted out the sun. Through the insulated suit, I felt waves of heat, then heard and felt shock waves coming from ground zero. After a few minutes, we were given the all clear to about-turn. I shall never forget the sight of that vast mushroom cloud as it grew in the distance, gathering up a dirty mass of earth, plants and debris. The beautiful solid metal tower and its enormous concrete base had vaporised – just disappeared. We were rendered speechless with awe and wonder at this massive and terrifying sight. We had just witnessed the success of one of the greatest moments in scientific history, carried out on Australian soil, and one that was to become its most contentious.

In the immediate aftermath of the explosion, I wondered how many people, whose lives had been saved when the atomic bombs dropped on Japan, had witnessed a replay of those historic events. And how many like me, had gone on to study nuclear physics? Very few, if any, I imagined.

Because of the inherent dangers in atomic testing, security checks, strict procedures and health controls for all those working at the site were in place right throughout the minor tests, in June 1956, until after the major event in September. Everyone had been issued with a pass showing name and photograph, and a photographic or film dosimeter, a kind of badge that measured radiation levels. It was read by a pen-like instrument and had to be worn at all times, even at night when dressed in our pyjamas. The badge did not retain the radiation reading, as it was not a cumulative dosimeter. It was not capable of registering a neutron particle, which has no electrical charge, or recording gamma radiation.

Other larger dosimeters recorded cumulative readings. Prior to the first tests in June, the dosimeters were read once or twice a week; after that they were read every evening. All results were recorded and cumulative results collated before we were cleared to go into the forward area again. Had we reached the cumulative dose limit we would not have been allowed into the contaminated area. No one wanted to reach that limit and, as far as I know, no one in our team did. All contamination checks were carried out under strict scientific controls of standard solution, standard temperature and other fixed conditions. There was a set limit on the number of integrated doses one could receive, which I believe was set at one tenth of the world background standard.

I recollect that patrols took place in the forward areas on a regular basis, both before and after the trials, including areas well outside possible contamination limits. All personnel had to go through roadside blockades to reach the forward areas and, unless accompanied by a recognised group leader, required written authority to enter. A key system also operated to ensure that no one was in the forward areas immediately prior to an explosion.

Health physics were controlled by the UK and it would have been impossible for anyone to accidentally enter the forward area. After an explosion, if I went out to the contaminated area I was transported in a yellow vehicle. Any equipment or bits and pieces brought back from this area went to a 'sterile' area for checking. On returning from the range, we showered and had radiation levels checked until an acceptable level was reached. On one occasion I was made to scrub and re-scrub my finger several times where a tiny split in my glove had let in a small amount of contamination. All ash-like dehydrated washing water and ash from any contaminated clothing burned was transferred to the United Kingdom. Reports that the UK Atomic Energy Commission was dumping waste back at Maralinga were completely false. In fact, the converse was true. Empty containers, sent from the UK, were returned with the radioactive waste. At all times, monitoring and checking was rigorously carried out and I am certain that no one could have eluded the restrictions and conditions in force at the time.

Prior to the main blast, only a very few top personnel had, for security reasons, been aware of the power of the device. I decided to calculate its strength myself using a fairly simple method. At the time, toothpaste and ointment tubes contained lead, which absorbs radioactive particles. I acquired some new, empty tubes, numbered them and placed them at various distances from ground zero, and plotted each one on a grid. After the blast, I collected them and measured the amount of radioactivity present in each. When my results were calculated, I innocently sent them to the UK Atomic Energy Commission, more as a matter of confirmation than for any other reason. All hell broke loose. The results were surprisingly accurate and the authorities were convinced there had been a security breach. When I assured them there had not, and revealed my simple experimental methods, I was invited to the Atomic Weapons Research Establishment (AWRE) at Aldermaston, to complete a course in nucleonics.

I flew in a Royal Air Force Hastings aircraft, piloted by Flight Lieutenant Smith, a dour Yorkshireman who kept his watch on Greenwich Mean Time and had his meals and rest breaks accordingly. In those days we stayed overnight at various

Commonwealth airfields and it was several hours after taking off from Colombo that Smithy noticed something was wrong with one of the engines. I happened to be in the cockpit at the time observing the communications and operating systems and generally enjoying myself.

'Well, I'll be booggured,' Smithy exclaimed. 'Port engine seems to be in trooble. Never mind, we've got another three to get us home.'

I resumed my seat and we cruised along happily for a few more hours when I detected an irregular noise in another of the engines.

'Sorry, folks,' Smithy announced to his passengers. 'We seem to have lost another bloody engine. Have to make arrangements for an emergency landing. But don't worry, we've still got two more left.'

Smithy was the only one who seemed unconcerned. He was cleared to land at an Italian Air Force base at Cagliari in southern Italy and made a perfect touchdown. As we walked across the tarmac to the base buildings, Smithy suddenly froze.

'Christ Almighty! Will you look at that!' An operator was refuelling an aircraft with the aviation fuel hose in one hand and a lighted cigarette in the other. 'I'd rather take my chances on two engines,' Smithy exclaimed. 'I didn't come all this way to be blown up by bloody foreigners.'

The facilities at the base were luxurious. Lots of marble, coffee machines, delectable food and far more amenities than we had in our own messes. We felt quite shabby among the Italian officers in their stylish uniforms but Smithy comforted us. 'No wonder we won the war! All show and no fight here.' We anticipated a week or more of pampering while replacement engines, engineers and a new crew were flown out from the UK and the engines installed. However, the RAF had other ideas and, once the engines and personnel were unloaded, we flew to England on the returning flight.

I eventually reported to the Foreign Office in London in late 1956. Nobody quite knew where to put me until I mentioned that

I had some work to do and indeed had some low-level equipment with me, the radioactivity of which had decayed to the general natural background level and been cleared for atomic research purposes. At the mention of the word 'atomic' they panicked and quickly found a spot for me in the old War Cabinet rooms under the Thames Embankment where I was happily ensconced, in between trips to Aldermaston in Wiltshire. During this time, I returned to Maralinga to conduct some investigations at the old test site, and at the end of 1957 returned to Australia to continue my career with the Department of Supply.

I had met many colleagues in England whose company and friendship I enjoyed on return visits to England, when I met them in other parts of the world or when they were posted to Australia. It was in the late 1950s when, after many years, I caught up with Rob Scott, now Sir Robert Scott, my former Outram Road cellmate. After the war, Rob worked in the Foreign Office as Assistant to the Under-Secretary of State, and at the British Embassy in Washington DC. More recently, he had returned to Singapore as Commissioner-General. I was distressed to learn that on the day of his investiture in August 1955, his only son, Robert, aged 18, had been killed in an accident while on National Service with the Royal Marines.

For the next two years I was posted Senior Inspector (Electronics) in the Army Inspection Service and travelled backwards and forwards between Australia and the UK. In August 1960, I transferred from the Regular Army to the Army Reserve to take up a position as a scientific officer for the Defence Department.

And so I embarked upon another career, even more exciting than anything I had ever done.

CHAPTER 16

MY CAREER TAKES OFF

Victoria Barracks, St Kilda Rd, Melbourne, 1970s, where Rod was based from 1960-77.

My work as a scientific officer in the Department of Defence involved attachments to the UK Ministry of Defence concerning classified research and development work on electronic equipment, especially for secure communications. As a result, I was responsible for selecting land for the construction of overseas diplomatic transmitting and receiving stations in the Northern Territory, a joint venture between the British and Australian Governments. Establishing such a site was not just a matter of building on any piece of land. Special parameters such as signal reception, absence of interference and large spaces on which to erect aerials, had to be taken into consideration. Also, because the area is subject to cyclones, the stations had to be away from the coast.

After several visits to Darwin and many hours spent tramping over the tropical terrain, I found two suitable sites at Howard Springs, 30 kilometres south of Darwin. I filed a report to the secretary of the department in Canberra and waited results. The government raised some objections to the chosen sites but I was adamant that, on all fronts, they were the only suitable locations. As a result, the department secretary arranged a meeting with the then Prime Minister, Robert Menzies. After asking me a few pertinent questions, the PM reached for the phone, made a couple of calls and then said, 'Well there, you've got your land.' If only all of my dealings with government had been as simple my life would have been much easier. Now that land had been secured for the aerials, offices and equipment, I had to let the contracts and was then responsible for construction.

Darwin, being the place it then was, became a battlefield with the contractors who regarded contracts as a mere formality and carried out the work as they saw fit. I had many tussles with them until it was completed to the required standards. The wet season also interfered with progress and I was not prepared for the activities of a couple of wild buffalo, which had become trapped inside the fenced area and whose favourite pastime was to rub against the mast supports, bending them out of shape. The administrator, Roger Dean, and his wife Ann were very helpful and kind to me on my many visits. Over the years I also met the various Officers in Charge at Larrakeyah Army Barracks, situated on a beautiful headland, and also spent some time at nearby HMAS *Coonawarra* base.

The Defence Signals Directorate (now the Australian Signals Directorate, based in Canberra) had been established in 1947, and I worked closely with its personnel in upgrading equipment during the 1960s. Another unit I raised during this time was 126 Signal Squadron from the former 301 Squadron. Its first home was at Albert Park, then in Watsonia Barracks, now named Simpson Barracks. All these undertakings needed the latest equipment and it was very satisfying to put my technical and organisational skills to practical use. In March 1961 I was involved with British colleagues in surveillance of a Soviet couple, which resulted in their arrest as spies.

Apart from the spies, this may sound unexciting to some, but for me it was a fascinating and enriching period. In 1962, I underwent special training in the UK for two years, when I met men and women who had spent their whole careers in special undertakings for their country – diplomats, service personnel, recruits and high-ranking public servants. I spent time in Milton Keynes, at Bletchley Park, the wartime communications and code-breaking establishment, and at Hanslope Park, Her Majesty's Government Communications Centre. On one particular course, I became very close to four or five other trainees, all with special talents. Jeffrey, with his swarthy complexion, was an expert on Arab affairs and when dressed in his robes could have been taken for one. Willie was immersed in Chinese and could read, write and speak the main dialects and get by in lesser ones. The German speaker was David, while John was fluent in French. I was the only technical specialist, as well as the only Australian and, apart from bazaar Malay, was short on language skills. However, we all got on famously and once again I made several good friends.

During one of my courses, I met Royal Signals officer, Major Jackie Hunter. As Chief Signals Officer to the British Prime Minister, Harold MacMillan, Jackie was heavily involved with his duties during and after the Cuban Missile Crisis of October 1962. It is perhaps not surprising that members of the same unit seem to naturally gravitate towards each other and signals personnel seemed to be exceptionally good at seeking out each other and keeping in touch.

In October 1962, Jackie became CO of 39 (City of London) Signal Regiment (Volunteers). In 1954, the regiment was adopted by the Worshipful Company of Skinners, thus reviving an old system of linking City Units of the Auxiliary Forces with Livery Companies. It became known as the Skinners Regiment and they met and trained at premises in Worship Street, East Central London. At Jackie's invitation I had sometimes visited the regiment and, in 1963, was delighted when he asked me to take over temporary command. At its annual dining-in night in the officers' mess that year, the regiment entertained Sir James Harman, Master of the Worshipful Company of Painter-Stainers and Lord Mayor of London. It was a wonderful evening, with its traditions and history reaching back for many centuries.

After the formalities were over, and the Lord Mayor had departed, one of the Royal Signals officers took a pen from his jacket and said, 'Think you're smart, don't you, Aussie?' and proceeded to write his name on the starched dickey front of my dress shirt. Others joined in until it was covered in signatures. Then they wrestled me to the floor, where they succeeded in removing it.

As I walked back to my digs, technically regimentally undressed, the first edition of *The Times* was on the newsstands. Under 'Lord Mayor's Engagements', I read with interest that the Lord Mayor of London had been entertained at dinner the previous evening by Major Wells, RA Signals, and members of 39 Signal Regiment. Some weeks later, when I was back in my office at Victoria Barracks, Melbourne, the duty security officer informed me, with a bit of a smile, that there was a top priority parcel for me from London.

Carefully wrapped was the framed shirt front with all of the signatures and the date, 25 July 1963. Strangely, this was the day which the Nuclear Test Ban Treaty was agreed on by American President John F Kennedy and Soviet Premier Nikita Khrushchev. It was an historic occasion in more ways than one. The framed shirt front still hangs on my office wall.

During the 1960s, I spent a lot of time in South-east Asia, especially Malaya. From the late 1940s until the middle 1960s, the Federation of Malaya, formed in 1948, faced two threats. The first, beginning that year and known as The Emergency, was infiltration by communists and the formation of the Malayan National Liberation Army. By the mid-1960s this threat had largely been contained but remained ongoing. My job was to train Special Branch Police in communications and surveillance techniques. Because of my wartime experiences, I felt very much at home there and developed close friendships with many of the Special Branch officers.

It was a proud day when I was invited to the official ceremony marking the union of Sabah (formerly British North Borneo), Sarawak and Singapore with Malaya to form the nation of Malaysia on 16 September 1963. This created the second threat, when tension over territory along the borders of Sabah and Sarawak with Kalimantan on the island of Borneo led to confrontation with Indonesia from 1963 to 1966. Malaysia had a lot of work on its hands to contain these threats and I was immensely satisfied to help, in some way, the people who had been so loyal to us prisoners during our captivity.

Soon after the formation of Malaysia, it became evident that political and economic differences between Malaya and Singapore could not be resolved. Accordingly, in August 1965, Singapore became a separate sovereign state. So many changes were taking place in this part of the world.

It was on my first visit to the British High Commission in Singapore in 1960 that I renewed my friendship with a Royal Signals officer, Major Peter May, whom I had met during the war. It would have been in 1963, on a subsequent trip to Singapore, that Peter met me at the airport. We headed off in the car, but not in the direction I had expected.

'Where are we going?' I asked him.

'You'll see,' he replied, quietly, as we travelled along familiar roads.

We finally stopped at a demolition site and, as we got out of the car, Peter approached the foreman.

'Here's the man you've been waiting for,' he announced.

Then I realised where we were. It was the site of Outram Road Gaol. I could scarcely believe that this evil place no longer existed except for a low wall of a few bricks, waiting for its final blow. I was handed a mattock.

'There you are,' Peter said. 'You can have the satisfaction of demolishing the last of your old home. Then we'll go and have a gin and tonic.'

I took to it with gusto and was applauded by the workmen for my efforts. Knowing that I was soon to visit the High Commission, Peter had arranged for the last part of the wall to be left standing until I could finish the job. He had to go to the Prime Minister, Lee Kuan Yew, to obtain permission; it was gesture that I truly appreciated. The site is currently open space, and the high embankments at the rear of the gaol are still very much in evidence.

Some time was also spent in Indonesia and the Philippines and I made several visits to colleagues in the US State Department in Washington. In 1964, I was appointed Chief Scientific/ Telecommunications Officer to the Australian Defence Department. This involved the security of our overseas missions in the Middle East, the Philippines, Indonesia, Thailand, Burma and

East Africa. I happened to be in Jakarta in 1965 when The Thirtieth of September Movement assassinated six Indonesian generals in an abortive coup, and spent some exciting times in Saigon and Phnom Penh. On one occasion we were taking off from Phnom Penh airport with Air Cambodia, known to its regular passengers as Air Cam-bodgie, a play on the slang term for something that is inferior. As the aircraft was about to lift off it suddenly bounced to a halt, lockers flew open, armrests were dislodged and passengers tossed about. My seat mate, a Cambodian, patted my arm reassuringly.

'Sir, I am engineer with this company. I will see what is the problem,' he said importantly.

A few minutes later he returned from the cockpit and settled comfortably into his seat.

'What seems to be the matter?' I asked.

He smiled confidently, 'Ah sir, we do not know, but we try again.'

It was one of many similar incidents I encountered in my constant travelling. Another that I particularly remember happened when I was helping to conduct communication trials with the RAF over the south-east coast of England. All air traffic, both military and civilian, had been banned from the area. We had completed the trials and I was in the tail of an aircraft, heading back to base, when I idly put on the headphones. To my horror I picked up a message from a plane requesting permission to land. I hastily notified our navigator who quickly confirmed that we were on a collision course with an unknown flight. Impact was narrowly avoided and we both landed safely. The aircraft involved was carrying wives and children of British servicemen stationed in post-war Germany who were returning home on leave.

It would have been sometime in the mid-1960s that I made my first trip to Japan. It was at first strange to be surrounded by Japanese faces and I did feel uncomfortable. I got through the work satisfactorily and was departing Tokyo airport when an airline official shouted and thrust at me a form that I had just completed

– the sort that requires lots of details to be recorded in a minute space. I instantly reacted with a string of Japanese words, of which I had no idea of the meaning and thought I had forgotten. He was so stunned that he let me through without further ado. I was on a diplomatic passport and should not have reacted so strongly but it was an involuntary reaction, even 20 years after my last contact with a Japanese.

In the mid-1960s I returned to Rangoon, Burma. I was fascinated to dine once again at The Strand Hotel, which I had visited while stationed in Malaya in 1941. The 24 ceiling fans still lazed overhead and the Burmese orchestra played their Viennese waltzes. I was the only diner. It was sad to see this once prosperous country being fought over by opposing communist forces. However, their security service surveillance was so clumsy that I turned around and waved to my shadow. Other places I visited that allowed me to experience different ways of life and cultures were Dar es Salaam, capital of Tanganyika (Tanzania), and Khartoum, the Sudanese capital. From Amman, the Jordanian capital, I was taken by American colleagues to visit the ancient city of Petra.

It was in mid-winter in the early 1960s, off the south-coast of England, that I took part in telemetry tests for the first British atomic powered submarine, HMS *Dreadnought*. It was my first experience of working in a submarine and I was fascinated by its equipment, arrangements for the crew, engineering and especially by the communications systems.

'Now, no funny business,' I requested as I entered the conning tower, where I proceeded to work on the instruments. Suddenly I was thrust upward. As the vessel rose to the surface, I was ejected into the freezing waters of the Atlantic Ocean with only my life jacket between me and certain death. However, the Royal Navy had things in hand. I was soon hauled back on board and given a tot of rum, whose restorative powers made it obvious why crews on sailing ships treasured their rum rations above all else.

The 1960s was a most eventful decade. As a member of the Naval and Military Club, Melbourne, I enjoyed reciprocal membership rights at the Naval and Military Club, Piccadilly, a most convenient place to meet friends and colleagues or stay during my many visits to England. One day, in the lounge, I saw Lieutenant General Percival, seated by himself and looking, I thought, rather sad and lonely. I introduced myself, gave him a brief history of my experiences of the war in Malaya and we had a long and interesting talk about the campaign. I expressed my views on several controversial episodes that had taken place at the time. He talked candidly of the unenviable task he had been given and the situation in which he found himself – to win the unwinnable. He is a figure who, I think, history has treated unjustly.

In August 1964, my father died from prostate cancer. I was based at Victoria Barracks in Melbourne at the time, which allowed me to arrange the funeral, attended by a huge crowd. A popular figure, Dad had been active in many local organisations and was a wonderful friend and mentor to me. Without his example and guidance, I would never have survived my wartime experiences or achieved so much in my own life.

Although my professional career had taken off, Linda and I were experiencing difficulties in our marriage. Once again, I felt a failure, but things had become intolerable between us and we could no longer pretend that the situation would improve. In the late 1960s, we separated by mutual consent, and with mutual relief.

CHAPTER 17

THE 1970S

Rod Wells' and Pamela Bennett's wedding, Scots' Church, Collins Street, Melbourne, 1974.

International travel, to check the security of our overseas high commissions and embassies, became more frequent in the late 1960s. I made dozens of trips to Singapore and Malaysia, mainly to the latter, where I was still training their Special Branch officers in surveillance and communication techniques. At the time, I was based in Melbourne at Victoria Barracks in St Kilda Road and living in Marne Street, South Yarra. Around the corner from Marne Street, in Toorak Road, was the headquarters of the English-Speaking Union, a club formed in 1919 to foster cultural and educational ties between peoples from English speaking countries. As a member, I found it very handy to sometimes have dinner there and to enjoy a range of social activities with people whose backgrounds were different from those of my scientific and public service colleagues.

It was at a New Member's night, sometime in 1972, that I was introduced to pharmacist Pamela Bennett, and my interest was immediately captured. I could talk to her about my life and careers and be understood reasonably well. When I asked for her phone number, she replied that I could look it up in the book. When I contacted her the next night with an invitation to dinner, she said she was too busy for a couple of weeks. I decided I could wait and, when we eventually had dinner together, I knew that at last here was a woman about whom I felt absolutely sure. Our backgrounds were similar: we had both had a country upbringing, Pam in Echuca, and a science-based tertiary education; our fathers came from modest backgrounds but had made good despite limited formal education and both had given their families a loving and stable upbringing and been active in local affairs. The fact that I was twice divorced and almost 21 years older than Pam did not bother her.

Having decided to marry we bought a home in Kew, where I lived while undertaking renovations. I put in lots of innovations and, on the morning of our wedding, 29 June 1974, I was up in the ceiling putting finishing touches to the alarm system. My best man, Bill Dwyer, just managed to get me cleaned up and to the church on time.

We chose Malaysia for our honeymoon. We arrived at Kuala Lumpur airport to the noisy, colourful, confusion of busloads of Malaysians heading off on pilgrimage to Mecca. Each coach of pilgrims seemed to have two or three more coaches full of well-wishers. It was a spectacular introduction to Asia for Pam.

As soon as the aircraft doors had opened, I was hit by the overpowering stench of ripe durian. Pam, with her very poor sense of smell, asked, 'What smell?' Her ability to eat the fruit without being put off by its aroma soon made her popular with my wonderful Malaysian friends. Sadly, there was one friend she was unable to meet – Tan Sri Abdul Rahman bin Hashim, Inspector General of Police – with whom I had worked closely during my time with the Special Branch. He had been assassinated in Kuala Lumpur on 7 June, just a few days before, by communist terrorists. Rahman was the third most highly-ranked police officer killed that year. Dato Sri Yuen Yuet Leng was another Special Branch police officer with whom I had become very friendly. He had narrowly survived several assassination attempts and was relentless in his aim of ridding his country of communist insurgents. As a result, the Malaysian Police Force was on high alert and an armour-plated car with armed police escorts was provided for our travels throughout Malaysia.

It did not take me long to realise how happy I was in my marriage. We fitted in well with each other's friends and families, had a busy working and social life, and enjoyed getting our new home in order. To top it all off, some friends in Tatura gave us a border collie/kelpie-cross pup which we promptly named Buster. He became a wonderful companion, despite his incurable habit of digging holes all over the lawns.

In November, I decided to carry out an inspection of the radio stations at Howard Springs. Pam came with me. On arrival at the stations, which were also cyclone evacuation centres for Darwin-based personnel, I found things had become rather slack, as people living in the top end had become a bit blasé about the wet season and severe weather warnings. I discovered that the fuel tanks were almost empty and the fridges and freezers for emergency provisions had found their way to the homes of staff in Darwin. I reminded the station manager that the cyclone season was already on us and ordered that the fuel tanks be filled, all equipment to be returned to the bases and emergency food supplies purchased. I also reinforced instructions that, if there should be a cyclone red alert, all staff in Darwin were to immediately evacuate south to the radio stations in Howard Springs.

On 11 November we attended the Armistice Day Ceremony at the Adelaide River War Cemetery where I meet up with Barry Tiernan, an Australian Federal Police officer I had come to know during my many visits to the Northern Territory. Barry, a member of the pipe band and dressed in full Scottish regalia, piped, drummed and sweated away in the tropical heat and humidity for the ceremony. His main claim to fame was that he was involved in the sensational rescue of Mrs Petrov at Darwin Airport, when Soviet agents were attempting to take her out of the country in April 1954.

Back in Melbourne, as Christmas approached, my deputy, Jim, offered to be on call over the Christmas break.

'You've always been on call in the past. Just go and enjoy your first Christmas with Pam and her family. We'll be fine, nothing ever happens over Christmas.'

On Christmas Eve we drove to Tatura to collect my mother, then on to Echuca. Christmas Day was the usual festivities with family and friends and it was not until late in the afternoon that Pam's father turned on the TV news.

'I see there's been a bit of a cyclone in Darwin,' he said.

It was Cyclone Tracy, and it had destroyed Darwin, killing more than 70 people. I was immediately on the alert and concerned about the radio stations. When I finally managed to get in touch with Jim at Victoria Barracks, he assured me that the stations had sustained only minor damage and were still up and running; in fact, they were the one reliable source of communication from the devastated area. Most of the staff had lost their homes, but thankfully had headed out of Darwin as soon as the cyclone warnings were issued.

In January, I inspected the stations and found that things were going smoothly and the fuel tanks held out for several months afterwards. Darwin, however, was unrecognisable. It was eerie not to be able to distinguish any landmarks; all was flattened, strewn with debris, and stripped of all vegetation. It was unbelievably quiet with no birds or animals to be seen and most of the residents evacuated south.

In March 1975, I had to undergo surgery to remove my gall bladder and decided it would be a good time to give up smoking, which I had taken up on joining the army. Of course, I had ceased during my imprisonment but, after the war, had resumed the habit and, due to all the stresses in my life, had become a heavy smoker. So, the night before my hospital admission I threw out the cigarettes and have never smoked since.

A few months later I undertook an official tour of the UK and USA. Pam was able to come with me. We began by travelling to Darwin, where I sorted out a few problems, before continuing on to the UK, via the Far East and Germany.

We spent a weekend at Peebles in Scotland where Rob Scott, now Lord Lieutenant of Peebleshire, and his wife Rosamond lived. Our paths had crossed briefly in 1965 when Rob, as Permanent Secretary of the Ministry of Defence, presented the Dyason memorial lectures in Australia. As always, it was fascinating to talk with him. Because of my current work in South-east Asia I was particularly interested to hear of his views on the end of the war in Vietnam. Would the communist takeover of South Vietnam extend further south through Thailand to Malaysia? My concern was that Malaysia might once again have to overcome the threat of terrorism as it had done during the Malayan Emergency (1948-1960) and which was still happening at a lower level. Our Australian Embassies and High Commissions in the region would be under more intensive foreign intelligence scrutiny. Communications' security, for which I was responsible, would need to be upgraded and diplomatic staff briefed on the need for extra vigilance. With Australia increasingly recognising its position as being part of South-east Asia, our strategic communications' bases, especially in the north, would also be under raised levels of intelligence attack. Political stability in several countries could also come under threat from communist influence.

During the Harvest Thanksgiving Service at the tiny Peebles Kirk, I thought very few, if any of the congregation, would have known the details of the intelligence activities or the imprisonment of this man who sat so modestly among them. I realised, sadly, that this would probably be the last time Rob and I would meet.

We arrived in London in early autumn, staying at the Naval and Military Club in Piccadilly, opposite Green Park. It was only because of a last-minute change of plans, that we missed being blown up by a provisional IRA bomb at Green Park Underground Station on the night of October 9.

In Putney, we had a reunion of the six members of the 1962 special training group and introduced our wives. Each member had gone on to a career in diplomatic and intelligence spheres. During the 1950s and 1960s, David Cornwell had worked for both the Security Service and the Secret Intelligence Service but was better known by his pen name John le Carré, a British author of espionage novels.

From London, we flew to the USA, where I had meetings with my US counterparts in Washington. At the time, the Labor Whitlam Government was in crisis at home and I was closely questioned as to what would happen should the Prime Minister be dismissed. Though fully conversant with their own political system, the Americans were rather vague about those of other countries, and their constitutional lawyers were unable to predict an outcome. Drawing on my early school lessons with the nuns, and a subject that used to be called 'civics', I outlined what I thought it would be. The Americans were in disbelief when I told them that the Governor General had the constitutional power to dismiss the Prime Minister and appoint the opposition leader as interim PM until elections could be called, and they confidently made a bet with me that such a thing would never happen.

After a week in Washington, we arrived home on 11 November, the day on which Prime Minister Gough Whitlam was dismissed from office by the Governor General, Sir John Kerr. A week later, two bottles of bourbon were delivered to our home for 'Constitutional Lawyer Wells' from the US Consulate in Melbourne: the nuns' civics course was spot on.

September and October 1976 saw us in the Philippines. Hospitality was lavish and flamboyant. We spent a couple of days at the seaside residence of President Marcos, though, I hasten to add, not when he was there. Pam was fortunate to attend a children's clinic run by the doctor wife of one of our Australian diplomats and found that, behind the façade of bright lights and glitter, conditions for the ordinary people were not very good. Malnourished children and mothers desperate for basic health support for their families were a sad sight.

In March 1977, we were invited to the re-consecration of Christchurch Cathedral, Darwin, destroyed in the cyclone. All that remained of the old building was the porch, now incorporated into the new building. The amount of reconstruction that had taken place in the three years since the cyclone hit was amazing, transforming the city into a modern, prosperous community. A few days after we arrived home, my mother died from complications during an operation. She had been a good wife and mother and I loved and admired her very much.

Later that year, we travelled again to the Far East. Visiting a restaurant in Tokyo one night, I was jolted back to my POW days when I encountered an elderly Japanese man, who I swear was one of the guards at Kuching. A vivid image flashed into my mind after all those years, when I thought such memories had been forgotten. It was a terrifying moment. I told myself that he could not harm me now and, with Pam's help, got through the evening.

On the same trip, at a consular reception in Kobe, some young Japanese people asked where I had learned my (very rudimentary) Japanese. I told them I had learned it from a book – they had not been responsible for the treatment I had undergone and I saw no need to enlighten them. Another guest, a Japanese businessman, showed me the itinerary for his forthcoming trade visit to Australia. Among pages of Japanese script, he pointed out the letters SPC (Shepparton Preserving Company). He would be visiting the factory in Shepparton, which had sent so many cases of fruit to our troops in Malaya, only to have them shipped to Japan as spoils of war. The world had indeed moved on.

By this time I was becoming restless in my career, although at last my home life was content and settled. Instead of fieldwork, which I loved, I was becoming increasingly bound to my desk. I had always enjoyed the practical aspect of my job, planning and creating something and seeing a tangible result. Besides, it looked as if the office would be moving to Canberra. As we were not keen to relocate, on 1 January 1978, my 58th birthday, I retired from the Department of Foreign Affairs, and in 1979 fully retired from the Army Reserve with the rank of Lieutenant Colonel, after a career of almost 40 years in the army and public service

Instead of a pension, I invested a lump sum, a decision that many years later proved to be a financial disaster. We also set up a business, R & P Wells Consultants, which was launched in March and was an immediate success. I had many contacts in the security and communications' industries who were happy to engage my skills or recommend me to others. I installed many domestic and business security systems, which was very satisfying, especially when several burglars were apprehended on the job. My speciality was checking boardrooms and offices for listening devices and, despite the fact that I did not advertise, I soon had as much work as I could handle.

At the same time, I became a consultant for the UK electronics' company Racal, at their Melbourne headquarters. I had met the original founders, Ray Brown and Cal Cunningham (hence the company name), who set up the business in the UK in 1950. In the 1980s they developed their Airstream Helmet for use in mining and heavy industry, which quickly became popular and kept me busy with new clients. One of the more unusual jobs I undertook was as security adviser to the new Jika Jika maximum security section being incorporated into Pentridge Prison – surely the first time a former inmate had been asked for advice on designing a prison security system but, after all, who else better qualified for the job?

It was on a winter morning, in 1979, that we woke to the sounds of heavy rain, early morning traffic and the prospect a cold day ahead. I remarked to Pam, 'I'd love to get out of all this noise and cold weather.' To my absolute amazement she immediately said, 'Yes, I could easily live back in the country.'

We decided there and then that northern Victoria would be ideal, and so began the search for a suitable property. After several false starts, my lifelong friend Jim Stewart, who had succeeded to his father Galloway's legal practice in Tatura, contacted me one day with the news that he had a property that might interest us. It was situated just eight kilometres out of Rushworth, on the northern shore of Waranga Basin, where Laurie and I had conducted the nitroglycerine experiment. It covered 48 hectares of dry, unproductive land with several rocky outcrops, clay soil and not much else. Fencing was poor, the land had been excavated for rocks and was badly eroded and only a few large old grey box trees remained. But it was perfect for what I planned. I was going to build a solar, self-sufficient home. We would have our own power plant, water supply and firewood. We would be free from the increasing power failures that Victoria was experiencing at the time. Above all, I would be able to put my talents to practical use and harness the sun, wind and rain, all available for free. I had found my retirement project.

In September 1979, we purchased what was known locally as 'Stony Rises', a very apt description of the property. We continued to live in Melbourne while we set about re-fencing, tree planting and deciding where to site the house and workshop. Planning for all the equipment and facilities took a few years but we were not in a hurry.

For the next three or four years I continued with my consulting work. Pam practised as a relieving pharmacist and we visited the Rushworth property, now named 'Kowandi', as often as we could.

In October 1980, when my friend Yuen from the Police Special Branch, now living in Ipoh, Malaysia, invited us to spend some time with him, it was the catalyst for a trip to Borneo, the first since my wartime experiences.

I have frequently been asked about my reactions and thoughts regarding the Japanese.

During my internment, I decided to make the most of my subsequent life, with related studies, careers, overseas postings and travel keeping me busy throughout the immediate post-war years. I saw a Japanese, for the first time since my release from Changi, during the 1956 Olympic Games in Melbourne when I was walking down Collins Street with a colleague. I absolutely froze with shock. Had I been in another country I doubt that my reaction would have been so extreme, but to see Japanese on my home territory was quite horrifying.

'What's the matter?' my colleague asked. It was some minutes before I could get myself together to explain.

'It's just that I've seen a Jap.'

'Well it's all over now. They can't do you any harm here.'

We moved on. The shock stayed with me for a few days afterwards but I decided, yet again, that I would not let negative events of the past define my future. It was my life and I would be fully in control of it. However, I still left Australia with mixed feelings about visiting Borneo, yet was keen to see what changes had occurred there and whether or not any of the local people, who had helped us, were still living.

In Ipoh we attended a charity dinner, where the Sultan of Perak and his beautiful young bride – wife number four – were also guests. We were amused to see that she dined under the watchful eye of the Sultan's number one official wife, who scrutinised her from the royal portrait hanging above the entrance doors. When Pam asked if the new wife had any choice in the marriage, our Malay friends were astonished; no one ever refused the Sultan. Even if the lady concerned refused, her family would ignore her views – this was an honour too important to decline.

Our time at Ipoh was eventful. Yuen was now Chief Police Officer of the state of Perak. A week before our arrival, a bomb had been found in a culvert outside his home and while we were there a raid took place at a police station in Malacca, so the compound was heavily guarded and well-lit at night. Then, all too soon our visit was over, and we were off to Borneo, to retrace my footsteps in what had been the most traumatic period of my life.

CHAPTER 18

RETURN TO BORNEO

Former fruit stall, Sandakan, 1980.

The small Fokker Friendship plane wobbled in the midday heat above the tarmac of Sandakan Airport. Then, after one or two trial bounces, we finally touched down with a thump. How ironic, I thought, that we landed on a runway where our POWs had sweated, laboured and suffered, razing two hills to make the original aerodrome. I leaned forward in my seat trying to recognise landmarks as the plane taxied to a halt, but the area had changed enormously since 1943. Nervous, excited and quite disorientated, I alighted from the aircraft to set foot, for the first time in 37 years, in Sabah – 'The Land Below the Wind'.

A police inspector greeted us and introduced Peter Ng, whose wife Winnie was a cousin of the Funk brothers. We found that wherever we went in Sabah, the Funk family was still very active in business and community affairs and highly respected. On the drive into town, I tried to recapture the scene in 1942 – the road had been widened; new buildings rose among the old ones, but it somehow looked familiar.

Peter directed the driver to the padang. On its edge, he pointed out a building, which he said had replaced the old Kempeitai headquarters, where we had been interrogated and tortured. I tried hard to remember the house, but could not recollect it being near the padang. What I did recall, however, were the twisting steps leading up a hillside and through a gateway to the colonial timber Mission School of a nearby stone church, where the officers were housed on our first night off the prison ship.

The view from a lookout above the town helped me gain my bearings. Hills bordered three sides of the harbour, flattening to a broad sweep of mangroves to the south. The town itself clung to a narrow strip of land on the northern shore while, to the east, the South China Sea was glazed and lifeless, throwing into relief dozens of islands, some of them no larger than a room. The largest of these was Berhala, with its towering red cliffs, guarding the harbour entrance.

My main objective was to find the site of the Japanese POW Camp, 13 kilometres beyond the town. We retraced our route along the airport road. I was still somewhat disorientated but then, about eight kilometres out of town, I suddenly saw it: the former fruit stall in a jungle clearing and in an instant all the memories rushed back – the shop keeper offering fruit, a prisoner running to buy a bunch of bananas, a poorly aimed shot fired by the Japanese guard, the column of prisoners marching grimly onward. We stopped to take a photograph of the hut, or rather its descendant now roofed in corrugated iron, before continuing for another four or five kilometres. Just beyond the airport turnoff, Peter indicated a large rubber plantation covering the side of a hill. He said that the camp site was on the far side.

I was not so sure. It was too close to the airport. Although the camp was on the northern side of a slope, I could not recall such a large hill being near the camp. The track to the camp had left the main road at the eight mile stone and certainly we were at a place known as 'Eight Mile', but it did not look familiar. Since it was late in the afternoon, we decided to return the next day, to try and confirm the position of the camp. The following morning, Peter Ng phoned from the foyer of the hotel in great excitement.

'I have someone who knows you,' he said.

'Who is it?' I asked. I could recall many local people who had helped us but most of them were no longer alive, or living elsewhere.

'I won't tell you who it is; see if you recognise him. Last night I thought very deeply about who might have been here during the war. I was worried that I could not positively identify the Kempeitai headquarters or the camp site. Then I thought of this person and he remembers you quite clearly. Come down and meet him.'

I was quite puzzled as to who it could be. Standing with Peter was a Chinese gentleman about my own age. It took me barely a second to recognise him.

'Chin!' I cried, seizing him by the hand.

Chin and Rod Wells, Sandakan, 1980.

'You remember me?' he asked.
'Of course, I do. And do you remember me?'
'Almost. But what happened to your red moustache?'
'I shaved it off years ago.'

It was wonderful to see Chin again. As a young man, he had smuggled secret messages to the camp and helped to hide a B Force prisoner who had managed to escape and reach Berhala Island, where he had joined the E Force escapees. Chin knew the exact location of both the Kempeitai headquarters and the camp. We set off in great excitement. Peter Ng was delighted that he had finally succeeded in finding someone who knew of the places I wanted to see. His persistence and kindness were typical of the many friends who helped us during our tour.

Chin directed us beyond the large hill we saw yesterday. The road had been re-routed slightly since the war, and the new mile markers did not correspond with the old ones. At the Sibuga Forest area we turned off the main road, following the track for about 400 metres to a shallow valley dotted with rubber and cinnamon trees, the site of the Government Experimental Farm. Beyond it was the camp.

It took us some time to establish the various areas of the Australian compound. The main landmark, the huge tree that stood at the main entrance gate, was no longer there. A housing estate encroached on part of the experimental farm but the camp area was untouched. We roughly established the perimeter, the huts, the vegetable gardens and the track leading across to the airstrip. The gullies and terrain were the same and helped link up my past memories of the camp. Near the cinnamon trees, still scattered around, I recognised the spot at the lower entrance to the camp, on the track leading to the airfield, where Hoshijima arrested me on that terrible evening. We spent some time taking photos, much to the interest of some residents of the housing estate: to them, it was just jungle; ghosts of people and events past had no part in their lives.

Returning to the main road we drove further west for a kilometre or two. I easily recognised the rice paddies and the areas where we were sent to collect wood. A small bridge over a culvert brought back another vivid memory – this was where I pushed a Japanese guard off a lorry one evening when returning to the camp.

I became very apprehensive about the next place I wished to see, the Kempeitai headquarters. On returning to Sandakan township, Chin directed us to the site, off Leila Road. I was greatly relieved that the place that had caused us so much pain and torment no longer existed. It was now the car park for a block of flats and shopping centre. Opposite was a large Toyota dealership and the irony was not lost on me. A short distance away were two old-style houses identical to the Kempeitai headquarters building, built of wood and raised well off the ground with large verandas all around, similar to our Queenslanders. Sandakan is not large and my wartime memories of it were not very clear – as prisoners we spent little time in the town itself – but, in just two days, I was surprised how familiar it became.

Altogether, the day had been a great success and the following day, when we farewelled Chin and his wife at the airport, he produced a letter, which I had written to him in 1946! The next two days were spent at Kota Kinabalu from where we were driven to Ranau and Mount Kinabalu. Although I had heard much about the death marches, it was disturbing to see the places where so many of my friends and colleagues had died. I thought of the punishments inflicted on them while on the point of death and remembered them with great sadness and pride. After all these years I was still acutely aware that, had I not been arrested by the Kempeitai, I would have shared their fate.

An early morning flight of 30 minutes, two days later, took us south to Labuan Island and the Commonwealth War Graves Cemetery. I was apprehensive about visiting the place where Lionel's remains, recovered from Kuching, were reburied, along with so many of our prisoners of war. Police Sergeant John Chin (there are many Chins in Borneo) met us and, while we waited for our luggage, introduced us to an Indian friend, Anup Singh, who was passing through the airport. After a few minutes of polite conversation, Anup asked, 'Are you here for business or pleasure?'

'It's a sentimental journey,' I replied. 'I was a prisoner at Sandakan during the war and I haven't been back since. I particularly wished to visit the grave of a very dear colleague and friend who is buried here.'

'Were you at Kuching?' he asked in astonishment.

'Yes. I was arrested at Sandakan and shipped down to Kuching for trial by the Kempeitai.'

Anup Singh, Labuan, 1980.

'Then you may have known my father.'

'Not Ojagar Singh?'

'Yes. We never saw him again after he was taken from Sandakan by the Kempeitai and I have never met anyone who was with him at Kuching.'

We were both quite overcome by this extraordinary chance meeting. Anup was a child of eight years when his father was arrested and the family had never heard any details of his trial. I was able to give Anup some information of Ojagar's imprisonment and trial but I spared him the shocking details of his torture, his broken bones and his shaved head, a great indignity for a Sikh. More importantly, I assured him that his father had died with courage and dignity. We invited Anup to accompany us to the cemetery; he was unable to do so but we arranged to meet at the golf club for lunch.

The Labuan War Cemetery is a short drive from town. The caretaker Mr Lim, and his wife, spent the morning showing us the graves and memorial columns. Like all war cemeteries, Labuan evoked feelings of sadness, pride and peace. We placed some flowers on the Cross of Sacrifice and then found Lionel's grave. Despite the passage of time, I was overwhelmed by a feeling of closeness to Lionel and all my comrades, who are buried or commemorated there. Mrs Lim informed us that on two of her royal tours the Queen had visited the graves of Lionel and two VC winners. We left more flowers on Lionel's headstone and continued to wander through the hundreds of graves and memorials. It was sobering to read the ages on the plaques – so many men lost, most of them just out of boyhood. Of the almost 4000 graves here, more than 2000 are inscribed as 'Known unto God'. Many were signallers or artillerymen, known to me and who perished at Sandakan and in

Captain Lionel Matthews' grave, Labuan, 1980.

dozens of unknown places in the Borneo jungle. On the drive to the golf club to meet Anup, we were each silent with our thoughts.

Over lunch, Anup again questioned me closely about his father and our treatment by the Kempeitai. We were both very emotional - me as I recalled Ojagar Singh, and his son on meeting someone who was with him during his incarceration. I could only reassure Anup that his father did his utmost to help us when the underground was up and running and was fearless during his imprisonment. Anup told us that, after moving to the outskirts of town after his father was arrested, the family travelled on foot and along jungle rivers to Lahad Datu, south of Sandakan, where they spent the rest of the war in a hut on land belonging to Ojagar's brother. His mother supported her family by gathering and selling coconuts.

That afternoon we flew to Kuching, more than 650 kilometres to the south. The flight to Sarawak's capital took us over fascinating jungle scenery. Wide rivers looped from the mountains through the rainforests and spilt their silt in huge red fan shapes into the sea. Kuching is a peaceful and pleasant city set on the banks of the Sarawak River. Rivers largely take the place of roads in this difficult terrain and boats are the main form of transport. On my previous 'visit' to Kuching, I saw only the docks, the two gaols and the convent school room where our trial took place, so I was pleased to at last see what lay beyond those confined areas.

Miss Wong, a very charming Special Branch police inspector, was our guide and had arranged for us to meet the governor of Kuching Central Prison, formerly the Kuching Civil Gaol. Now situated in the heart of the city, it was rather small and not as forbidding as other such establishments but, as we entered the yard through the main gate, I felt that it was only a short time since I had been here. It had altered very little. Several new cell blocks and workshops had been added and the prisoners were at work. The old prison block and the Governor's office still stood squarely in the middle of the yard. We entered by the narrow outside stairs into the office, a privilege not extended to me as a prisoner. I became very nervous and unsettled, steeling myself to go through the door. After some chat with the Governor over morning tea Pam asked if we would be able to see where I was imprisoned, to which he readily agreed. I was both interested and reluctant; interested to see my old home but reluctant to face what memories it might trigger. However, since we had come so far and were unlikely to ever return, I accepted the invitation.

At the time of my imprisonment there was one large area set aside for the Kempeitai and divided into smaller cages, with a passage running around the perimeter of the room. Each cage was divided into two and six prisoners were held in each partition. Two inmates now occupied a space measuring about 3 metres x 4.5 metres though they were out on working duties and the cages were empty. As was the case during my imprisonment, light and air came through several unglazed openings in the outer wall. 'My' cage was number four. Although the pens were now larger it was uncanny to see that things had changed so little – silver-frosted wire mesh, raised wooden sleeping platforms, locks on the doors and latrine buckets in the corners – the same as when I last saw them on 3 March 1944. The only things missing were the lice and bedbugs that caused so many sleepless nights. It felt totally surreal. I am here. I am not here. So much had changed yet was exactly as I remembered it. I am a free man but was back in the cage. It was now a quiet place but I was hearing the cries of my colleagues. It was eerie and disturbing but I was fascinated that it had scarcely changed in 36 years. I allowed these sensations to come and go until eventually we moved on – out into the tropical heat and humidity, away from the place where I spent many days of my imprisonment. I was relieved to be outside and thankful that I was able to overcome my fears.

Just over a kilometre away stood St Joseph's Cathedral. We had walked there chained together for our sentencing after our trial at the adjoining St Teresa's Convent School. I could recall very little about the cathedral itself. There were two things that I now wanted to do: find the room in the school where the trial took place and to find the grave in the cemetery where the executed Borneo civilians were buried.

Miss Wong, who had been a pupil at the convent, was an excellent guide. While making enquiries at the cathedral office we met an Australian priest, Monsignor Eugene Harley, who had served as a padre in the Australian Army in the 1960s during the Indonesian Confrontation. He was making a return visit to the area and asked if he could accompany us on the search. I was comforted by his presence and eventually we found the 'Heroes' Grave' in a back corner of the cemetery. It was sad to see it overgrown and neglected, the names on the slab almost indecipherable. The Monsignor offered a prayer at the graveside. It was a very sad and emotional moment for me.

At the convent, I immediately recognised the storeroom where we were kept for a short time on the day of our trial. I had hoped to see the science room that had been used as the courtroom but, unfortunately, the school was closed for Saint Teresa's Feast Day and we could not enter. I gazed through the windows long enough to take it all in and confirm that the present-day art room was indeed the courtroom. Apart from the absence of taps, equipment and Bunsen burners, it looked much the same as I remembered. Between the store and the art room was the walkway where Lionel and I said our final farewell before he was led away for execution. It was a humbling experience to stand on that spot again.

My trip from Kuching to Singapore was much more comfortable this time and the fresh memories of Sandakan, though tinged with sadness, were very happy. The arranged meetings with descendants of the Funk family, Peter Ng and Chin and their families at Sandakan, Anup Singh at Labuan, and Monsignor Harley at Kuching had all happened at just the right time and at places where I was at my most vulnerable. But, most of all, I had at last put some unhappy memories to rest and paid my respects to the many friends who had so valiantly and selflessly contributed to my survival.

St Teresa's School, Kuching, 1980.

By 1980, the room in St Teresa's School, Kuching, used as a Kempeitai courtroom for Rod's trial in 1944, had been converted to an art room. (Photo unknown source.)

CHAPTER 19
COUNTRY LIVING AND BEYOND

Kowandi, Rushworth, 1986.

Early in 1981, I was invited to become communications and security consultant for the Commonwealth Heads of Government Meeting, held in Melbourne later that year. The Queen would be attending, along with a huge contingent of prime ministers, diplomats and staff from all of the Commonwealth countries. Planning meetings were held throughout the year with State and Federal police and we were all relieved when the event went off safely during the first week of October.

Shortly afterwards, Pam and I attended a POW reunion in Sydney where I and several others were interviewed on ABC radio by journalist Caroline Jones. When the interview was over, one of the technicians introduced himself and said he had met me when working at the Australian High Commission in Rangoon in the 1960s. Johnnie, a Burmese, was now a proud Australian citizen.

In June of that year, another ABC journalist, Tim Bowden, stayed with us in Melbourne to document my experiences. The eight tapes recording my time as a soldier and POW were then transcribed, by a very diligent ABC typist, into 200 pages of text for research and study purposes.

In preparation for our move to the Waranga Basin property I began preliminary planning. We had decided to excavate one side of a hill into a flat area large enough to build a home and workshop, which would give maximum orientation to the north for the solar panels and hot water systems. The workshop needed to accommodate a lifetime's collection of tools, storage for a large array of batteries, a work pit for car maintenance and a diesel engine to back up the power system. Had it been feasible, I would have built an atomic power station! As it wasn't, I had to make do with sun and wind. I believe that clean, efficient and cost-effective power, given Australia's abundant source of uranium rich minerals, is the long-term solution to our energy problems.

The workshop started out reasonably small but, each time I thought of something else that was needed, I added three or four metres to the plan and finished up with a huge space. However, this also gave us a big roof area for rainwater collection and where eventually 22 solar panels were mounted. With the existing dam enlarged and several storage tanks installed, the basics were in place by the end of 1982.

In March 1983, we sold our home in Melbourne, packed up our belongings and set off behind the moving van, Buster's kennel tied to the tailboard. With our goods and chattels stored in the workshop, we began the building project. Unfortunately, we had a robbery. Among several items stolen from the workshop was my officer's sword (a replacement of the original, surrendered to the Japanese) which I intended to donate, with other memorabilia, to the Signals Museum. I was very upset that this was not to be.

With a great deal of planning, help from like-minded friends and a competent builder, the house soon began to take shape. I sourced a lot of equipment needed through industry contacts, and an old mate from Canberra, Ted Howell, was a tremendous help with making up printed circuit boards and control equipment for the electronics involved.

While construction took place, we lived about a kilometre away in a house owned by Jim Stewart. Being so close to the building site was a huge advantage for what became a very complicated project. Of course, I could have designed a conventional home and paid a huge amount of money to have the usual utilities connected, but that would have been too easy. Besides, I wanted to be free from power failures and have full control over my own environment. The only outside facility coming in was the telephone. I was working at the site one day when a power company representative called. We discussed a few things then he asked, 'When do you want the power connected?'

'I don't,' I replied and elaborated on my plans for our own power supply.

'Well,' he said, 'I bet that in twelve months' time, you'll be asking me to connect the power for you.'

'No, I won't. I'll be asking you if I can put some of my excess power into your grid.'

The building proceeded pretty much to plan and, two days before Christmas, we moved into 'Kowandi'. Despite the upheaval, Pam managed to put up the Christmas decorations and we ate meat pies and plum pudding for Christmas dinner. A few days later, we had an unexpected deluge with 80 millimetres of rain. The tanks overflowed, the pool was filled and we were in business. Settling into our new life at Waranga Basin was easier than I had anticipated. Several cousins and friends from my schooldays lived in the district and Tatura became the focus of our social life. Although both my parents were by this time deceased, many people remembered our family, and I joined the Rushworth RSL, Shepparton Legacy and Jubilee Masonic Lodge. The consulting business took up a large amount of time and Pam undertook work as a locum at pharmacies in nearby towns. We all loved it, especially Buster who was kept busy chasing rabbits, hares and kangaroos.

While living in Melbourne, a lot of interstate and overseas friends had stayed with us, and after moving to the country we welcomed many to our new home. My cousins, friends and colleagues from England, Malaysia, US and around Australia all found their way up to Rushworth. It wasn't long before I was elected president of the Rushworth RSL and later became a state councillor.

In 1983-84, I was called to testify about the safety procedures at Maralinga in the case of Johnstone vs the Commonwealth of Australia and also at the Royal Commission into British nuclear tests in Australia, conducted by Mr Justice J McClelland. In the latter case, because my evidence was not favourable to the Commonwealth's case against the British government, it was not taken into account.

We always looked forward to visiting the Signals Headquarters at Simpson Barracks and in late November 1986 were invited to see the Governor General, Sir Ninian Stephen, present the Princess

Anne banner to the Corps. The Princess Royal has traditionally been Colonel-in-Chief of both the Royal Signals and the Royal Australian Corps of Signals, so the presentation of the banner was a significant event in our Corps' history and one of great pride to all members.

Sometime in 1987, it was suggested I should become Master of the Rushworth Jubilee Lodge. I had always declined taking on senior roles in the lodge due to work and travel commitments but decided that now was a suitable time. The installation was set for 31 October and there was a lot of ritual, which I had never been very good at. Preparations were complicated by the fact that the lodge was celebrating its centenary year, so we had to conduct a re-consecration just prior to my installation. It would be a long day starting at 2 pm and finishing just before midnight. It was an exceptionally hot day for that time of year, ventilation in the lodge rooms was very poor, and I was required to wear evening dress with all the trimmings of Masonic regalia. Just after the installation ceremony concluded I was overcome by the heat and passed out.

When I came to, a Freemason doctor friend was leaning over me, an ambulance had been called and I was rushed to Shepparton hospital, having suffered a massive heart attack. The next few weeks were uncertain until I was finally allowed to go home. In the meantime, Pam had notified our clients that I would not be returning to consulting work – the decision to finally retire was taken out of my hands.

Years of anxiety, smoking and damage caused by broken ribs, because of my ill-treatment as a POW, had resulted in an aneurism on the left ventricle of the heart. I was too frail to undergo surgery immediately; in fact, I think I was expected to die. Subsequently, I suffered two more heart attacks at home and Pam revived me on both occasions. By March 1988, I was back in Rushworth hospital, my blood pressure was so low it could not be measured, oedema had set in, I was delirious, and I'm told that Father Treacy, parish priest from Rushworth with whom I had become friendly, said the prayers for the dying over me on Good Friday.

Once again, my life balanced on the edge of a dark precipice. Again, I was pulled back from death, this time by the skill of the dedicated nurses at this small rural hospital, led by Dr Rodney Payne, an ex-Royal Navy Surgeon, my GP and good friend. Pam later told me that the nursing staff asked her if she had thought about funeral arrangements. Sadly, the day before I was declared well enough to go home, our much-loved Buster died from a stroke. By July, I was strong enough to undergo surgery, a risky operation to repair the aneurysm, carried out at St Vincent's Hospital in Melbourne.

After a period of convalescence I was allowed to return home - that safe and peaceful place we had created and where I could now relax and enjoy the rest of my life. Not too relaxed though. I had several projects planned, which I knew I could manage without too much physical exertion but would keep my brain working.

Recovery was steady and, although my stamina was much reduced, I felt more at ease than I had in many years. Like so many perfectionists, I had not realised how driven I had become and what a toll it had taken on my health. However, I was able to maintain my interests in the RSL, Lodge and Signals Association and we continued to have many friends stay.

In April 1990, Yuen, now retired from the police and living in Kuching, invited us to visit him. As it was two years since my heart attack, I was feeling quite fit, so we decided to extend the trip to Kuching and once again visit the UK, before continuing to Ottawa, Canada, to see an old army friend.

During the week spent at Kuching with Yuen and his family, we revisited the Heroes' Grave at the cathedral with Victor, Yuen's secretary, as our guide. I was touched to see that the grave was fully restored and well kept; the curator told us that family members and local people who remembered those terrible days were frequent visitors. Victor also took us to the convent school and arranged for us to see the old courtroom, which we were unable to do on our previous visit. It was disused and rather dingy but was basically the same as in 1944, except that the door leading to the walkway was a window. Victor showed us a memorial in the grounds of the Teachers' College, formerly the Kuching Camp, erected to the memory of military and civilian POWs. Then, quite unexpectedly, Victor headed off to the river. Suddenly, there it was – the riverside landing where I was unloaded on our arrival from Sandakan and where I had been nailed into a crate for transport to Outram Road Gaol. It was a shock to see it. Although I had no detailed recollection of the actual place, the sights and smells of long ago, which I thought I had forgotten, were overwhelming.

Rod Wells and Dato Sri Yuen Yuet Leng, Malaysia, 1980.

Heroes Grave, Kuching, 1986.

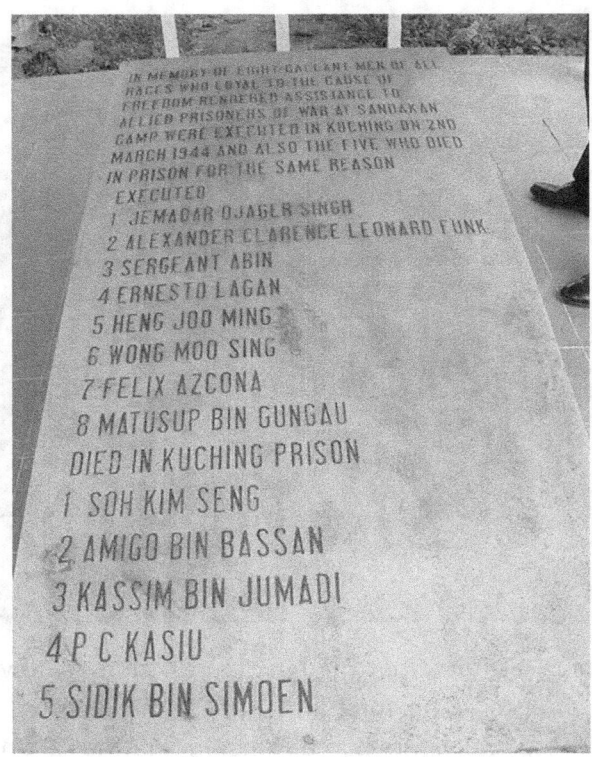

Inscription on the Heroes' Grave, Kuching.

From Malaysia, we flew to London. We spent ten days or so catching up with people before setting off for Trieste, Italy, returning to the UK for another month, then finally flying home via Canada. After the heart surgery I had not expected to undertake such a long trip and the following year it soon became evident that things were not well with me.

The heart surgeon discovered that one lung was infected, probably from the Teflon tape that had been put in place to keep the wound closed from the previous heart operation. We were sent home for a week to prepare for yet another risky procedure, and one that the surgeon had not previously carried out. We arrived at the hospital full of doubts and anxieties but everything went to plan and the offending lung was successfully removed. This time,

Capt Lionel Matthews' portrait by Robert Anderson, unveiled at Simpson Barracks, 1994.
L-R: Rod Wells, Mrs Lorna Ransom (Matthews) and Lionel's son David Matthews.

my recuperation was slower. I realised that I would never regain my full stamina and, although life at Kowandi was still full of interest, I was forced to curtail my RSL, Masonic Lodge, Legacy and the Royal Australian Signals Association activities.

In 1993, the Royal Australian Corps of Signals commissioned artist Robert Anderson to paint a portrait of Lionel, to commemorate the 50th anniversary of his death in March the following year. I was invited to give the keynote address and became involved in the planning for this significant event in the Corps' history. In July, the artist and I travelled to Adelaide so that Lionel's widow, Lorna, now Mrs Ransom, could view the completed portrait and any adjustments made. It was an emotional reunion, both of us moved by the Signals members' honouring Lionel in this way.

On 2 March 1994, at Simpson Barracks, Melbourne, in front of a large crowd that included many of my old colleagues, who had come from all over Australia, Lionel's son David and General Francis John Hickling, General Officer Commanding Training Command, unveiled the finished work. After the formalities were over, we inspected the latest buildings and equipment at the School of Signals. It was quite a revelation to the old timers, who had never previously visited the school, to see the amazing array of equipment with scarcely a battery in sight – transistors had taken over.

Life at Rushworth continued at a reduced pace for me, and an increasing workload for Pam, when I decided to give up driving. However, we frequently had friends to stay and I was always happy to find something to do in the workshop or at my indoor workbench in the office. Ted Howell was a regular visitor and we spent many happy hours designing printed circuit boards and the like. I also mentored a local lad who was interested in electronics and was always on hand as a Legatee when one of the Legacy widows needed advice. I can't remember what prompted us, but in 1995 we decided to put aside July, August and September and return to the UK.

A month before we set out on our trip, I was interviewed by Ray Quint, well-known film producer and director, for a proposed documentary entitled *True Stories*. Although Ray had hoped to do an entire program on my POW experiences, the project did not come to fruition. However, the DVD of the interview is an excellent summary of my experiences and the only time I have been filmed.

The few days spent in Singapore were rather disappointing. It had altered so much in the five years since our last visit and was almost devoid of the shophouses, street vendors and markets. Local colour had almost disappeared and Raffles Hotel had been redeveloped into a tasteless, garish and sad travesty of its previous charming, peaceful atmosphere.

We arrived in England on 5 July and immediately travelled to Blandford in Dorset for the 75th Anniversary celebrations of the Royal Corps of Signals. Princess Anne attended the church service and opened the museum extension. At a breathtaking display of motorcycle events in the afternoon we felt quite at home with broiling sun, flies, dust and scorched grass and fields. It was the hottest summer on record and continued until the end of August.

While visiting friends in Suffolk, we happened to see a BBC television program about Eric Lomax, the Royal Signals officer whom I had met at Outram Road Gaol. Over the years I had tried to trace him but had no luck. On contacting the BBC, we were put in touch. When we learned that his book, *The Railway Man*, was to be launched that night at Camden Town, we drove back to London and just made it in time to attend the book launch. It was a very emotional reunion for both of us.

Eric had become quite withdrawn over the years, but writing his book and meeting Takashi Nagase, the Japanese Kempeitai interpreter and his tormentor, many years later, had helped him overcome some of his demons. Although our contact at Outram Road had not been of long duration, the bond of those shared experiences was still strong; for me, it was stronger than any bond forged with my army or POW comrades. Outram Road survivors were special to each other. No one else could fully understand what we had been through. It was a relief to be with someone to whom you did not have to explain things. It was an eventful, nostalgic and moving night for Eric and for me, 50 years after our shared torture and deprivations.

Two days later, on 19 August, we attended the Victory in the Pacific (VP) Day celebrations. We had an excellent view of the choir, service band and the official party, including the Queen and many members of the royal family. The most moving part of the commemoration was when the huge crowd, numbering into the hundreds of thousands, stood absolutely still, heads bowed, for the two-minute silence. The solemnity was broken by a distant droning sound, then a deafening roar, as a Lancaster bomber flew at low level straight down The Mall and over Buckingham Palace, fluttering a million red poppies onto the crowd below. It was a never-to-be-forgotten moment. A parade of bands, floats, armed forces, veterans and various wartime organisations concluded this colourful celebration of the Allied victory in the Pacific, which saved thousands of lives, including mine, but which also commemorated the many lives lost. It was as if I had finally laid to rest my army comrades who had suffered and died, and now, at last, I felt at peace.

We also visited the RMCS at Shrivenham and it was wonderful to show Pam the place where I had spent so much time studying and enjoying the company of like-minded students. A day at the museum at Blandford was followed by an interview at Bournemouth University, which had recently established a Centre for the History of Defence Electronics (CHiDE). The manager, Brian James, was keen to record for posterity the smuggling in of the parts and the building of the receiver and transmitter at the Sandakan Camp. It was very satisfying to finally have these details officially recorded.

A few days before we left London, Pam and I took a stroll along the Thames Embankment. As we neared the Wartime Cabinet rooms, where I had been established on my arrival from Maralinga in 1956, we were confronted by a larger than life bronze statue simply inscribed OUTRAM – Sir James Outram, the distinguished Victorian soldier, colonial administrator and hero of the Indian Mutiny of 1857, for whom Outram Road and the Gaol were named. As we paused to look at Sir James, gazing eternally towards infinite horizons, we wondered what he would have made of the war in the Pacific, of the suffering and sacrifice of so many brave men who fought so valiantly to preserve the freedoms we enjoy today. It was a quiet moment of shared reflection on the broader picture: that we lived in a democratic country and would be returning home to our Australian spring.

EPILOGUE

Prior to our trip to England in 1995, our doctor, Rodney Payne, confirmed what I had suspected for a year or two – that Rod was developing dementia. He really enjoyed seeing his family and friends, the VP Day ceremony, re-visiting the RMCS, meeting up with Eric Lomax again and the CHiDE interview. However, his increasing anxiety and insecurity concerned me greatly and we were pleased to be home after three months away. Rod was much more settled once he was back to the security and routine of home life.

At the end of November, we were contacted by British author, Christopher Somerville, who was compiling a book on the contribution made by Commonwealth service personnel and civilians during the war. He travelled to Rushworth and, after the interview was over, began to chat to Rod about his post-war career. Incredibly, they discovered that Rod and Christopher's father had worked together at the Government Communications Headquarters in Cheltenham, Gloustershire, many years previously.

In March 1996, Rod was awarded life membership of the Royal Australian Corps of Signals and in April we drove to Canberra as special guests for the ANZAC Day National Ceremony at the Australian War

Memorial. A month afterwards, I underwent knee surgery so Rod went into respite care at Rushworth for a couple of weeks. Several days later, I had to break the news to him that Bill Dwyer, one of his oldest friends and best man at our wedding, had been killed in a car accident. On the same day his good mate, Ted Howell, had suffered a massive stroke and was unable to move or speak. Both of these events affected him deeply as they had been trusted and valued friends for many years. In September, Rod received his Fifty-Year Jewel at Army Lodge – a very proud day for him. The following month the Odyssey Foundation presented him with an 'Australian Achiever' award, at a gala dinner in Melbourne.

It was about this time that Rod became concerned about the future of our power supply. It was working extremely well but he realised that, if I had to face looking after it by myself, I might know what was wrong, but did not have the expertise to solve any problems. So he began long and complicated negotiations with the power company, which drained his already low stamina.

In November, we entertained 40 or so Totally and Permanently Disabled veterans at Kowandi for afternoon tea and also travelled to Benalla for the unveiling of a bronze statue of the town's well-known and much respected POW doctor, Sir Edward 'Weary' Dunlop.

It would have been about this time that we were contacted by the Probert brothers, Sherriff and John, who were researching a book about their father Jack who had died at the Sandakan Camp. Rod, who knew Jack quite well, had written a letter to his widow after the war and the Proberts had used it to trace Rod to Rushworth. Luckily, on the day of the interview, Rod recalled a lot about their father and it was touching to see these two men in their sixties absorbing every detail he could recall of a man they had scarcely known.

January 1997 saw the power connected to the main supply. This was quite a relief to both of us, though rather sad for Rod as he realised that he was no longer able to cope with the upkeep of our own system. In May, he was diagnosed with Parkinson's disease, fortunately in his case rather mild and with very little tremor. In August, he managed to attend the annual 'Guests of Nippon' lunch at the Naval and Military Club in Melbourne and, in October, we enjoyed a week's holiday at Lord Howe Island. However, osteoporosis had caused fractures in several of Rod's vertebrae, which gave him considerable pain and discomfort. A visit from a UK cousin cheered him up considerably in March 1998, and later that year in August we drove to Canberra to attend the launch of Sandakan, a Conspiracy of Silence *by Lynette Ramsay Silver, who had developed a good rapport with Rod and interviewed him in depth. Her book details the experiences of the Borneo prisoners with great accuracy and involved the author in many years' research.*

Although Rod's dementia was progressing, he still managed to communicate and enjoy the company of many friends. This changed in January 1999 when we suffered a huge setback in our finances. The 'friend' with whom Rod had entrusted his retirement funds had defrauded us of more than $230,000. Rod had always been conscious of leaving me financially secure and this setback brought a change in his mental state. When I broke the news to him and he said, 'Forget about it,' I knew that he would never be the same again. His decline was rapid and complete.

The next few months were spent looking after Rod and travelling to Echuca to see to my father, whose health was becoming increasingly frail. At the same time, I set about dealing with the business side of the impending proceedings against the failed investment company. I told myself that we owed no money, owned our home and property, still had an income from Rod's pensions and that, when things settled down, I could always take on more relieving work.

On the morning of 3 June, Rod fell and broke his hip at home. For various reasons we decided not to have it replaced but to have conservative treatment and let it heal naturally. Two weeks later, leaving Rod convalescing in hospital, I travelled to Melbourne for the final hearing of the case against the finance company. The outcome? We would receive 13 cents in the dollar, if we were lucky. I returned home late that evening to learn that my father was not expected to live through the night and early the next morning received the news that he had died. In the space of two weeks, Rod had been admitted to hospital, we had lost a large amount of our savings, and my father had died. I can truly say that losing the money was the least of these disasters, but I did resent the fact that, when I should have been in Echuca with my father, I was dealing with the duplicity of a friend whom Rod had trusted implicitly for almost 40 years. I also learned a lot about the ins and outs of receivership. In my innocence, I had expected that the receivers would be working to achieve as good a deal as possible for the investors. In the event, they were simply intent on obtaining a good outcome for the banks to whom the company owed money. There was always something to learn.

On 29 June, Rod and I celebrated our Silver Wedding Anniversary. The hospital provided a special afternoon tea, I packed up the silver teapots, bone china tea sets, flowers and champagne, to take into the hospital and we celebrated with 20 or so friends. It certainly helped dispel the gloom of the previous few months. Rod had always enjoyed a party and, although he was not quite sure what the fuss was about, he didn't stop smiling all day.

Early in July, a permanent place became available in the adjoining nursing home and I had to make the heartbreaking decision to have Rod admitted into full-time care. We were so fortunate to have a very small ten-bed nursing home with excellent care, just a few minutes' drive away and where Rod could still be under the care of Dr Payne, whom he knew and liked so much. The nurses loved looking after Rod. Despite his frail state of physical and mental health, they declared he was always a gentleman.

In January and February 2000, two of Rod's friends helped sort out his lifetime collection of electrical, electronic and radio equipment, much of it out of date. We held a successful sale and were amazed at the number of purchasers who went off happily with their treasures, most of which I had thought was junk. On the same day, a buyer dismantled the wind generator, the last item to be sold from our self-sufficient lifestyle – it was heading to a remote community in the Gulf of Carpentaria.

In July, I was invited as a VIP guest to represent Rod at the 75th Anniversary of the Royal Australian Corps of Signals at Simpson Barracks. Princess Anne was present for a happy reunion of over 300 members of the Signals Corps and their families. In September, I purchased a van with wheelchair restraints and lifter, which allowed Rod to travel comfortably in his special flotation chair/bed. He loved coming home, visiting friends, and having lunch at the golf club. 2001 turned out to be the year of the books. I attended the launch of the Bryce Courtenay book, Four Fires, *for which Lynette Silver was the historical consultant and which included several chapters on the Borneo experiences of Australian POWs, including Rod's. In March 2001, UK friends David Cornwell, better known to most people as best-selling spy novelist John le Carre, and his wife Jane, made a quick trip to Rushworth when they were in Australia to promote his latest book,* The Constant Gardener. *Then, late in September the Probert brothers' book,* A Prisoner of Two Wars *was launched in Griffith, NSW.*

In April 2002, I went to Melbourne to receive a certificate of Life Membership of the RSL on Rod's behalf. It was a particularly memorable day, as it was presented by former Victorian premier, Jeff Kennett, and marked the retirement of the outspoken and unique RSL President Bruce Ruxton. No one who has heard either of these men speak would soon forget their very individual and colourful style of oratory.

During our marriage, Rod and I had sometimes discussed setting up a charitable fund and, in August 2002, the Rod and Pamela Wells Community Fund was established. As a result, several organisations have been able to set up permanent means of ongoing finance and I continue to take a keen interest in their activities. Rod's health, although frail, remained stable and, in October 2003, I was encouraged by our doctor to go on a three-week garden tour of Greece with a girlfriend for a much-needed holiday. A week into the trip, when we were in northern Greece, I received news that Rod's health had deteriorated. I flew back to Athens and on arrival at the airport suddenly burst into tears. An hour later, my sister phoned to say that Rod had died an hour previously. It was also my birthday – Sunday 12 October. The return trip was a nightmare of bungled bookings and many regrets that I had deserted Rod when he needed me most. My two sisters, Jenni and Pru, made the trip to Rushworth and were with him when he died for which I have been forever grateful.

Dementia is an overwhelming condition; it brings on a regression to childhood when independence diminishes. Mobility, speech, cognition, continence, the ability to feed oneself are all lost until, in the final stages, the patient is like a newborn infant, totally reliant on others for life. Rod had survived death on many occasions and faced many setbacks with courage and hope; he was always grateful for the happy times and for the countless friends who had illuminated and enriched his life. His death was a great loss but, although I had known for many years I would have to face the future without him, his life example gave me the strength to do so.

Rod's funeral service was held at All Saints Anglican Church, Tatura, where he had been christened and confirmed, had attended Boys' Club and where his mother had been a regular worshipper. An overflowing congregation of family, friends, RA Signals personnel, government representatives and many former colleagues attended the service and the burial at Tatura cemetery. We subsequently held a memorial service in the chapel at Simpson Barracks and another at the Rushworth Nursing Home for the residents, staff and local friends.

Soon after Rod's death I contacted the CO of Simpson Barracks offering to sponsor an annual award for students at the School of Signals in Rod's memory but was disappointed not to receive a reply. However, in September 2007, a new building of 126 Signal Squadron at Holsworthy Army Barracks was opened and named the Rod Wells Wing. I gave an address at the celebrations and donated his medals, Morse-code key and other memorabilia. They are now on permanent display – an ongoing tribute to Rod's dedication to the Royal Australian Corps of Signals and to the service he gave his country in war and *peace for more than 40 years.* In Adelaide the following April, David Matthews launched his book, The Duke: a Hero's Hero at Sandakan, a tribute to his father; a memorable event for Lorna and David and for all members of 8 Division Signals who had known and admired Lionel.

In an odd twist of fate, Rod's grave overlooks the part of the Tatura cemetery reserved for graves of German prisoners of war who died at the district internment camps. As he was not involved in the European war I don't think that this would bother him, but his attitude towards the Japanese was that, although we should try to forgive our enemies, we should never forget the death and suffering the Japanese inflicted on hundreds of thousands of ordinary people.

Rod's outstanding talents and abilities were always put to practical use; his whole life was tirelessly, modestly and selflessly devoted to the peace and security of the country he loved. We still have, always will have, the Sandakan prison camps of this world with us, though they may be in other guises. If Rod were here today, I think he would have two messages. The first would be to always have a project in hand, something to enthuse over, something to keep you motivated and your mind stimulated. The second would be to pursue your ambitions to the utmost of your ability. You may be emaciated, oppressed, weak, and suffering, but keep hope in your heart; and never, ever, give up.

Tatura, March 2022

APPENDICES

APPENDIX A – Report on Clandestine Radio 1945............ 256

APPENDIX B – Fall of Singapore Surrender letter 259

APPENDIX C – Kuching Trial Records 260

APPENDIX D – Eyewitness Statement for Matthews' George Cross recommendation 269

APPENDIX E – Wells' Self-Sufficient Home 271

APPENDIX F – Rod Wells ChiDE interview 1995.............. 276

APPENDIX A –
Report on Clandestine Radio 1945

CONFIDENTIAL
Signal 8 Aust Div, AIF

Singapore
10 Sep 1945

CO Signals 8 Aust Div

REPORT ON ILLEGAL RADIO TRANSMITTER OPERATING IN JOHORE BAHRU AREA DURING THE MALAYAN CAMPAIGN

1. INFORMATION OF THE PRESENCE OF A TRANSMITTER:

As telegraph liaison officer attached to the Johore P & T [Post & Telegraph] Dept frequent contact with the Johore Police Commissioner C P Morrish, and the Assistant Supt end Security Officer H Donaldson was made regarding civil communications. Information was received from Morrish during early January regarding a transmitter reported to him by F E C B and Security. The Johore Police reported the matter as no progress was being made, and it was obviously a matter for Military investigation.

2. ACTION TAKEN BY THE UNIT:

A verbal report containing the above Information was made to Lt Col Kappe through Major Jacobs and orders from the CO to investigate immediately were received. Owing to the absence of suitable DF equipment Improvisation was made. Two AWA Interceptor receivers with Unit made DF aerials commenced operations within four hours of receipt of the information. The transmitter was picked up, but owing to the fact that Japanese code was used, no intelligent messages were received.

Application was made to Malaya Comd and the use of two DF sets with operators from Malaya Comd Signals was granted. Numerous coded messages were received and forwarded to Intelligence Malaya Comd. One message deciphered announced the arrival of 30 Hurricane aeroplanes two days before they landed. Times for the termination or transmission and the resumption of traffic were Tokio time and always accurate. DF activities were continued for ten days for reasons outlined below.

3. JMF AND POLITICAL OBSTRUCTIONS:

Attempts were made to obtain permission from Malaya Comd to search the Area in the proximity of Tunku Ahmat's (the Sultan of Johore's son) residence, but it was refused on the grounds that the disloyalty of the JMF may result from any "incident" with the Sultan's family. However it was stated that a search could be carried out when the enemy was driven from the Johore border.

The JMF and in particular the Signal Section was watched by the AIF. A radio set operated by JMF Signals was left at Mersing, intact with notes of frequencies, code names, etc. In addition messages giving Unit names etc were sent in clear. As a result of these activities, the Unit took control of the Johore Signals. This fact combined with Tunku Ahmat's interest in radio and associations with the JMF may have been the cause of the above activities.

From information received from HQ 8 Aust Div In early January a recording of all telephone communications to and from the residence of Mr F M Still Inspector of Prisons, Accountant PWD and security Johore International Club was made. No actual evidence pertaining to the transmission of information was received, but numerous incidents showing Still's disloyalty and leanings towards the Sultan's policy were cited, especially by the Johore Police.

4. TECHNICAL PROBLEMS CONFRONTING DF AND ACTION TAKEN:

After initial bearings were taken the conclusion was reached that two or possibly three transmitters connected by land line to synchronize transmission, and operated on the same frequency were used spasmodically opening and closing transmission to prevent DF detection. Variation in Signal strength obviously intentional, added to the difficulty of detection.

One transmitter was operated from somewhere in the jungle between Kranji Naval Radio Station and the causeway. The second was somewhere in the vicinity of Tunku Ahmat's residence and a possible third was in the Skirdar Area. The location vehicles were not accurate within approximately ¼ sq mile, and after application was made to Malaya Command, a cable was sent to Middle East Command for "ferret sets" which never arrived. As a last resort the electrical power supply was interrupted on the circuit feeding the area of Tunku Ahmat's residence, and a distinct variation in signal strength was recorded.

5. STATEMENT BY SGT YATES:

Information from Yates reveals that in late 1941 radio equipment was supplied by him to Tunku Ahmat. Yates had a radio shop at Nos 1 & 2 Orchard Road Singapore under the name of "Techlab", but during the campaign joined the SSVF.

The equipment was installed behind panelling in Tunku Ahmat's residence. More information is obtainable from Yates from whom a statement has not been obtainable owing to his absence from Changi on radio installation duties in Singapore. The equipment included a transmitter made to Ahmat's order and other apparatus about which Yates has details.

6. ADDITIONAL AVENUES OF INFORMATION:

The OC Police Depot Johore Bahrn Mr W C Carbonnel has reported this matter to Lt Col J C Barry i/e Police Administration and Security with the present Military Administration. Lt Col Barry has additional information regarding the activities of the Johore Royal Family during the Jap occupation and is anxious to get in touch with the Unit according to the former Commandant C R Morrish.

(signature) Lt R G Wells
Signals 8 Aust Div.

APPENDIX B –
Fall of Singapore Surrender letter

TO THE HIGH COMMANDER OF THE BRITISH ARMY IN MALAYA

10th February 2602

Your Excellency,

I, the commander of the Nippon Army in Malaya, based on the spirit of Japan's chivalry, have the honour of presenting this note to Your Excellency, advising you to surrender the whole of your forces in Malaya. My sincere respect is due to your Army, which, true to the traditional spirit of Great Britain, is defending Singapore, which now stands isolated and un-aided. Many fierce and fearless fights have been fought by your gallant men and officers to the honour and glory of British warriorship. But the development of the general war situation has sealed the fate of Singapore, and the continuation of futile resistance would only serve to inflict direct harm and injuries to thousands of non-combatants living in the city and would certainly not add anything to the honour of your army. I expect that Your Excellency will accept my advice, will give up this meaningless and desperate resistance, and promptly order the entire front to cease hostilities and will despatch at the same time your parliamentaire according to the procedure shown at he end of this note. If, on the contrary, Your Excellency should reject my advice, and the present resistance be continued, I shall be advised, though reluctantly, from humanitarian consideration to order my army to make annihilating attack upon Singapore. In closing this note I pay my respects to Your Excellency,

(Signed) Lt.-Gen Yamishita Tamayaki,
High Commander of the Nippon Army in Malaya.

N.B. The parliamentaire shall bear a large white flag and the Union Jack. The parliamentaire shall proceed along Bukit Timah Road.

[This note is a copy of one shown to me by a British staff officer after the Japanese surrender in 1945. R G Wells]

APPENDIX C – Kuching Trial Records

Kuching Trial Records sourced from Attorney General's Department, Court Martial files, Trial of Yamawaki and others, Australian Archives CRSA471 Item 81957

This is an accurate copy of the original, translated from the Japanese, which was amongst Rod's papers. Grammar and spelling of names, places etc have been left as per the document. Square brackets with corrections have been added, where necessary, for clarification.

REGARDING THE CASE OF MR. WELES [WELLS]

June 1947

I read the stenograph record No. 212 of Far East Military Tribunal which was distributed lately, and found that Documentary Evidence No. 1998 mentioned in my cross-examination by Prosecutor Commins Carr on the same day, the statistics which I submitted under the title of "List of Prisoners Sentenced at the Court-Martial From 8 Dec. 1941 to 15 Aug., 1945" at the request of Prosecutor Monahan, was prepared by a secretary under me, based on copies of Written Judgments at court-martials submitted by various armies to the War Ministry and that these copies are now under the custody of this Bureau.

I also add that the judgment for Mr. Weles is enclosed in the Attached copy of "Written Judgment of the Case of the Co-Accused Weles and Other Four Persons."

OYAMA, Fumio
Chief of Legal Investigation Division,
1st Demobilization Bureau

Judgement

Native place: Stepny [Stepney], Suburb of Adelaide, South Australia, Australia.
Former Unit: Signal Corps, 8th Division, Australian Army
Prisoner Capt. Raionel [Lionel] Collin [Colin] Matthews 31 years
Native Place: Tatchera [Tatura], Victoria, Australia
Former Unit: Signal Corps, 8th Division, Australian Army
Prisoner 2nd Lt. Rodelic [Roderick] Graham Weles 24 years
Native Place: Perth (others unknown), Western Australia, Australia
Former Unit: A Company, 4th M.G. Corps, 8th Division, Australian Army
Prisoner Sgt. Alfred Steevens [Stevens] 30 years
Native Place: Caura [Cowra], New South Wales, Australia
Former Unit: 22nd Inf. Rgt. Hg., 8th Division, Australian Army
Prisoner Cpl. John Allan MacMillan 38 years
Native Place: John Street, Beasly [Bexley], New South Wales, Australia
Former Unit: 84th Auto. Repair Corps, 8th Division, Australian Army
Prisoner Cpl. Walter Joffley [Geoffrey] Roffy [Roffey] 30 years

This Court Martial, participated with Prosecutor Legal Capt. WATANABE, Harmo, tried, The accused case of espionage, preparation for external safety of the State, violation of Prisoner of War Regulations and spreading of rumours against Matthews; the accused case of spreading rumours and violation of Prisoner of War Regulations against Weles and Steevens; the accused case of violation of Prisoner of War Regulations against MacMillan and Roffey, And gives judgement as follows:

Text of Judgement

Undermentioned defendants are sentenced as follows:
defendant   Matthews to death,
    "   Weles to 12 years' imprisonment
    "   Steevens to 5 years' imprisonment
defendants MacMillan and Roffy to 1 year and 6 months' imprisonment.
The seized six-shooter (Evidence No. 1) is confiscated.

Reason

Five defendants, belonging to their respective units, participated in the Greater East Asia War, taken prisoners by the Japanese troops at Singapore on 15 February 1942, and were being held in 1st Branch of Borneo POW Camp at Sandakan, East Sea, Borneo.

Defendant Rionel Collin Matthews, who had a hostile feeling for the Japanese troops even after surrender and dislike for the life of a prisoner, was watching for a chance to escape. Since arrival at the Camp he worked in the attached farm outside the stockade everyday. Around August 1948, he, taking advantage of relaxed watch came to contact with Abin, a Dosun and Head of the Eight Mile Branch Office of Sandakan Police Station, in Rabok Street [Labuk Road], several policemen under Abin, Matosap [Matusup], a Dosun [Dusun] and watchman of attached ranch to the East Sea Provincial Agricultural Experimental Station, a Chinese farmer Alexanderfan [Alexander Funk] in Seven Mile of Rabok Street and several local natives thereabout. Although he knew that the correspondence and contact with the local natives outside the stockade was forbidden by order or Lt. HOSHIJIMA, Susumu, Chief of the Camp, about October the same year, he still continued contact with the above persons and agitated Abin and others suggesting that those who assist the action of the defendants, prisoners, would warmly be received upon the resurrection of the British administration. From the middle of March to July of 1943 he, with continual criminal untent, selected the neighbourhood of above farm as a place of contact and secretly met with Abin generally once a week, and, as undermentioned, not only made him mediate correspondence between him and those outside the stockade hut but, also met and consulted with the local natives referred above. About August 1942 he requested Alexanderfan to draw maps of British North Borneo and Sandakan to use some day and received them. Then he was told by Alexanderfan that there was a rumour that a large number of the U.S. troops were stationed in Sulu Arch., and that they would shortly make a landing at Sandakan. He believed it would be possible and intended that in the event of landing of the U.S. and Philippine troops at Sandakan he would collect all the prisoners in the Camp, destroy it ad cooperate with the troops. He asked and received from Alexanderfan a pistol [revolver] and six [five] rounds of ammunition and arranged with him to notify the former immediately by blowing a whistle outside the stockade in case the Allied troops made a landing. He asked Alexanderfan to hand over a letter addressed to the Commanders of the Allied troops, in which he asked their rescue of the prisoners and enclosed a map of environs of the Camp. He told his intention to Policeman Abin and made him consent to hand over 6 rifles and 150 rounds of ammunition to the prisoners, in case they started up. He, in order to report to the Allied troops in the event of their landing, tried to know and collect the information concerning the Japanese troops. About the end of August 1942 he asked Alexanderfan to draw a map of Sandakan and its neighbourhood jotted down in details the strength and disposition of the Japanese troops and in December of the same year also asked Maginal, a Dosun and clerk of abovementioned Agricultural Experimental Station, to draw a map of the neighbourhood of the Station and the Camp, and received both them. At the end of September 1942 he made Masosop persuade Lai Kueifu [Pheobe Lai], a nurse of the Sandakan Citizen Hospital, to draw a map mentioning the billets and number of Japanese troops and Japanese residents there and obtained it. Whenever he met with Abin, several times, he got information concerning the removal of the Japanese troops, and Englishmen and Americans detained in the Camp, the movement of Japanese fleet and ships in Sandakan Port and matters of supplies to the Japanese residents in Sandakan.

About November 1943 Prisoners Weynton and Rikers [Rickards] in the Camp secretly constructed a radio set and listend to a broadcast from U.S.A. and England, which they promulagated among the prisoners there. He, taking advantage of unfavourableness of the news to the Japanese troops, intended to transmit them to Americans and Englishmen intained in the Camp or detained thereabout in order to stir up feelings of hostility. Conjecturing that the news would be promulgated among the local natives there through Americans and Englishmen, he asked Weynton to give every piece of news and received it. When he met with Policeman Abin and others, he transmitted through them more than ten times in the period from the middle of November 1942 to the end of February 1943, to Mr. Smith, Governor-General of former British North Borneo, and other Englishmen detained in Bahara [Berhala] Island the mouth of the Bay of Sandakan, unfavourable news to the Japanese troops that the severe battle was fought between the Japanese and American fleets with a result of heavy loss on the former side and that the Japanese troops suffered heavy loss in New Guinea. He transmitted more than twenty times in the period from December 1942 to July 1943 to Mr. Teller [Taylor], a British Doctor who had been ordered to serve in the Sandakan Citizen Hospital and under surveillance, news unfavourable to the Japanese troops that the U.S. Air Force attacked the Japanese transport ships and sunk 22 warships and ships and brought down many aircrafts in the sea near the Bismark Is,. He sent to Philips, an Englishman who was under surveillance in his house at Five Mile, Rebok Street, suburb of Sandakan, letters telling the news concerning the situations in the Solomon Sea and New Guinea unfavourable to the Japanese troops several times from May to July 1943. About May 1943 he intended to construct a radio set after Weynton to listen to broadcast from America and England and told Weynton and accused Weles his intention and they, in collusion with, asked Policeman Abin to get parts of radio set and received them one after another and tried to assemble it secretly under the guidance of Weynton until about June 1943, when they were detected before having finished it.

Accused Rodelic Graham Weles also had hostile feeling Against Japan and dislike for being a prisoner. He knew that correspondence and contact with local natives outside the stockade were forbidden for prisoners by order of the Chief of the Camp in about October 1942, but about May 1943 when he was told by accused Steevens that Mavar [Mavor], an Englishman under surveillance, was in the service of the Sandakan Power-Generation-Station as an electric technician, Intended to raise Mavar's hostile feeling by secretly transmitting news broadcasted by America and England generally once a week in the period from that time to the middle of June of the same year, and, with continual criminal intent, came into contact with him through the good offices of Steevens and Chien Pei [Chan Ah Ping], a worker in the power-generating-station attached to the Camp, and exchanged a letter written in cipher in Roman letters and figures and transmitted about ten times news unfavourable to the Japanese troops that the U.S. Air Force attacked a large group of Japanese transport ships and sunk most of them and shoot down many aircrafts, About May 1943 he was invited by the accused Matthews to Cooperate in constructing a radio set and consented. From that time to

July, 1943 he was engaged in assembling secretly the radio in cooperation with Matthews under the guidance of Weynton. About the beginning of June 1943, while Weynton was subjected to discipline and detained in the guard room, he listened to the broadcast from America and England with Weynton's radio in place of him and each time he promulgated orally or in writing the news unfavourable to the Japanese troops that the Japanese troops in Ragoon suffered a heavy loss due to the bombing of the U.S. and British Air Forces and that the Japanese troops in China were counter-attacked by the Chinese troops and were fighting desperately.

The accused Alfred Steevens had been in the service of the power-generating-station attached to the Camp since the end of October 1942, where he was ordered to operate the machines there. Notwithstanding that the prisoners were forbidden to come into contact or communicate with the natives outside the stockade by order of the Chief of the Camp, he, with continual intent, told Wu Kokuang [Ng Ho Kong], Chien Pei, etc., Chinese electric workers in the power-generating-station, several times during the period from January to July 1943, news unfavourable to the Japanese troops that the U.S. Air Force attacked the large group of the Japanese transport ships and sunk the most of them in the sea near the Bismark Is. and so on. About twenty times during the period from around May to July 1943 he sent letters between the accused Weles and abovementioned Mavar, and several packages containing parts radio set sent by Mavar to Weles, through the accused MacMillan, Roffy and Chien Pei. He also acted as intermediary of correspondence and contact between prisoner Matthews and policeman Abin three times in the end of June 1943.

The accused MacMillan and Roffy, the former from about September 1942 and the latter from about February 1943, were engaged in collecting wood outside the stockade and knew that prisoners were forbidden to contact and correspond with natives outside the Camp. MacMillan, taking advantage of relaxed watch and with continual criminal intent, twice in the end of May and also in the middle of June 1943, handed to Weles letters and packages sent by abovementiond Mavar through the accused Steevens and Chien Pei and forwarded to Mavar letters sent by Weles through them.

Roffy, thrice every month during the period from the middle of June to that or July 1943, received from Weles letters addressed to Mavar and sent them to him through Steevens and Chien Pei, and received from Steevens letters and packages addressed to Weles by Mavar handed them to Weles.

The abovementioned facts, excepting each continual criminal intent, are acknowledged by statements of the five accused made at this Court, the accused Matthews' deposition examined by a military police official; Weynton's deposition examined by a military police official mentioned in the trial record of Alexander Golden [Gordon] Weynton and other four persons for the case of violation of prisoner of war regulations, spreading of rumours, etc. (T.R. No. 16, 1943); depositions of the accused Abin Angon, Matosop Binganao, Alexanderfan, Teima Jinal [Dick Majinal], Lai Kueifu, Wu Kokuand and Chien Pei, examined by a military police official mentioned in the trial record of Earnest Trakan [Ernesto Lagan] and other 38 persons for the case of violation of military discipline which was obtained from the Military Discipline Tribunal of Nada No. 9881 (T.R. No. 21, 1913); depositions of Mavar, James Teller, Alfred Phillips, examined by a military police official mentioned in the trial record of the accused Jerald [Gerald] Mavar and other three persons for the case of violation of military discipline (T.R. No. 22, 1943); confiscated six-shooter, radio set with 18 parts and a copy of diary. Each continual criminal intent is also acknowledged by the repetition of similar crime in a short period.

According to the Law, the act mentioned in I-(1) in the case against the accused Matthews comes under Clause 1, Article 5 of the Prisoner of War Regulations; the act of espionage mentioned in I-2) comes under Clause 1, Article 85 and Article 60 of the Criminal Law, and the act of preparation for external safety of the State comes under articles 88 and 86 of above Law; the act mentioned in I- (3) comes under Article 99 of Military Penal Code and article 100 of Naval Penal Code; and the act mentioned in I-(4) comes under the latter part of Article 11 of the Prisoner of War Regulation. The offence mentioned in (1), (2) and (3) in I respectively constitute an act and they are also correlated with several other offences, while the offences mentioned in (1) and (3) concern with continual criminal intention, so the former part of Article 54, Article 55 and Article 10 of Criminal Law are applicable, therefore he is sentence to death for espionage, most severe penalty according to the above Articles. Espionage and penal for violation of Prisoner of War Regulations are concurrent offences mentioned in the former part of Article 45 of Criminal Law, but as he is sentenced to death, other penalties are exempted in accordance with clause 1, Article 46 of the same Law.

Among the acts mentioned in the case against the accused Weles, the act mentioned in II-(1) comes under Clause 1 Article 6 of Prisoner of War Regulations, Article 99 of Military Penal Code and Article 100 of Naval Penal code; the act mentioned in II-(2), comes under the latter part of Article11 of Prisoner of War Regulations; and the act mentioned in II-(3) comes under Article 99 of Military Penal Code and Article 100 of Naval Penal code. The offences mentioned in (1) and (3) respectively constitute an act and they are also correlated with several other offences. Moreover, the above two offences concern with continual criminal intent, so a penal servitude for a limited term is selected for violation of Prisoner of War Regulations, most severe penalty according to The former part of Clause 1, Article 54, Article 55 and Article10 of Criminal Code and penal servitude is also selected for the offence mentioned in (2). The above two offences are concurrent offences mentioned in the former part of Article 45 of Criminal Code, so Articles 47, 10 and 14 of the Code are applicable, therefore, the accused Weles is sentenced to 12 years' penal servitude, the most severe penalty according to the above Article with legal increase within the term of the penalty.

The acts mentioned in III-(1) and (2) in the case against Steevens come under Clause 1, Article 5 of Prisoner of War Regulation; the act of spreading of rumours mentioned in III-(1) comes under Article 99 of Military Penal code and Article 100 of Naval Penal Code. The offences mentioned above are respectively constatute an act and they are also correlate with several other offenses. Moreover, the above offences concern with continual criminal intent, so a penal servitude for a limited term is selected for violation of Prisoner of War Regulations, most severe penalty, according to the former part of Clause 1, Article 54, Article 55 and Article 10 of Criminal Law, there fore the accused Steevens is sentenced to 5 years' penal servitude within the terms of penalty provided by the above Articles.

Each act mentioned in IV case against the accused MacMillan and Roffy comes under Clause 1, Article 5 of Prisoner of War Regulations and Article 55 of Criminal Code so a penal servitude for a limited term provided by the above Articles is selected for each act within the term of penalty, therefore, the above two accused persons are sentenced to one year and six months' penal servitude with the term of penalty thereof.

The seized six-shooter (Evidence No. 1) was obtained by the accused Matthews for preparation for external safety of the State mentioned in his case and does not belong to anyone except the offender, so it is confiscated in accordance with Article 19 of Criminal Law.

Therefore, sentence is given as mentioned in the text.

2 March, 1944

Exordinary Court Martial, Nada 9801 Unit

Presiding Judge Lt.-Col. EGAMI Sobei
Judge Leg. Maj. NISHIHARA Shuji
Judge Capt. TSUTSUI Yoichi

APPENDIX D – Eyewitness Statement

Concerning Award of 'GEORGE CROSS' to VX24597 8 Australian Division:

I Roderick Graham Wells of 3 Holyrood Av, North Essendon, In the State of Victoria, and ex Lieutenant Signals 8 Australian Division, do take oath and state:—

The appointment of Captain L C Matthews to the position of Intelligence Officer on the death of Lieutenant Sligo, RAN, was made at Matthews' request to Lieutenant Colonel Walsh to be allowed to do some useful work for the [B] Force and Allies in general. He argued that his knowledge of the Malay language would assist initial contacts, and the responsibility of any interference from the Japanese should be borne by him alone.

Regardless of the then unknown risks of being caught, he first contacted Malays on the officers' garden party and by sheer determination and organisation arranged weekly communiques to the civilian internees on Berhala Island, and similar contacts resulting in the delivery of medical supplies from Dr Taylor in Sandakan.

Captain Matthews ran grave risks in smuggling notes and news bulletins past the guards at the gate to the above contacts, as well as bringing in some radio parts. The copying of news bulletins in the camp where a search was likely at any moment, and organizing the delivery of firearms to a secret rendezvous, required a courage that few would challenge.

After his arrest Captain Matthews showed courage that was both admired and an inspiration to all to remain silent under the most severe torture. When stretched on an improvised rack and severely beaten he still denied facts, the admission of which would have probably involved Senior Officers of the Force in the same fate as himself.

Although he fully realized what his ultimate fate would probably be, he steadfastly refused to make admissions under torture, other than to confirm some facts which had been admitted by natives under severe torture. This ability of knowing what to admit made the Japanese believe his efforts to prevent others being involved.

When the transport which conveyed us to Kuching spent some time in Kudat Harbour, and an opportunity was available for escape, (although only a meagre one) Matthews stated that he would not leave the responsibility of our organisation to anyone else, and was determined to see it through.

During the period of 5 months in Kuching Gaol, he indicated that if the work done by the organisation was of any use to the Allies his life was not in vain. When the death sentence was passed, Matthews had full control of himself, he shook me by the hand, wished me good luck and stated that he was pleased to be going with such loyal friends – the natives who had worked with us. Later Japanese guards stated that he was shot after refusing to be blindfolded.

(Sgd) R G Wells

SWORN BEFORE ME THIS 17 DAY OF JANUARY, 1946

(Sgd) ....J P

APPENDIX E –
Wells' Self-Sufficient Home

Wells, Pamela (June 1986) 'Wells' Self-Sufficient Home', *International Solar Progress*, Vol.7, No 3, pp.12-13

The northern shore of Waranga Basin, near Rushworth in northern Victoria, was the site chosen for this solar, self-sufficient home by Lt-Col Rod Wells and his wife Pamela when they opted for a return to rural living. The property of 52 hectares comprised mainly clay soil with some rocky outcrops, a few mature grey box trees and one small dam. Large areas of the land had been degraded by rock removal and washaways; erosion was significant. A small hayshed was the only building and no facilities were connected. The climate is semi-arid with hot, dry summers of low humidity, and a winter climate of sunny days and frosty nights. Most of the 400 mm rainfall comes in late winter or early spring.

The property was purchased in September 1979, and a program of planting 2000 eucalypts and acacias began; the dam was enlarged to hold 5 mega litres of water and fenced off to prevent muddying by stock. A large workshop and undercover parking area were completed in November 1982 and the side of a hill excavated, and the overfill compacted to produce a flat area of about one hectare for the house site. In the plan the house is a large rectangle with a flat comprising two bedrooms, living area and bathroom at the east end. Linking the flat to the main house is the indoor heated pool room. This room, roofed with translucent fibreglass with full length windows either end, traps the sun in winter to help heat the house; it also provides thermal stability in the summer. The main area of the house comprises open-plan kitchen/living area, study, main bedroom/en-suite, laundry and boiler room. Building began in mid-February 1983. The owners moved from Melbourne to a rented neighbouring property in April 1983 to supervise construction and to allow Rod to install the pipes and wiring needed for the special features of this complicated project. Building went ahead smoothly and was completed by Christmas that year.

Entrance to the home is via the pool room which acts as an airlock. No doors open directly to the outside from the living areas. Wide verandas run on the east, south and west sides of the house. The unsheltered north face receives maximum winter sun with eaves designed to eliminate summer sun. The building is angled from north at 17 deg. to the east to obtain maximum winter sun. Its area totals 52 sq m.

Building Materials

The north wall is brick veneer and other external walls and pool room walls are of painted Hardi-Plank (asbestos/cement 'weatherboards'). The north-facing roof is pitched at 45 deg. to obtain maximum sun for the solar hot water panels. The long low-pitched south roof is of plain metal decking. All external walls, pool room walls and the ceiling area are insulated with foil insulation and R1 rockwool bats. Windows and sliding doors are white aluminium-framed; south windows are double glazed and open at the bottom; north windows open at the top. In summer a cool breeze from the basin comes in through the south windows and is expelled through the north; ceiling fans also help cooling.

Heating

The slow combustion stove in the kitchen is used for winter cooking and domestic hot water.

A 'Burning Log' carousel fire in the living area is freestanding with glass panels. Heat is given out via the glass, the double enamel hood and flue. It gives the maximum amount of heat for the minimum amount of wood and burns so efficiently that there is very little ash to remove.

A wood-burning boiler located in the boiler room has an output of 30kW and heats eight wall-mounted water radiators in the flat and the rest of the house, including a laundry airing cupboard. It is also used for winter pool heating. An abundant supply of good quality burning wood is available on the property.

The four thermal storage walls, built into the north walls of the lounge and study areas are the most effective source of heat. Winter sun shines through the glass, heating the bricks and cavity. At night insulated shutters are lowered to keep the heat in; during the night heat is given out into the house. In summer the shutters are kept permanently closed. Vents are placed at top and bottom of the thermal walls to allow quick ingress of warmed air if required, control being by means of manual flaps.

Cooling

This is achieved by:
Minimising summer heat gain (good insulation etc)
Ceiling fans
Through ventilation at night
External awnings on north and west windows
No west facing windows
Solar Water Heating
Two glass panels provide domestic hot water.
Lay-on panels heat pool. Both of these on north roof.
Two pumps for this system are thermostatically controlled so they run for the minimum of time. On frosty nights a differential controller monitors the water pumps to prevent the solar water panels from falling below 4 deg. thus preventing damage due to freezing and eliminating the use of a heater element.

Power

Main source of power is the bank of 22 photo--voltaic cells (3 amps, 48V) mounted on the north facing workshop roof.
Three cupboards were specially built to each house 24 batteries of 2V, 200 amp.hr. These 72 batteries are charged via a 2KW ex-Telecom battery charger. These keep the three refrigerators and four solar pumps working unattended. Refrigerators are programmed so that they do not all start up at once, thus preventing a high demand on the batteries at one time.
An `Antelope' wind generator, sourced from Holland, also feeds into the batteries. This is a 1+ kW 48V DC generator and the most economical source of power.
An 8.5kV lister diesel generator is used as a backup to charge the batteries or when extra power is needed for heavy loads e.g. the inbuilt vacuum system, washing machine or iron.

The brains of the power system is a 48V, 3kW static inverter which converts DC from the batteries to 240V AC. This allows lights, refrigerators, freezer and appliances to be used on demand without having to start the diesel engine. Where acceptable fluorescent light tubes are used and recently developed Philips low wattage globes, although expensive, give maximum incandescent light for minimum power consumption.

Facilities

An alarm system, intercom to all rooms and the workshop, radio and TV rediffusion to all areas of the house and flat as well as short wave and international TV facilities ensure that none of the urban comforts are missing. The boiler room is the 'ship's engine room' within the house and contains pool filter, Trojan wood boiler, domestic hot water tank, vacuum motor, switch board and control panel. The diesel engine, situated in the workshop, can be started from the boiler room. This makes servicing very easy.

Water

From the dam, a windmill pumps water to a 45,000-litre tank on top of the hill which gravity feeds back to the stock trough and garden taps. In the workshop, this dam water pass through a filter to use in the three toilets; in the unlikely event of there being no rain water available, filtered dam water can be diverted through the taps for domestic use.

House and workshop provide a roof area of some 800 square metres, so a rainfall of 10 mm yields 80,000 litres of water. Two 45,000-litre concrete rainwater tanks, partly underground, provide ample storage and are interconnected to prevent water loss; any overflow is diverted back to the dam. On top of the hill another two 45,000-litre rainwater tanks can be filled by pumping from the lower two tanks.

Four pumps are required to keep the water system running. The two solar pumps, already mentioned, cope with hot water from solar panels for the house and pool. The third, a heavy-duty pump, sends water from the lower rain water tanks to a 4,500 litre header tank, mounted on one of the larger tanks on top of the hill. Gravity feeding this back to the house avoids fluctuation of water pressure when more than one tap is turned on. The fourth pump circulates water through the boiler for the water radiators in the house.

Builder

Mr Ray Wilson, Colbinabbin. Plumbing and wiring carried out by qualified tradesmen to comply with building regulations and for possible connection to mains power in the future.

Comments

The design, installation and operation of the electrical, power, water, communications and heating systems required an enormous amount of meticulous planning. They were all designed by the owner, a highly qualified electrical and electronics engineer. All pipes, cables, wires etc had to be connected from the workshop to the house, pool, wind generator and outdoor tanks before the actual house could be started. Sourcing photo-voltaic panels, insulated shutters, wind generator and batteries was not easy in the early days of domestic solar undertakings. Many `experts', especially the power company, were quite sceptical about the project. The owner, with great prescience, even suggested to them that in a few years' time they would be paying him for the extra power he would be able to feed back into their grid. However, the experts have been proved wrong. The house is very comfortable with even summer and winter temperatures between 22 and 25 deg. C. The best features are the passive stored heat walls and the heavy insulation, which greatly reduce the need for artificial heating and cooling. Some problems arose due to lack of practical knowledge by sales people and equipment (eg. the wind generator, solar panels) not producing the results claimed by them.

The success of this project is quite a work of art and is a tribute to the vision, energy, patience and ingenuity of Rod Wells.

APPENDIX F – ChiDE interview by Rod Wells 1995

Transcript of a tape-recorded interview conducted by Brian James, with Lieutenant Colonel R.G. Wells, Royal Australian Signals Corps (retired) at the Centre for the History of Defence Electronics, Bournemouth, UK, on 13 September 1995. Interview in relation to the construction of radio equipment by then Lieutenant Wells whilst held in a Japanese Prisoner of War Camp at Sandakan, British North Borneo, after the fall of Singapore.

RGW: It was about the beginning of 1942, when I was a prisoner of war of the Japanese, when I was ordered to go on a working party which eventually finished up in Sandakan in British North Borneo. 2,000 odd, of us, were on this work party and it wasn't long before we noticed the absence of information as to the international situation – what was happening in the outside world, and the whole camp had a real craving to get news by whatever means. Escape parties were being organized, but none of these was very successful. The next thing people turned to was a means of getting some radio news, and this is where the building of a radio set became an urgent requirement.

The main thing, of course, was that we didn't have any components and although we had some contacts outside which later on were helpful in the building of this receiver, it limited our requirement to a regenerative receiver as distinct from a super heterodyne receiver and the decision to do that was borne out by the results. The high frequency spectrum during that time of the war was fairly quiet in that part of the world and the BBC, we hoped, would be able to be received. This was aided by the fact that the Japanese, in their wisdom, called a friend of mine out one evening to repair their radio set and he took the opportunity, of course, to switch over to the short wave bands, with headphones while doing that, and picked up the BBC successfully. That day was memorable because it was the day that the BBC broadcast the death of the Duke of Kent in an aircraft crash. That was the only news we had of the outside world for something like six months.

The problem building the set, or course, was the need to build components. So, until we could build some components there was nothing much we could do. A look at the circuit diagram of a regenerative receiver indicates a number of capacitors – about two or three are required –low capacitors to make the oscillating part of the system work, and in fact from memory we needed in the grid circuit at least one .01 microfarad capacitor and there was no chance we could get this anywhere, or any other components. So we hit upon the idea of taking some tin foil or aluminium foil from the tea chest which the Japanese supplied with rice rations, then by the well-known equations for calculating capacity and the relationship of the distance between the plates and the area of the plates, we built a capacitor, at least, I built a capacitor which according to calculations should have been about .01 microfarad. If I could put an aside here, I built a replica of this capacitor some years ago, and it went out to Simpson Barracks where we had some friends in the testing laboratory, and with great excitement, the Warrant Officer concerned said, 'We will see how good your calculations were.' So he put it on his equipment which was accurate to many decimal points and read on his display unit .009 microfarad, so we thought we were pretty good. I said 'Touché' to him because he didn't think we could do it. I made two or three of these, and I still have one of them that would work. If I built the receiver again, which I have been thinking about doing, but there's always something else, like a lot of other projects, which one has, as one gets older.

The resistors were another problem. We found out that we could use the impurities in some of the tree wood and the bark, particularly cinnamon bark which was available by getting through the wire only about 2 feet, and we could normally pinch that while the Japanese sentry was moving around. We used a piece of string with the material rubbed on it from the burning of the cinnamon bark which had some impurities in it (we didn't have a chemical analysis.) We weren't very fussed because most grid-leak detectors were about a megohm or thereabouts and we had no means or any way we could measure a megohm, so it was largely a trial and error thing to see if it would work. We made a number of these bits of string and tied them round different things to dry them out to get the thing going. Eventually, about an inch, three quarters of an inch to an inch, was about the right order of things to get about a megohm resistance. They were the two main things.

Now the things we couldn't provide, couldn't do. We had to make coils. They were largely trial and error. One could calculate the inductance of these if one had access to some means of measuring the wire gauge and the space between them. So that was largely a trial and error business.

The two biggest components, or two biggest requirements, we needed were some headphones and we needed a valve, and I thought that the rest could be made locally with a bit of luck. On the question of the headpiece, an outside contact smuggled in one headphone, which was better than no headphone, and a valve – no valve holder – but one can't have everything in this life. The other trouble was the power supply. The Japanese main around the camp, which provided the power, was 110 volts roughly, according to the power station meter, which we couldn't help but see, because we delivered the wood there while the power station was running. I switched over when no one was looking and the frequency was about 60Hz, not 50Hz as we thought – not that this worried us anyway, but to know that it was manageable. So two problems remained for the power supply. The first one was the A-battery or low voltage supply necessary for the filament of the valve. We started with a couple of dry cells, but these didn't last very long and we had to make something then. Through being friendly with the pharmacist with the party, we got some potassium bichromate, and made up a bichromate cell, which is probably well known in text books, but not of very practical use. It's fairly hungry for zinc and it needs some sulphuric acid which one can't throw around or hide easily but it served for some time and was quite successful but, in the end, had the operations lasted very long, we would have been in trouble for that. Two of these cells provided about 3 volts to 4 volts, and 6 volts was a bit too much because each cell was running at a bit over 2 volts, about 2.2 volts.

The biggest problem was a rectifier to rectify the AC into DC of sufficient voltage, without dropping it to a low voltage, because remember in those days we needed high voltages for the B supply, or anode supply, but in these days we bring everything down to small DC voltages; we needed to get them up as high as we could. That was a partial failure in that using aluminium foil again and oxidizing one piece of it, or length of it folded over, with some weak acid and then using the two electrodes, one of clear aluminium, we could make a rectifier. We wouldn't be so audacious as to call it a rectifier now, because it had a reverse voltage of something like 30 or 40 volts, which wasn't exactly ideal, but for DC we had no option. The result was that I made a bridge rectifier, but the only problem was that after 15 minutes the electrolyte began to boil, so it was really passing current in both directions but a little bit more one way than the other. So a single call, an extra rectifier cell, was the only way I could close this down a bit, and some smoothing. This we achieved with part of a fish plate from the railway line which was being used at the aerodrome to move the dirt from one place to another by man-power, about six men on these, and the odd fish plate used to disappear anyway for various reasons. I dropped one off at the power station and asked the Chinese, under my breath, if he could cut it into three little sections, which he did. He didn't want to know why. Then again using some palm oil and some bee wire, which was in fairly plentiful supply, which we stole – it was a bit risky because the Japanese were cultivating a couple of beehives outside the wire and of course this wire used to disappear for various things unrelated to radio – and we put the palm oil along the wire stretched out and rubbed this palm oil on it, thickening it with a little bit of flour and then heating it: the flour bound the palm oil together and formed a fairly good insulation over the wire. Good, but lucky, and with a lot of travelling.

I should come back to the capacitors on that, because we had to insulate the layers of those which we did by putting a layer of newspaper (a few people had newspaper and various things, for other reasons than newspaper of course, but then we had no other toilet requisites in the party) and by soaking this in some coconut oil we could insulate each layer after we wound it, and with a piece of this bee wire – we had something like fifty feet of it – wound round this part of the fish plate, we made a fairly good choke coil. And then a bigger capacitor, which was no trouble, having had success with the small one, to just wrap as much tin foil as we could round another sheet of newspaper which finished up about 18 inches long by about three quarters of an inch in diameter. We didn't even try to measure the capacitance of it, because we couldn't do anything about it anyway, except put more wire on. And that in effect was a fairly good rectifier – a very dangerous one because we had the 110 all right, but we had a bit over that by the time we had rectified it, and we don't know because we had no means of measuring it.

Finally, the valve; we joined the valve by winding the clean bee wire around it and then plugging it with any insulating material we could get to make it stick – no valve holder, of course. So eventually we produced a receiver or sorts, except it wouldn't oscillate. We tried building more, another choke coil, and this went on for ages; there was no possibility we could get this valve to oscillate. I think it's recommended according to a friend of mine who had an amateur licence, he thought that about 120 volts was the best we could get and there was no way we could get that by trying to smooth this any more. So, the only avenue open was to bribe one Chinese working at the power station, who was very much our way, and of course in those days, was a nationalist Chinese. The Capital of China in those days was Chungking, and I told him we could get him some overseas news from Chungking if he would slowly wind his field coil power up on the generator every night starting at about 9 o'clock niche by niche, and to get it up to about 130 volts on his meter. He understood, and after that I said half an hour to drop it again, very quietly and slowly because it may affect the lights '…and you no speak about that because you get chopped, you known, and we will give you Chungking news.' This was duly done, and for about six months we had reliable communication. The first trial on air had too much hum, and we had to modify a few things two or three times in attempts to get it right, and in the end, we had a workable situation which was worth exploring.

Capacitors right, choke coils right, one head phone, we had some old rag so we tied it round the head and tied it on, or string, or whatever we could get. With the hope of recording something we took some paper, which wasn't in plentiful supply, but the odd piece of paper we could get. Running notches down the left hand side, about a quarter to a half inch apart down the paper, and bending it over so that these little pieces stuck up in the air, and in the pitch darkness one could then put the headphones over one's head with eyes looking out for possible interruption by the Japanese. We had some lookouts, or cockatoos as the Australians called them, around the place, to warn us at the oncoming of the Japanese, and with great trepidations we heard Big Ben chiming one night. Of course, only one of us heard it, but we were so full of enthusiasm. It was the BBC all right; it was quite a clear signal but it was somebody talking about growing hops in Kent. This broadcast went on for something like three quarters of an hour without any interruption, but ultimately the signal faded out and I was very annoyed. I was asked the next morning by my senior officer what was the news, and I said, 'We've got good news. I can't talk here, but come this way.' So he came along and said, 'What's this news you're talking about?' I said, 'I didn't actually hear any news.' And he became very annoyed with me and said, 'What the hell did I mean?' And I said, 'If the British primary producing experts are capable, and able to spare the time to talk about growing hops in Kent, Britain must still be alive and floating with their thumbs up, and as far as I'm concerned that's the best news I could hear!' That's the outline and maybe there are some questions I haven't covered properly.

BJ: The first question I would like to ask you is, 'What did you have in the way of tools, if any? And how did you connect the components of the wireless without, presumably a soldering iron?'

RGW: No soldering iron, no solder of course, and no other system really available but to twist and wrap with some coconut oil paper, or cardboard or something, and very gently lift it. It was on a platen of wood we obtained somewhere; it was about a foot by a foot, or something, so we just mounted the components on that. A meat skewer on the capacitor – oh we had a capacitor too, a capacitor, a valve and a headphone, which were external to camp components we had. We didn't have any tools at all, except someone obtained the use of a sledge hammer, for what purpose I don't know, because one of those would not be needed to escape; other than cutting up the soft iron of the fish plate which was about the only reason we needed anything, the rest were just twisted wires. We just wanted to get one usable because we didn't know whether it might be blown up or captured. We weren't worried, the main thing was initially a short-term aim (as well as a long-term aim) that it might last. Fortunately, it lasted for over a year – 16 months until the arrests took place, but that's another story.

BJ: Can I ask you – the components for the low voltage battery cells that you produced. Where did you get all the components from?

RGW: Well, zinc wasn't hard. There was some sheet zinc lying on the aerodrome and we pinched quite a bit of that because that would be eaten away during the use of the cells for the low voltage. I don't know what would have happened when that ran out. I think someone produced two lantern cells which did for a while, but it was mainly on the home-made cell system, which wasn't efficient, but nowhere near as inefficient as the rectifier was. We must have been consuming. Ah Ping said he had to turn up a lot of power to keep the lights they wanted. We were dissipating such an amount of power in this four test-tube rectifier for the high tension.

A variable capacitor was another component we had to bring in. We couldn't make a variable capacitor. It was impossible. We had to take two plates off the one we had to get a high enough frequency. Yes, I can't remember why we didn't go up a bit in inductance. It was largely a trial and error business really. Except that in a regenerative receiver you had some idea when you were near a station because the receiver was so sensitive, as all regenerative receivers are. It had a piece of meat skewer type wood which I had a hole drilled in by a pen knife, and we glued this in with some flour glue or something, into the capacitor shaft so that we could tune it by holding a little stick across it, fixing it at about six inches because one couldn't get one's hands any closer to the set because it was in a state of very near oscillation where it has the maximum sensitivity. Just before it bursts into oscillation, the regenerative receiver is at maximum sensitivity. With a fairly clear HF band, it wasn't long before we knew roughly by putting a couple of marks on the stick, where it was. We knew that the Voice of America was about a quarter of an inch away from the BBC – I don't think we ever knew the frequencies because the BBC didn't announce frequencies. They just came on the air and broadcast.

BJ: What did you use for an aerial?

RGW: A clothes line. All the huts had a clothes line of some sort, so we just took a thin wire from that and wrapped it round the edge, knowing that a normal sentry wouldn't take any notice of it, and we just dragged that across to the side of the hut and brought it in, and odd people with our permission would put their loin cloths out and hang them over this when they washed so it looked as if it was being used. The toilet in the sleeping block was a hole in the ground and it was verboten to be used by anybody except to put our radio set in when it wasn't in use. Everybody respected our wishes in that regard! I think that the best thrill was, well two or three thrills, which were momentous, I suppose, and of great excitement, almost excitement of crying with excitement, and the first was I think when we heard a full news bulletin of something like 400 aircraft over Dresden or somewhere, pounding the place to pieces. We were very pleased about all this. But from the land point of view, from the beginning of '42 I think, I can't remember, but sometime just before the Battle of Alamein, and we heard some of the troop movements in preparation for that. The bulletins in those days were fairly long and gave a lot of detail.

Unfortunately, the first lot of rectifiers blew up about 2 days after this, so we were out of business for something like 5 or 6 weeks. Of course, the rumours started to flood in as to what was happening, what wasn't happening. The war would be over in 5 minutes and all these mainly optimistic things; but there were a few super pessimists who said we would never get off the island and would die there, and that sort of thing. But the thrill, I think, was when reception was restored again and we had to do another little bit of fine tuning because everything you changed seemed to affect something else. The whole thing was very sensitive and wouldn't have stood up to present day quality assurance bump tests!

So back on air on the first night we missed the BBC for some reason, and the next thing was the Voice of America which had a headline which ran something like this: 'The war is over in North Africa. Rommel is knocked to pieces. He's out of the Middle East and the Middle East is finished. The future for this and that …' That was the end of the American news in about three sentences! No other detail, so I said we would go back at about 12.30, and hope that Ah Ping hadn't pulled the voltage down too far, to see what we could hear. Again, the BBC was a little low, but it suddenly came quite bright and lifted in volume, and Big Ben chimed again and there was a voice in the wilderness calling. It was a lovely sensation to hear Big Ben playing in those days and every time I hear it now I become excited. The announcement, initially in a most depressing vein, described all about the 8th Army's movements, and it was here that it did this, and this regiment drew up and did that, on and on this went for something like 15 to 20 minutes, and we tried not to follow it because we had our eyes on too many other things, look-outs and so on. But a lovely flow of English and if you had a tracing board you could have traced out exactly where everything was 'in situ', but of course that wasn't the aim of our exercise which was to get news. At the finish of the news the polite sentence said, 'It must be considered now that as all resistance in North Africa has been overcome, the Allies victory must be assured' or something like that. And that was all he said, but took a few minutes to describe everything that happened, so you had a clear picture. But the Americans seemed to be creating for a public that just wanted the headlines, three headlines and that was all; no other interest in anything else. That was one of the happy moments of the system.

We had the problem, or course, of writing the news because naturally a lot of people wanted to know it and a lot of people could be told it, without its origin. This is why we used the piece of paper we took with us (Gordon Weynton and the other officer who used to share some of the work) and as soon as we heard about 30 bombers over Dresden or something, you just put 30BD, or B for Berlin, and feel the paper down when you felt it coming to the end, and pick up the next little bit of bend and write along that in the pitch dark, hoping that you've got something in the morning. Surprising how legible it was, just triggered a couple of words like that. Unfortunately, I was in the deep custodianship with the Kempeitai when the Atom bombs were dropped and I didn't hear that news on the BBC; it was relayed to me. We didn't keep these things, of course.

Getting off the technical side now, the radio set didn't betray itself. Some criticism could be levelled at us I suppose. We trusted too many people. We had no intelligence training then, of course, or anything like that and we were inclined to trust every Asian we met who smiled at us and who said he was one of us. Anyway, while this was going at the aerodrome, and once the troops heard, we had to tell the troops the good news of course. We said we had heard from an unknown source that the war is getting better, or something like that – we had to give them a sanitized version. It was probably all they wanted, but naturally, two or three senior officers wanted to know as much as they could because they may be the ones who would have to take some decisions one day about it.

Unknown to us an Indian – I don't like saying this and I'm not being racist, it could have been any nationality, blackmailed a Chinese who was helping us on the aerodrome picking up bits of iron for us and various other things. He blackmailed him, but the Chinese wouldn't talk, so the Kempeitai arrested the Chinese and put him on a rack. He mentioned in the course of his cries for help, which was not a nice thing to think about, but I don't blame him. He mentioned Captain Matthews and a couple of other people, I think I would have done the same thing at that stage.

The Japanese then decided to make a raid on the camp, which they did, and I was then charged and taken away by Captain Hoshijima. He wanted the receiver and I gave it to him in the end after a lot of leading him round the camp with his soldiers. I could almost laugh at some of the things that happened. He must have told them he was looking for a radio set. A Jap soldier came running up to him with a piece of metal which looked like a piece of horse harness or something. The Captain almost kicked him and told him what to do. So, in the end I decided that I couldn't talk to anybody, because the rest of the troops were on the parade ground and I felt so conspicuous. He walked back and said, 'Are you to tell me because we want the wireless set?' So, I said, 'Yes, I've just thought where it might be.' So, I went across and told him where the hole was, and they dug the hole up and, of course, there was the transmitter. He said, 'Ah, you've been sensible at last,' so he took the transmitter and they took it away.

From that day on, I was worried about this because I knew that the receiver was ok and the troops would be happy about that. They would still be able to get news. And then he took me up to the platform where he stood and addressed everyone. All he said in English was, 'You all look at this man. You will never see him again,' and led me off. I had a sort of a dying wish, going in on the vehicle to Sandakan to be interrogated, that somehow or other this set (the receiver) could be preserved and, of course, unknown to me, it was. They continued using it, but not until after about a week or so. Their nerves were a bit shaken. But they used it for some months afterwards, until the big moves came and it was a successful source of morale lifter.

During the trial, that was when the shock came to me when this transmitter was brought out by the prosecution as evidence that we had been using a receiver, but the Court accepted it. It was never mentioned after that because, had it been, I don't think either of us would have been alive, because we had planned to get some crystals from the Philippines and try and fit them in this set, then we could call them on CW and give them some news about ourselves. But we did get some news by other means, via an agent taking a sandalwood vessel across, that British and Australian authorities knew where we were, and it was proved at the end of the war that they knew exactly where to come for us. They had guerilla parties in behind the lines, but they couldn't contact us and they had to watch some of our people just die virtually, because they were there and there would have been trouble otherwise.

BJ: Could I just take you back and ask you to fill in a few details about the transmitter. You talked a lot about the construction of the receiver and I would be very interested to know where the transmitter fitted into this. Were you developing that alongside?

RGW: No, the receiver first. We had that, and then we started the transmitter as a rather low priority of course, but one it would be nice to have. I had finished the two 6L6Gs to make a push-pull amplifier that was the RF output to be, and the oscillator, and we had the capacitor, but were missing a few more components and that was about where we were. In other words, in the course of events, had he been an expert with some sort of knowledge of electrical engineering, we would never have got away with two 6L6Gs sitting up on a block of wood with a few capacitors and things hanging on them, but obviously the court martial officers were normal, without disrespect to infantry officers, and they had no knowledge of telecommunications.

BJ: Again, the valves you used in the receiver were?

RGW: Only one, that's all we had, which was brought in by Mr. Mavor. He smuggled in a pipe to me. A smoking pipe with some tobacco. Lovely gentleman. Unfortunately, I never had long with him. He died soon after being arrested. His widow lived at Hove with her sister. The two are deceased now.

BIBLIOGRAPHY

Bennett, Lieut-Gen H Gordon, *Why Singapore Fell*, Angus & Robertson, Sydney, 1944

Bowden, Tim, *Prisoners of War: Australians Under Nippon*, sound recordings and transcript, ABC, Ultimo, NSW, 2007

Chin, Aloysius, *The Communist Party of Malaya: the Inside Story*, Vinpress, Kuala Lumpur, Malaysia, 1994

Firkins, Peter, *From Hell to Eternity*, Westward Ho Publishing Co, Perth, 1979

Firkins, Peter, *Borneo Surgeon: a Reluctant Hero: the Life and Times of Dr James Patrick Taylor*, Hesperian Press, Perth, 1995

Leng, Dato Sri Yuen Yuet, *Nation Before Self: and values that do not die*, Dato Sri Yuen Yuet Leng, Ampang, Selangor, Malaysia, 2008

Matthews, David, *The Duke: A Hero's Hero at Sandakan: Captain Lionel Matthews, GC, MC,*, Seaview Press, West Lakes, SA 2008

Nelson, Hank, *Prisoners of War: Australians Under Nippon*, ABC Books, Sydney, 1985

Quint, Ray, video recording interview with Rod Wells, 23 June 1995

Russell, Lord of Liverpool, *The Knights of Bushido: a short history of Japanese war crimes*, Cassell, London, 1958

Silver, Lynette Ramsay, *Sandakan: a Conspiracy of Silence*, Sally Milner Publishing, Bowral, NSW, 1998

Silver, Lynette Ramsay, *The Bridge at Parit Sulong. An investigation of mass murder, Malaya 1942*, Watermark Press, Sydney, 2004

Somerville, Christopher, *Our War: How the British Commonwealth Fought the Second World War*, Weidenfeld & Nicholson, London, 1998

Tsuji, Colonel Masanobu, *Singapore, the Japanese Version*, Mayflower-Dell, UK, 1966

Wells, Pamela, 'Wells' Self-Sufficient Home', *International Solar Progress*, Vol.7, No 3, pp.12-13, June 1986

Wigmore, Lionel, *The Japanese Thrust*, Australian War Memorial, Canberra, 1957

LIST OF ILLUSTRATIONS, PHOTOGRAPHS AND MAPS

Chapter 1 – In the Beginning

Frontispiece: Dick Wells, just before leaving for WWI – Donovans Studio, Brighton. Pamela Wells' archives

Cuthbert Hall, Tatura, 2018 –
Photo by Ken O'Connor. Permission John Basile 8

Map showing the Wells' farm, Cuthbert Hall, Tatura –
Image courtesy K Seppings/Google Maps 8

Map of Shepparton, Tatura – K Seppings/Google Maps 9

Map of Victoria with Melbourne and Shepparton –
K Seppings/Google Maps 9

Ch 2 – Birth, School, Experiments

Rod Wells, early 1922 – Pamela Wells' archives 10

Rod, Maggie, Madge and Dick Wells, 1920s –
Pamela Wells' archives 13

Madge and Rod Wells, 1928 – Pamela Wells' archives 18

Convent of Mercy, Tatura, now St Mary's College Hall, 2010 –
Photo by Kaye Watson 19

Ch 3 – A Scientist's Life

Rod Wells' schooldays, 1930s – Pamela Wells' archives 36

Williams' shop interior, circa 1920 – Hill family archives 40

Williams' shop exterior, circa 1910 – Hill family archives 45

The Wells' jinker and horse, Codger, 1930s –
Pamela Wells' archives 48

Ch 4 – Apprenticeship, Enlistment, Training

Rod Wells 1938 – Pamela Wells' archives 57
Rod's ship SS *Sibajak* at Fremantle – Silver Papers 67

Ch 5 – Malaya

Map of Malaysia and Borneo – *The Herald* 29 May 1968 68
Clifford Pier, Keppel Harbour, Singapore, 1941 –
Pamela Wells' archives 69
Rod Wells, Malaya, 1941 – Pamela Wells' archives 70
Map of Japanese landings in Malaya, January 1942 –
Silver Papers 81

Ch 6 – In The Bag

The destruction of the oil reserves at Kranji, Singapore city,
February 1942 – Silver Papers 82
Pre-war photo of buildings in Selarang Barracks, Changi –
Silver Papers 89

Ch 7 – Sandakan

Sandakan waterfront, municipal buildings and Jubilee Clock
Tower 1935 – Silver Papers 90
Interior of officers' huts, 8 Mile POW Camp, Sandakan, by POW
artist F Woodley 1942-43 – Silver Papers 95
Johnny and Paddy Funk c 1941 – Silver Papers 98

Ch 8 – The Underground

Ojagah Singh and his children; Anup is 2nd from right –
Silver Papers 104

Ch 9 – Arrest and Interrogation

Map of Kuching, 1945 – Silver Papers 116

St Teresa's School, Kuching, 1980 – Pamela Wells' archives.... 128

St Teresa's School, Kuching, 1980 – Pamela Wells' archives.... 129

Lionel Matthews, 1940 – David Matthews' archives 133

Ch 10 – Outram Road Gaol

Entrance to Outram Road Gaol – Silver Papers..................... 134

Billy Young, on enlistment, aged 15 – Silver Papers 144

Ch 11 – Back to Changi

Changi Gaol as POW Camp – Silver Papers 154

POW hospital hut in the grounds of Changi Gaol, September 1945 – Silver Papers... 156

Ch 12 – War Ends

The day of liberation, September 1945, Changi POW Camp – Silver Papers 161

Lt Col John O'Neill, 2/15 Field Regt, c 1940 – Pamela Wells' archives... 166

Ch 13 – Homecoming

Japanese Judge Chief Sobei Egami – David Matthews' archives.. 169

Japanese Judge Junior Yoichi Tsutsui – David Matthews' archives.. 169

Japanese Judge Prosecutor Watanabe Haruo – David Matthews' archives.. 169

Ch 14 – Fresh Start

Rod Wells, 1-56 Australian Regular Army FD Officers Course, 1952 – Pamela Wells' archives 188

Ch 15 – Maralinga

Rod Wells, Maralinga, 1956 – Pamela Wells' archives 194

Ch 16 – My Career Takes Off

Victoria Barracks, St Kilda Rd, Melbourne, 1970s –
Pamela Wells' archives 202

Ch 17 – The 1970s Simpson Barracks, 1994 –
Rod Wells' and Pamela Bennett's wedding, Scots' Church, Collins Street, Melbourne, 1974 – Pamela Wells' archives 211

Ch 18 – Return to Borneo

Former fruit stall, Sandakan, 1980 – Pamela Wells' archives ... 222
Chin and Rod Wells, Sandakan, 1980 –
Pamela Wells' archives 225
Anup Singh, Labuan, 1980 – Pamela Wells' archives 228
Captain Lionel Matthews' grave, Labuan, 1980 –
Pamela Wells' archives 229
St Teresa's School, Kuching, 1980 – Pamela Wells' archives.... 233

Ch 19 – Country Living and Beyond

Solar house, Rushworth, 1986 – Pamela Wells' archives 234
Rod Wells and Dato Sri Yuen Yuet Leng, Malaysia, 1980 –
Pamela Wells' archives 240
Heroes' Grave, Kuching, 1986 – Pamela Wells' archives 241
Inscription on the Heroes' Grave, Kuching – Silver Papers 241
Captain Lionel Matthews' portrait by Robert Anderson unveiling, Simpson Barracks, 1994 – Pamela Wells' archives 242

INDEX

A

ABC (Australian Broadcasting Commission) 235
Abin, Sergeant 98, 106, 109, 117, 132, 179, 262-6
Adelaide, SA 182, 214, 243, 252, 261
A Force 91
Ahmat, Tunku 257, 258
Aldermaston xv, 199, 201
Allied Forces xv, 73, 75, 77, 78, 83, 85, 96, 105, 115, 159, 165, 168, 171, 269, 270, 284
    surrender 80, 82-4, 86, 89, 159
Anderson, Charles 76
Anderson, Keith 55
Anderson, Robert 242, 243
Andrews, H Lyell 24-6, 63, 69
ANZAC 93, 247
Ashby, Ellen Ethel xiv, xv, 65
Australia iii, xv, 1, 4, 26, 111, 128, 142, 150, 165, 168, 171-2, 177, 180, 182-3, 195-7, 201, 215-6, 218, 221, 235, 237, 243
Australian Army xv, 63, 69, 75, 174, 181, 186, 188-190, 193, 196, 201, 204, 232, 261
    Army Reserve/Militia xv, 5, 60, 201, 218
    Artillery –
    2/10 Field Regiment 91
    2/15 Field Regiment 65, 68, 166
    4 Anti-tank Regiment 69
    Australian Imperial Force (AIF) xiv, 5, 24, 60, 66, 77-8, 87, 101, 160, 181, 256-7
    Signals –
    Royal Australian Corps of xvi, 24, 62, 75, 180, 205, 238, 243-4, 247, 251-2, 276
    8 Australian Division iii, xii, 63, 67, 71, 74, 86, 229, 253, 256, 258, 269
    9 Division Signals 171
    39 Signal Regiment 206
    Army Headquarters Signal Regiment, Melbourne xv, 90
    Australian Defence Signals Directorate 204
Army Lodge, Melbourne 186, 248

Australian Defence Department xv, xvi, 201, 207
Australian General Hospital (AGH) 69, 156, 171
Australian War Memorial 247
Azcona, Felix 106, 132

B

Baba, Masao 171
Barker, Peter 39
Barker, Roy 63
Barnett, Ben 67
Barry, J C 258
Bathurst, NSW xiv, 63-5, 97
BBC (British Broadcasting Commission) 26-7, 107, 112, 114, 244, 276, 280, 282-4
Bennett, Henry Gordon 76, 168
Bennett, Pamela (see also Pam Wells) ii, xvi, 211-2, 292
Berhala Island, British North Borneo 94, 103, 115, 223, 225, 269
B Force xiv, 91, 97, 115, 180, 225
Blain, Macalister 184
Borneo xii, xiv, 94-5, 100, 103, 106, 129-30, 166, 170, 171, 177, 181, 183, 206, 220, 221, 227, 230, 249, 251, 262, 263, 276
Bowden, Tim iii, 235, 287
Brighton, England 1-3, 6
Brighton, Vic, Australia 54, 58
British North Borneo (Sabah) 95, 103, 106, 171, 206, 230, 262, 263, 276
British Army 259
British Signals' Headquarters, Singapore 79
Brooke, Rajah 125
Brown, Ray 219
Bukit Timah, Singapore 83, 259

C

Chan, Ah Ping 102, 110-114, 131, 264-6, 282, 283
Changi POW Camp, Singapore xv, 85-89, 91, 93, 96, 113, 122, 138-9, 145, 147, 151-2, 154, 155-62, 220, 258
  discipline 87, 93
  rations 87,
CHiDE (Centre for the History of Defence Electronics) 245
ChiDE interview v, 247, 276
Chin, Piang Sin 224-7, 232
Chin, John 227
China 69, 72, 111-2, 115, 159, 184, 223, 265, 280
Christison, Philip 163
Commonwealth of Australia xvi, 85, 190-1, 237

Commonwealth (British) 85, 190-1, 200, 235, 247
Commonwealth Heads of Government meeting xvi, 235
Commonwealth War Graves Cemetery 191, 227
    Cross of Sacrifice 229
communications/wireless/signals xi, xii, xvi, 20, 22, 24, 62, 64, 69-71, 74-5, 77,
    79, 97, 105, 143, 189, 193, 200, 203-4, 206, 209, 216, 218, 235, 256-7, 275
Cornwell, David 216, 251
Criminal Law 266-8
Cunningham, Cal 219
Cuthbert Hall, Tatura, Vic v, 7-9

D

Dar es Salaam 209
Darwin, NT 172-4, 203, 213-5, 217
Davis, Private Eric 108
Dean, Penrod 138-9
Dean, Roger 204
Department of Supply, Department of Defence xv, 193, 201
Department of Veterans' Affairs 175
Dhurringile, Vic xiv, 4-5, 7, 12, 46, 48, 60, 176, 189
Diamond, Laurie 31, 32-5, 45-7, 49, 219
Donaldson, H 256
Double Tenth Trial, Singapore 178
Dudley, Ray 23-4
Dunlop, Edward 'Weary' 248
Dwyer, Bill 60, 212, 248

E

Eaton, Charles 54-5, 58
E Force 103, 115, 225
Egami, Sobei 169, 177, 268, 291
Eight Mile Police Post, Sandakan 98, 224, 262
Electronic Target and Response Team (ET) 196
Ewin, Rus 102, 117
executions xiv, 132-4, 178, 182, 232

F

Firkins, Peter xii
Fremantle, WA xiv, 66-7
Fuh, Jackie Lo Ah 117
Funk, Alexander 98, 107, 132, 262-3
Funk, Johnny 131
Funk, Paddy 131
Funk brothers 98, 106, 223, 232, 290

G

Galleghan, Frederick 'Black Jack' 91, 160
Gambier-Parry, Michael 192
Gemencheh Bridge, Malaysia 74
George Cross 180, 269
Goudie, Lex 175
Great Britain iii, xv, xvi, 3, 5, 7-8, 11, 17, 22-3, 26-7, 55, 68-9, 73, 105, 111, 113, 159, 167-8, 186, 190-3, 196, 198-201, 203-6, 208-10, 215-6, 219, 237, 239, 242-5, 247, 249, 251, 259, 263-5, 276, 281

H

Hall, Maggie 2-3
Harley, Monsignor Eugene 232
Harman, James 205
Haruo, Watanabe 126-7, 130, 169, 178, 291
Hashim, Tan Sri Abdul Rahman bin 213
Heroes' Grave, Kuching 232, 239, 241, 292
Hickling, Francis John 243
Hill, Stan 63
Hitchcock, Robert 55
HMAS *Coonawarra* 204
HMAS *Sydney* 176
HMS *Dreadnought* xvi, 209
HMS *Sussex* 163
Holmes, Edward Barclay 160
Holsworthy Army Barracks, Sydney, NSW xvi, 65, 166, 252
Hoshijima, Susumi 96-7, 100-1, 117-8, 177, 179, 226, 262, 285
Howard Springs, NT 213-4
Howell, Ted 236, 243, 248
Hunter, Jackie 205

I

Imperial Japanese Army (IJA) xiv, xix, 67-9, 72-80, 83-8, 90-2, 94-103, 105-7, 109-11, 115, 117, 119-20, 122-7, 133, 135-7, 139, 147, 149-51, 155-6, 158-60, 162-9, 171-2, 177-8, 180, 184, 186, 224, 226, 236, 253, 259, 262-5, 269, 270, 276-80
India 69, 72, 167
Indonesian Confrontation 232
Ipoh, Malaysia 72, 220-1
Itagaki, Seishiro 164

J

Jakarta, Indonesia 208
James, Brian 245, 276
Japan xv, 90, 94, 96, 100, 102, 128, 159, 162, 168, 184, 197, 208, 218, 259,
Japanese Civil Administration 135
Japanese Military Law 127
Japanese surrender xv, 96, 159, 160, 163-4, 168, 259
Japanese War Crimes Tribunal 171, 177-8
Jemaluang, Malaysia 70, 72-3, 167
Jesselton (Kota Kinabalu), Malaysia xii, 103, 227
Johor, Malaysia xii, 70-1, 73-8
Johor Police 256-7
Johor P & T [Post & Telegraph} Department 256
Johor Royal Family 258
Jones, Caroline 235
Julius, William 75

K

Kappe, Gus 67, 72-3, 77, 157, 189
Keating, Ted 126
Kempeitai (Japanese military police) xii, xiv, xviii, 117-20, 122-3, 126, 128-30, 135, 145, 147, 149, 151, 155, 158, 173, 177-9, 187, 223-8, 230-1, 233, 244, 284-5
Kempeitai headquarters, Sandakan 118-9, 223-7
Kempeitai Military Prison, Kuching 124-5
Keppel Harbour, Singapore 67-9, 91, 135, 163, 290
Kerrins family v, 18, 37, 38
King, Linda Barton xv, xvi, 189-90, 210
Kingsford Smith, Charles 55
Kookaburra 55
Kormoran 176
Kota Bharu, Malaysia 72, 167
Kota Kinabalu, Malaysia (see Jesselton)
'Kowandi', Rushworth, Vic 220, 234, 237, 243, 248
Kranji Naval Radio Station 258
Kranji War Cemetery 166
Kuala Lumpur, Malaysia 69, 72, 213
Kuching POW Camp, Malaysia xiv, xv, 100, 102, 105, 116, 124-6, 128, 131, 133, 144, 165, 170-1, 177-8, 180-1, 218, 227-8, 230, 232-3, 239-41, 260, 270
    rations 125-6
Kuching Civil Prison 125, 230

L

Labuan, Malaysia 170-2, 227-9, 232
Labuan War Cemetery 229
Lagan, Ernesto 106, 117, 132
Larrakeyah Army Barracks 204
Leng, Dato Sri Yuen Yuet 213, 220-1, 239-40, 287, 292
Lim, Mr 229
Lloyd, David 196
Lomax, Eric xvi, 145, 151, 244, 247
Lovell, Charlie 58-9, 193
Lush, Doug 67

M

MacMillan, John Allan 127, 131, 261, 265, 267
Malacca, Malaysia 69, 221
Malaya/ Malaysia iii, xiv, 64, 69-75, 78-9, 83, 85, 95, 97, 155, 165-8, 173, 180, 187, 206, 209-10, 212-3, 216, 218, 220, 240, 242, 256-9
Malaya Command Signals 257
Malayan Emergency (1948-60) 206, 216
Malayan National Liberation Army 206
Malaysian Police Force 213
Mansergh, Robert 163
Manunda 170
Maralinga, SA xv, 193-6, 199, 201, 237, 246
Matthews, Lionel C xiv, xviii, 97-8, 105-7, 115, 117, 119-20, 123-4, 126-33, 166, 177-80, 182, 227, 229, 232, 242, 253, 255, 261-2, 264-6, 268-70, 285, 287, 291
Matthews, David 242, 252-3, 287
Matusup bin Gungau 106, 108, 117, 132, 262
Mavor, Gerald 98, 106, 108-9, 119, 124-5, 127, 151, 286
May, Peter 207
McClelland, J 237
McIntyre, Ernie 37-8
McIntyre, Jack 21, 28, 37, 45-6, 48, 50, 59
McNamara, Bernard 39
Melbourne, Vic ii, xiv, xv, xvi, 4, 9, 35, 53, 58-62, 65-6, 121, 124, 135, 173-4, 176-7, 182, 184, 190, 193, 202, 206, 210-2, 214, 219-20, 235-7, 239, 243, 248-9, 251, 271
Mersing, Malaysia 70, 72, 257
Ming, Heng Joo 106, 132
Miura 120

Montgomery, Bernard 190-1,
Morrish, C R 258
Morrish, C P 256
Morse code 23-4, 74, 76, 115, 123-5, 143,
Mount Kinabalu, Sabah, Malaysia 227
Murchison, Vic 1, 4, 7, 8, 12, 25, 53, 60, 69

N

Nagasaki, Japan 160, 184
Nagase, Takashi 244
Naval and Military Club, Melbourne 66, 249
Naval and Military Club, Piccadilly 210, 216
Negeri Sembilan, Malaysia 70
New South Wales, Australia 6, 62, 65
Ng, Peter 223-5, 232
Nishihara, Shuji 178, 268
Northern Territory, Australia 172, 184, 203, 214
Number 3 POW Camp 103

O

O'Byrne, Paddy 1, 53, 66, 174
O'Byrnes 53-4, 58, 121
O'Neill, John 65, 166-7, 291
Odell, Robert William 3
Okasaki, Lieutenant 89
Oliphant, Mark 196
Outram Road Gaol xv, 134-9, 142, 144-7, 149-50, 152-3, 155-8, 161, 163, 165,
    170-1, 178, 181, 201, 207, 240, 244-6
  discipline 139, 163, 170
  escapes 138, 144
  rations 137-9, 149-50, 161, 170
Outram, James 246
Oyama, Fumio 260

P

Parker, George 171
Parit Sulong, Malaysia 75
Patani, Thailand 72
Patmore, Charles 63
Payne, Rodney 239, 247, 250
Pearl Harbour, USA 167
penal servitude xiv, 132, 150, 158, 267-8
Penang, Malaysia 72

Penney, William 195
Pentridge Prison, Melbourne 135, 219
Percival, Arthur E 77, 83, 85, 210
Petrov, Mrs 214
Philippine Liberation Army 115
Philippines 105, 107, 115, 167, 207, 217, 286
Phnom Penh, Cambodia 208
Point Cook, Vic 54-5, 58
Port Hacking, NSW 3
POW (prisoner of war) iii, xii, xiv, 83, 86, 88-9, 91-3, 95-103, 107, 109, 113, 115, 117-20, 122, 124-7, 129-30, 132, 135-40, 143-65, 168, 171, 173-4, 176-9, 181, 183-6, 206, 218, 223-4, 227, 235, 238, 240, 244-5, 248-9, 251, 253, 260, 262-8, 276
Princess Anne 237-8, 244, 251
Prisoner of War Regulations 261, 266-7
Puckapunyal Army Base, Vic 189

Q

Queen Elizabeth II 190, 229, 235, 245
Quinn, Miss 29-31
Quint, Ray iii, 244, 287

R

Raffles Hotel, Singapore 71, 77-8, 244
Ranau, Malaysia 171, 227
Rangoon, Burma xii, 71, 209, 235
Ransom, Lorna 242-3
Red Cross 76, 172-3,
Returned Servicemen's Rehabilitation Scheme 176
Rice-Oxley, A 105
Roberts Barracks, Darwin, NT 86
Robbins, George 45
Roffey, Walter Geoffrey 127, 131, 261
Royal Air Force (RAF) xv, 162, 199-200, 206
Royal Australian Air Force (RAAF) 26, 55, 77, 174
Royal Australian Signals Association 182, 239, 243,
Royal Corps of Signals 77, 238, 244
Royal Engineers 79
Royal Johor Military Forces 74, 257
Royal Marines 201
Royal Military College of Science (RMCS) xv, 190-1, 245, 247
Royal Navy (RN) 163, 190, 209, 239
Royal Radar Establishment (RRE) 192

Returned Soldiers League (RSL) xvi, 12, 183, 237, 239, 243, 251
Rushworth, Vic ii, xvi, 53, 60, 219-20, 234, 237-9, 243, 247-8, 251-2, 271
Rutherford, Ludovic 192
Ruxton, Bruce 251

S

Sabah (British North Borneo), Malaysia 206, 223
Saigon, Vietnam 72, 178, 208
Sandakan POW Camp xiv, 94-9, 103, 105-11, 115, 117-9, 122, 126, 136-7, 144, 165, 171, 177-8, 180, 184, 190, 224-5, 227-9, 245, 248, 253, 269, 276, 279, 285
  arrests xiv, 117, 119, 227-8, 262-5, 285-6
  boiler 99, 112
  discipline 102, 264-5,
  escapes 101-3, 105, 107, 115, 171, 225, 262, 276,
  rations 109, 119, 196-7, 277
  torture 117, 119, 121-4, 137, 269-70,
  underground movement xii, 198-9, 105-6, 115, 187
  wireless radio 105-9, 111, 113, 115, 118, 126-7, 130, 158, 160, 165, 190, 256-8, 263-6, 269, 276, 279, 281-2, 284-5
Sandakan, Malaysia xii, xiv, 90, 94-5, 97-8, 103, 105-6, 118, 124, 126-7, 129-31, 171, 222-3, 225-7, 230, 232, 240, 249, 262-4, 269, 276, 285
Sarawak 100, 125, 206, 230
Scott, Robert 143, 145, 201, 215-6
Secret Intelligence Service 216
Sekiguchi, Colonel 86-7
Selarang Barracks, Changi POW Camp 86, 89, 290
Seymour Army Camp, Vic 62
Shepparton, Vic iv, xv, 9, 12, 80, 177, 189, 218, 237-8
Shrivenham, England xv, 190-2, 245
Silver, Lynette Ramsay v, 171, 249
Simpson Barracks, Melbourne 204, 237, 242-3, 252, 277
Singapore xiv, xv, 66-9, 71-3, 77-9, 82, 85-6, 88, 94, 97, 103, 106, 122, 135, 143, 150, 163, 165-8, 171, 174, 178, 180-1, 201, 206-7, 212, 232, 244, 280, 282-3, 262, 276
Singh, Anup 104, 227-8, 230, 232
Singh, Ojagar 98, 106, 132, 228, 230
Sleeman, Colin 178
Sligo, Norman 97, 269
Smith, Flight Lieutenant 199-200
solar 220, 235-6, 271-5,
Soldier Settlement Scheme 4-5,
Somerville, Christopher iii, 247, 288
South China Sea 115, 223

South-east Asia 26, 68, 158, 167, 184, 206, 215
Southern Expeditionary Army Group 164
SS *Katoomba* xiv, 66
SS *Sibajak* xiv, 66-7, 290
St Andrew's Anglican Cathedral, Singapore 86
St Joseph's Cathedral, Kuching 126
St Teresa's Convent School, Kuching xiv, 126, 128-9, 231, 233, 291
Stark, Jock 25, 42
Steen, Jock 39
Stephen, Ninian 237
Stevens, Alfie 108, 127
Stewart, Galloway 63, 76, 219
Stewart, Jim 39, 219, 236
Stewart, John 39, 63, 176
Strand Hotel, Rangoon, Burma 71, 209
Strathnaver 190
Suga, Tatsugi 100, 102, 128-30, 132
Sugama, Yoshiro 127, 130
Sugita, Ichiji 89
Sultan of Brunei 125
Sultan of Perak 221
Sydney, NSW xiv, 63, 66, 105, 172, 174, 183, 235

T

Takeo, Ishikawa 178
Tampin, Malaysia 69-71, 74
Tanglin Barracks, Singapore 78
Tatura, Vic ii, iii, v, xiii, xiv, 8-9, 12, 18-9, 23-4, 29-32, 37, 42, 46, 48, 52-3, 56, 58-62, 65, 76, 172-4, 213-4, 219, 237, 252-3
Taylor, James 98, 105-6, 117, 125-7, 179-80, 269
Terauchi, Hisaichi 164
Thai-Burma Railway xii, 145
Thailand 73, 207, 215
Thirtieth of September Movement 208
Thyer, James Hervey 63-5, 76-7, 93, 189
Tiernan, Barry 214
Titterton, Ernest 196
Tokyo, Japan 128, 143, 160, 208, 218
Toolamba, Vic 4, 53, 61
Treacy, Father 238
trials, Kuching 127-32, 227, 230-3, 260, 266, 285
Trumble, Ken 67
Tsutsui, Yoichi 169, 178, 268, 291

U

Ulm, Charles 55
UK Ministry of Defence 203, 215
UK Ministry of Supply xv, 191
US Air Force 264-5
USS *Missouri* 160

V

Victoria, Australia ii, xiv, 9, 12, 39, 173, 175, 219-20, 269, 271, 289
Victoria Barracks, Melbourne, Vic 181, 202, 206, 210, 212, 215
Victoria Cross 76, 180
Virtch, Miss 11
vitamin B 87, 163

W

Walsh, Alfred Walker 91, 97, 101-2, 269
Wands, Hugh 117
Waranga Basin, Rushworth, Vic xvi, 32, 219, 235, 237, 271
Washington, USA 201, 207, 216-7
Watson, Stan 24
Watsonia Barracks, Melbourne, Vic 204
Wavell, Archibald 82
Webb, William 176
Wells' farm iii, v, xix, 1, 5, 7-9, 12, 14, 16-7, 20, 29, 37, 39, 46, 51, 55, 60-2, 77, 122, 142, 149, 165, 176, 189, 192
Wells, Dorothy Margaret xiv, xvi, 14, 16-18, 27, 32-3, 35, 37, 39, 48, 52, 61, 63, 122, 174-5, 190, 193, 214, 217, 252
Wells, John George 15, 32
Wells, Richard (Dick) John xiv, xvi, xix, 1-8, 11-7, 22-4, 26-9, 32, 35, 37-8, 42, 45-6, 49-56, 58, 60-2, 66, 77-8, 94, 121-2, 174-6, 182, 186, 192, 210
Wells, Roderick (Rod) Graham iii, iv, v, viii, ix, x, xi, xii, xiii, xiv, xv, xvi, 10-11, 13, 15, 18, 21, 31-4, 36, 45, 49, 57, 67, 69-70, 118, 129, 132, 155, 157, 166, 174, 188, 194-5, 202, 206, 211, 225, 240, 242, 247-53, 258, 260, 269-72, 275-86
  arrested, Sandakan xiv, 137, 178, 226-7
  imprisonment, Changi POW Camp iii, 89, 131, 137, 139-41, 148, 151, 155, 165, 181, 215, 231, 261
  Rod Wells Wing, Holsworthy Army Barracks, NSW xvi, 252
  solitary confinement xvi, 119-20, 150, 132, 181
  trial, Kuching 227, 260, 285

Wells, Madge 13, 15-6, 18, 27, 40, 45, 53, 77, 175
Wells, Pamela ii, v, xiii, xvi, 211-12, 251, 271, 288
Weynton, Gordon iv, 107, 109, 112, 114, 118-9, 123-4, 127, 180, 183, 263-6, 284
White, Glyn 86, 155, 157
Whitlam, Gough 216-7
Williams, Mr 39-45
Wiltshire, England 190-2, 201
wireless radio iii, xi, xii, xiv, 20, 22, 24-9, 39, 45, 62, 71, 74, 76, 105-9, 111, 113, 115, 118, 126-7, 130-1, 143, 158, 160, 165, 170, 190, 213-4, 245, 250, 256-8, 263-6, 269, 274, 276, 279, 281-2, 284-6
Wireless Telegraphy (WT) 74-5
With, Mrs 17
Wodehouse, P G 96
Wong, Moo Sing 132
Workman, John 101
World War I xii, 12, 15, 24, 54, 60, 77, 93, 100, 175
World War II xii, 56, 115

Y

Yamashita, Tomoyuki 83, 259
Young, Billy 144-5, 291
Yubi Maru xiv, 91, 93